BEST of the BEST
from
TEXAS

Selected Recipes from Texas'
FAVORITE COOKBOOKS

BEST
of the BEST
from
TEXAS

Selected Recipes from Texas'
FAVORITE COOKBOOKS

EDITED BY
Gwen McKee
AND
Barbara Moseley

Illustrated by Tupper Davidson
Glossary by Carol Mead

QUAIL RIDGE PRESS

CONTINUED

CONTINUED

First printing - September 1985
Second printing - February 1986
Third printing - September 1989
ISBN 0-937552-14-3 (ringbound)
ISBN 0-937552-34-8 (hardcover)
Manufactured in the United States of America
Designed by Barney and Gwen McKee
Chapter opening photos and cover photo courtesy of
Texas Tourist Development Agency

Some of state's highest peaks are in Guadalupe Mountains National Park. West Texas near New Mexico border.

CONTENTS

PREFACE

Eighty of the Lone Star State's leading cookbooks are represented in this edition of the Quail Ridge Press "Best of the Best" cookbook series. From all over the vast area of Texas, these cookbooks were submitted and recipes selected that would record Texas' special brand of cooking. We are deeply grateful to all the individuals, organizations and publishers who allowed us to reprint recipes from their cookbooks. This comprehensive collection of Texas recipes could not have been achieved without their cooperation.

Compiling such a cookbook as this was a massive project. Texas with its vastness and diversity is the source of a great number of excellent cookbooks. The process of becoming aware of these books and then assembling a collection of recipes that captures the state's diverse cuisine was quite demanding. It was, however, a delightful undertaking, due largely to the many friendly and helpful Texans we met along the way. In a few cases, some books we wanted to include are not a part of this collection because of publisher's restrictions or organizational policies, or books going out of print. And we beg forgiveness for any that might have been included that we inadvertently overlooked.

The eighty books that are included among "the best," are each outstanding in their own way. Besides excellent recipes, many feature historical sketches as well as photographs, drawings, kitchen hints, Spanish translations, and humorous stories and anecdotes. We have attempted to reproduce the recipes as they appear in their own books, changing only the typeset style for uniformity. A complete catalog of the contributing cookbooks begins on page 323.

We are especially appreciative of the food editors at various Texas newspapers who recommended cookbooks for inclusion; to the bookstore and gift shop managers who gave us their knowledge of the most popular cookbooks in their area; to Barbara Jones of Southwest Cookbook Distributors in Bonham who shared with us a list of the

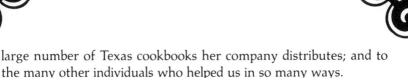

large number of Texas cookbooks her company distributes; and to the many other individuals who helped us in so many ways.

As was the case with the Cajun influence on Louisiana cooking (in *Best of the Best from Louisiana*), the Mexican influence on Texas cooking has been substantial. "Tex-Mex" has become a term that symbolizes a delicious culinary combination. For compiling a glossary that defines the many Spanish words and phrases that appear throughout the book, we are deeply grateful to freelance writer Carol Mead. Thanks also to illustrator Tupper Davidson for her delightful drawings, and to associate Waynell Harris of Lubbock who provided us with insight into the nature of West Texas. Richard Reynolds and Mary Schnell of the Texas Tourist Development Agency shared with us the resources of this agency including the beautiful photographs that appear throughout the book. For their assistance, we are grateful.

We are pleased to have the publication of this book coincide with the occasion of Texas' Sesquicentennial Celebration and we invite you to celebrate in the magnificence of her cuisine.

Gwen McKee and Barbara Moseley

CONTRIBUTING COOKBOOKS

The Adolphus Cookbook
Amarillo Junior League Cookbook
An American Gumbo
Becky's Brunch & Breakfast Book
The Blue Denim Gourmet
Bravo, Chef!
Calf Fries to Caviar
Chinese Cooking the American Way
Collectibles II
Company's Coming
Cook 'em Horns
Cooking Texas Style
Cookin' Wise
The Cottage Kitchen Cookbook
Cowtown Cuisine
Creative Mexican Cooking
Crème of the Crop
Cuckoo Too
The Dallas Pecan Cookbook
The Dallas Symphony Cookbook
A Different Taste of Paris
A Doctor's Prescription for Gourmet Cooking
Easy Does It
Elegant Elk-Delicious Deer
Enjoy!
Entertaining at Aldredge House
Entertaining in Texas
Flavor Favorites

CONTRIBUTING COOKBOOKS

Flavors
From My Apron Pocket
Gallery Buffet Soup Cookbook
Galveston Island Cookbook
Guten Appetit!
Hospitality
Houston Celebrity Cookbook
Houston Fine Arts Cookbook
Hullabaloo in the Kitchen
"I'm Glad I Ate When I Did, 'Cause
I'm Not Hungry Now"
It's a Long Way to Guacamole
Keepers!
La Galerie Perroquet Food Fare
Lagniappe
La Piñata
Leaving Home
March of Dimes Gourmet Gala Cookbook
The Melting Pot
Micro Quick!
Microwave Know-How
Morning, Noon and Night Cookbook
Mrs. Blackwell's Heart-of-Texas Cookbook
Nature's Kitchen
Noted Cookery
Of Magnolia and Mesquite
The Only Texas Cookbook
Our Favorite Recipes

CONTRIBUTING COOKBOOKS

The Pride of Texas
Rare Collection
Ready to Serve
Repast
Rolling in Dough
San Angelo Junior League Cookbook
San Antonio Conservation Society Cookbook
San Antonio Cookbook II
Scrumptious
Seasoned With Sun
Spindletop International Cooks
Square House Museum Cookbook
Sweets. . . . From Marina With Love. . . .
Tasteful Traditions
A Taste of Victoria
Tastes & Tales From Texas . . . With Love
Tempting Traditions
Texas Celebrity Cookbook
A Texas Hill Country Cookbook
Texas Historic Inns Cookbook
The Texas Microwave Cookbook
Through Our Kitchen Door
Trading Secrets
Wild-n-Tame Fish-n-Game
The Woodlands Celebrity Cookbook

Appetizers

Texas bluebonnets (state flower) roam statewide, as here in the Hill Country of
Central Texas near New Braunfels.

Mint Tea

4 tea bags
8–10 sprigs mint
1 quart boiling water
⅔ cup lemon juice

⅓ cup orange juice
1¼ cups sugar
3 cups hot water

Put tea bags, mint and boiling water in a covered container. Let set for 15 minutes. Mix all other ingredients in another container. Mix all together, serve over ice. Yields ½ gallon.

Scrumptious

White Sangria

½ gallon dry white wine
2 apples (cored, sliced and
  unpeeled)
½ lemon, sliced thin
1 orange, sliced thin
1 lime, sliced thin

2 fresh peaches, sliced (when
  available)
½ gallon (2 quarts) soda water
½ cup frozen lemonade
  concentrate or ½ cup sugar

This is a refreshing summertime drink and it won't stain carpets or linens like red wine sangria.

It's a Long Way to Guacamole

Festive Holiday Spiced Tea

Juice of 12 lemons or 2 cans Minute Maid lemon juice concentrate	9 cups boiling water
	3 teaspoons whole cloves
	3 teaspoons whole allspice
1¼ cups sugar (or same amount NutraSweet)	4 sticks cinnamon
	1 cup red hots (cinnamon drops)

Put sugar, spices, red hots, and lemon juice in boiling water. Let boil until cinnamon drops dissolve and until mixture is spicy enough. In separate pot, make 2 quarts medium strength tea, using tea bags; strain spicy mixture and add to tea. Pour into containers and refrigerate; heat as wanted and keep indefinitely. Makes 4 quarts.

Spindletop International Cooks

Glühwein

This is a hot, spiced red wine served in Germany and Bavaria. It gets its name from the afterglow that is present when a soft red light is just turned off. The bulb remains glowing for a few seconds, and this wine, served in a crystal mug, glows in a similar way.

6 cups sugar	¾ teaspoon ground nutmeg
2 tablespoons ground cinnamon	Burgundy or other dry red wine
2 tablespoons ground cloves	Cinnamon sticks (optional)
1 tablespoon ground allspice	

Combine first 5 ingredients in large bowl. Stir well. Store mix in airtight container.

To serve: Mix 2 teaspoonfuls of dry ingredients to ½ cup water in small saucepan. Bring to boil. Reduce heat. Add 1 cup wine and heat thoroughly (do not boil). Serve with stick of cinnamon, if desired. This makes 2 servings; the dry mixture produces a total of 72 servings.

Company's Coming

Wassail

Old family secret recipe for Mulled Cider, or Wassail, as it was called to interest the children. This is the recipe used by the Harris County Heritage Society.

2 quarts apple cider	**1 quart orange juice**
1 cinnamon stick	**3 tablespoons lemon juice**
¼ teaspoon nutmeg	**1 teaspoon lemon rind**
¼ cup honey	

Place apple cider and cinnamon stick in saucepan, cover, bring to boil, reduce heat and simmer 5 minutes. Never boil again. Add remaining ingredients and simmer 5 minutes uncovered. Cool and place in container in refrigerator. Heat as needed for family use. Yields about 3 quarts. Serves 18–20.

For a crowd this recipe is tripled, put in a large coffee maker and allowed to perk. No worry about the boiling this way. Be sure to stir well. Honey plugs the holes in the basket for coffee grounds, or it could stick to the bottom of the pot and scorch. Cinnamon stick can be used over and over if washed and dried.

Repast

Hot Buttered Rum

THE BATTER:

1 stick butter	**¼ teaspoon ground nutmeg**
1 pound dark brown sugar	**¼ teaspoon ground cloves**
¼ teaspoon ground cinnamon	

Mix softened butter with brown sugar and add spices. Keep in glass jar, covered in refrigerator. Will keep for a long time.

THE DRINK:

Dark rum	**Boiling water**

Into each cup or mug, place one heaping tablespoon of batter. Add 1½ ounces dark rum and fill with boiling water. The batter may be made up and put into a decorative jar with the recipe for Christmas gifts or for holiday bazaars.

Entertaining at Aldredge House

Slush Punch

1 large package Jello
½ cup sugar
1 small can frozen lemonade

2 small cans frozen orange juice
1 large can pineapple juice
1 quart ginger ale

Mix Jello as on package. Let cool some. Mix frozen juices with water, minus 1 can of water per juice and add to Jello. Add pineapple juice; mix and freeze in large Tupperware bucket. Thaw until slushy. Add ginger ale.

Note: Our favorite flavor is made with apricot Jello.

The Pride of Texas

Tequila Slush

1 (6-ounce) can frozen lime juice
2 (6-ounce) cans frozen limeade
1 (6-ounce) can orange juice
6 (6-ounce) cans water

1 quart bottle Wink or similar
  drink
⅓–½ bottle tequila

Mix ingredients and freeze. Remove from freezer 30 minutes before serving and stir until slushy with a spoon. Can be refrozen and kept indefinitely.

La Piñata

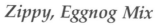

Zippy, Eggnog Mix

1 (3-quart) package (9.6-ounce)
  instant nonfat dry milk powder
2 (4½-ounce) packages no-bake
  custard mix

1 (6-ounce) jar non-dairy coffee
  creamer
2 teaspoons ground nutmeg

Combine all ingredients thoroughly. Store in tightly covered container. For each serving, stir ½ cup eggnog mix into a coffee cup or mug of hot water. To serve cold, in blender container place 1 cup cold water and 1 cup of the eggnog mix. Cover and blend until smooth. Add 1 cup ice cubes, one at a time, blending until slushy. Yields 5 cups dry mix.

Cowtown Cuisine

Libba's Bloody Marys

1 (46-ounce) can tomato juice
1 can beef consommé or beef
  bouillon soup, undiluted
1 cup lemon juice
2 tablespoons Worcestershire
½ teaspoon sugar, if desired

2 teaspoons celery salt
½ teaspoon pepper
1 teaspoon salt
1 teaspoon Tabasco
1½ soup cans vodka

Mix all together and serve over ice with fresh lime wedge and celery sticks. Also can add 1 slice cucumber to glass for an extra flavor! Serves 8.

Spindletop International Cooks

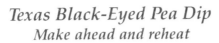

Texas Black-Eyed Pea Dip
Make ahead and reheat

A winner—from Athens, Texas, the Black-Eyed Pea Capitol of the World!

¼ bell pepper	3 chicken bouillon cubes
8 jalapeño peppers	¼ teaspoon nutmeg
2 stalks celery	¼ teaspoon cinnamon
1 large onion	2 (No. 202) cans black-eyed peas
1 teaspoon coarse black pepper	1 cup canned tomatoes
2 tablespoons Tabasco	1 teaspoon granulated garlic
½ cup catsup	½ cup bacon drippings
1 teaspoon salt	3 tablespoons flour

Chop finely the peppers, celery and onion. Add the next seven ingredients, and bring to a slow simmer. Then add the black-eyed peas, the tomatoes, and garlic. Cook for 30 minutes. Blend together the bacon drippings and flour, and heat with cooked mixture for 10 minutes. Stir well to prevent sticking. Serve hot with tostados or Doritos. Fills the bill for a New Year's party.

Collectibles II

Black-Eyed Pea Dip

2 cups cooked black-eyed peas	1 clove garlic
1 stick oleo, melted	4 ounces grated Cheddar cheese
1 jalapeño pepper	¾–1 cup milk (if needed for
½ teaspoon juice of pepper	consistency)
1 medium onion, chopped	

Mix in blender first 6 ingredients; then place in saucepan. Add cheese and milk as needed for consistency. Stir over heat until cheese melts. Serve hot or cold.

The Pride of Texas

International Bean Dip
Best bean dip ever tasted

1 (15-ounce) can refried beans
4 ounces cream cheese, softened
12 ounces sour cream
1 bunch green onions, finely
chopped
½ (12-ounce) can Ortega salsa
1 (1¼-ounce) packet taco
seasoning

½ (4-ounce) can diced green chile
peppers
Dash oregano
Salt and pepper to taste
1 cup grated Monterrey Jack,
Longhorn or Cheddar cheese

Combine all ingredients except grated cheese in ovenproof dish.
Sprinkle top with grated cheese. Bake 1 hour at 300°. Serves 15.

Cook 'Em Horns

Broccoli Dip

1 box frozen chopped broccoli
1 (10-ounce) can Rotel tomatoes
with green chilies

1 can cream of celery soup,
undiluted
1 cup shredded Cheddar cheese
(or more, if desired)

Preheat oven to 350°. Cook broccoli as directed on package. Drain
well. Put in bottom of baking dish that can be used for serving.
Drain and chop tomatoes. Sprinkle over broccoli in even layer.
Spread celery soup evenly over other ingredients. Sprinkle cheese
over top. Bake until bubbly, 20–30 minutes. Serve hot with your
favorite dipper. Corn chips are especially good.

A Texas Hill Country Cookbook

Dill Dip

Serve with fresh vegetable strips.

½ pint Hellman's Mayonnaise
1 tablespoon grated onion
½ pint sour cream

1½ teaspoons chopped parsley
1½ teaspoons dill weed
1 teaspoon cumin

Serve with fresh asparagus spears, sliced zucchini, green onions,
cherry tomatoes, celery, carrot sticks, cauliflower or radishes.

Square House Museum Cookbook

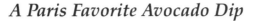

A Paris Favorite Avocado Dip

3 large avocados, mashed
1 (8-ounce) jar picante sauce (I use Pace)
1 cup Cheddar cheese, shredded
1 pint sour cream (room temperature)
3–4 green onions, chopped

Mash avocados in a 9 × 9-inch dish. Layer picante sauce and then sour cream. It spreads better at room temperature. Shred enough Cheddar cheese to cover the dish (about 1 cup) and top with chopped green onion. Serve with Doritos or any other Mexican chip. Good! Refrigerate until ready to serve. Serves about 6–8.

A Different Taste of Paris

Picante (pee CAHN tay)—A Spanish word meaning spicy hot.

Guacamole de Suzanne
(Avocado Sauce)

3 large avocados, chopped
1 medium-sized onion, peeled and chopped
1 medium-sized tomato, peeled and chopped
2 small chilies, chopped
1 tablespoon olive oil
1 teaspoon wine vinegar or lemon juice
2 teaspoons salt

Mix all ingredients (except ½ avocado) until creamy then chop the remaining half avocado in cubes and add. Taste for seasoning. Chill. If made in advance be sure to store in refrigerator with the avocado *seeds* placed in the sauce and sprinkle with lemon juice to prevent its darkening. Serve as a dip with toasted tortillas, or for a salad in lettuce cups. Serves 8.

Variation: If chilies are not available, use canned Mexican hot sauce to taste.

From My Apron Pocket

Guacamole (gwa cah MOH lay)—A paste made from avocados. It is served on lettuce as a salad, as a filling, or as a dip.

Tex-Mex Dip

3 ripe avocados
2 tablespoons lemon juice
½ teaspoon salt
¼ teaspoon pepper
1 cup sour cream
½ cup mayonnaise
1 package dry taco seasoning mix
  (I use McCormick's)
2 cans plain bean dip

3 green onions with tops,
  chopped
3 medium tomatoes, coarsely
  chopped
2 (3½-ounce) cans ripe olives,
  drained and chopped
8 ounces Cheddar cheese,
  shredded

Peel, pit, and mash avocados with lemon juice, salt, and pepper. Combine sour cream, mayonnaise, and taco seasoning in bowl.

Spread bean dip on a large, shallow serving platter. Top with seasoned avocado mixture. Layer with sour cream and taco mixture. Sprinkle with chopped onions, tomatoes, and olives. Cover with shredded cheese. Serve chilled or at room temperature with round tortilla chips. This recipe makes a HUGE amount!

Company's Coming

Sombrero Spread

2 teaspoons salt
2 pounds ground beef
2 cups chopped onion
1 (14-ounce) bottle Heinz hot
  catsup
5 teaspoons chili powder

1 teaspoon comino seed
1 pound cooked pinto beans, or
  1–2 cans
2 cups shredded American cheese
1 cup chopped stuffed olives
Corn chips or tostados

Spread salt in frying pan and heat. (Oil may be used, if preferred). Add beef, stirring with fork. When moist, add 1 cup of onions. Continue stirring until beef and onions brown. Stir in catsup, chili powder and comino seed. Mash and add pinto beans. Heat until blended. May be refrigerated or frozen. More salt, Tabasco, Worcestershire, or sugar to taste may be added. When ready to serve, heat and place in a large chafing dish. Pile olives in the center and surround with a large ring of onions and an outer ring of cheese. Olé–a sombrero! Serve with corn chips or tostados. Serves 40.

San Antonio Cookbook II

 Tostada (tohs TAH dah)—A crisp, fried tortilla that is garnished.

Hot Artichoke Spread

1 (14-ounce) can artichoke hearts, drained and chopped
1 cup real mayonnaise

1 cup Parmesan cheese, grated
⅓–½ teaspoon garlic powder (according to taste)

Combine all ingredients and put into a lightly greased, small casserole. Bake for 20 minutes at 350°. Serve with assorted crackers. Yields about 3 cups. Freezes.

La Piñata

Easy Nacho Spread

1 (8-ounce) carton avocado dip (or 4–5 avocados, mashed, mixed with ⅛ teaspoon garlic powder, ⅛ teaspoon garlic salt, 1 tablespoon lemon juice, and 2 tablespoons mayonnaise)
1 bunch green onions, chopped, tops included or 1 (4-ounce) can chopped green chilies

3 peeled and chopped tomatoes
1 (8-ounce) jar Picante sauce
1 (8-ounce) carton sour cream
1½ cups shredded Monterrey Jack or Cheddar cheese
Optional layers or substitutions:
1 (10½-ounce) can bean dip
1 (4½-ounce) can chopped ripe olives

1. Layer in bowl or 8 × 8-inch dish in order listed. 2. Serve with tortilla chips.

Easy Does It Cookbook

Monterey Jack—A mild, semi-soft cheese generally classified as a Cheddar, but also very similar to Muenster cheese. Although Monterey Jack originated in Monterey County, California, its name is sometimes spelled like the name of the Mexican city of Monterrey. Also called just Monterey or just Jack.

Nachos

No, the jalapeño is not the state vegetable of Texas, but it is a versatile little critter, popping up fresh, pickled, stuffed, chicken-fried, jellied, in lollipops, jelly beans, and daiquiris. How about jalapeño wine? (No kidding, folks.) For those of you with delicate constitutions, the Aggies have developed a flameless jalapeño, but it has yet to catch fire on the open market.

6 corn tortillas
Oil for frying tortillas
½ cup refried beans

¼ pound Monterrey Jack,
Cheddar or Longhorn cheese,
grated
Sliced pickled jalapeños to taste

Cut tortillas into quarters and fry in hot oil until crisp. Spread with refried beans, sprinkle with grated cheese and top with 2–3 slices jalapeño chiles. Broil until cheese melts. Guacamole and sour cream can be used to top nachos after broiling. Variations are limited only to your imagination. (If you're in a hurry, tortilla chips can be used to eliminate frying the tortillas.) Yields 24.

Tastes & Tales From Texas . . . With Love

Nachos (NAH chohs)—A popular Tex-Mex snack. They are fried tortilla chips that can be topped off with melted cheese, slices of pepper, or refried beans.

24

Sausage-Cheese Balls

10 ounces grated sharp Cheddar cheese   3 cups buttermilk biscuit mix
1 pound hot bulk sausage

With hands, mix all ingredients. Roll into marble-sized balls. Freeze. Bake while still frozen at 325° until toasted, about 20–30 minutes. Yields 100 balls.

These freeze before or after baking. Great for appetizers, served hot. These are served on a stick by the Republican Women of Comal County at their booth at the Wurstfest (sausage celebration) in New Braunfels every fall.

Keepers

Cream Cheese Puffs

4 ounces cream cheese
¾ teaspoon grated onion
¼ cup homemade mayonnaise
1 tablespoon chopped chives
⅛ teaspoon cayenne
⅛ cup Parmesan cheese
½ small loaf white bread

In a small bowl combine first six ingredients and mix well. Cut bread into circles (1½-inches round) and spread each with cheese mixture. Bake in 350° oven for 15 minutes: longer for crisper puff. The bread may be cut and spread with cheese mixture and then frozen. Bake when ready to use. Yields 2 dozen puffs.

Amarillo Junior League Cookbook

Catherine Lee's Cheese Spread

8 ounces mild Cheddar cheese
8 ounces sharp Cheddar cheese
8 ounces Mozzarella cheese
1 bunch green onions, chopped
5 ribs celery, chopped
1 (4-ounce) can ripe olives, sliced
2 (2-ounce) cans chopped pimiento
1 (4-ounce) can jalapeño peppers, washed, seeded, and chopped
½ cup mayonnaise

Grate and combine cheeses. Add onions, celery, ripe olives, pimiento and jalapeño peppers. Mix well with mayonnaise. Serve with crackers. Serves 20–30.

Entertaining in Texas

Fried Swiss Gruyère Cheese

4 tablespoons sweet butter	½ pound Swiss Gruyère cheese,
5 tablespoons flour	grated
1½ cups scalded milk	1 egg, beaten
Salt	¼ cup scalded milk
White pepper	1 tablespoon olive oil
2 egg yolks, well beaten	Bread crumbs

Melt butter over low heat. Remove from heat and add the flour. Return to heat and cook the roux for about 3 minutes, stirring constantly. Remove from heat and slowly add 1½ cups scalded milk. Stir with a whisk until smooth, then return to heat and bring to a boil, stirring constantly. Cook sauce over low heat for 10 minutes until it is smooth and thick. Season with salt and white pepper to taste. Add about ⅓ of the sauce to the beaten egg yolks and mix thoroughly, then add egg yolk mixture to the remaining sauce. Using a rubber spatula fold in the grated Swiss cheese. Spread mixture in a well-buttered shallow dish (9 × 6-inch), cover, and chill for at least 2 hours, or overnight. Combine one beaten egg with ¼ cup milk and olive oil. Cut equal portions of cheese mixture and form into balls or croquettes. Roll the croquettes in flour, then in the egg mixture. Drain and roll in fine bread crumbs. Deep fry croquettes in 370° oil for 45 seconds to a minute. Serve with Tomato Sauce.

TOMATO SAUCE:

1 tablespoon chopped yellow	Salt
onion	White pepper
1 tablespoon olive oil	2 tablespoons tomato paste
1 (28-ounce) can pear tomatoes,	Cayenne pepper to taste
crushed	1 clove garlic, crushed

Heat oil in saucepan. When hot, add onion and sauté for 1 minute. Add tomatoes and salt and pepper. Cook on high heat for 5–6 minutes to evaporate some of the liquid. Add garlic and tomato paste. Cook 3–4 minutes. Season with cayenne.

Bravo, Chef!

Fried Camembert

Only a Texan would fry French cheese.

1 (6-inch) round Camembert, medium soft, not too ripe
1 egg, beaten

1 cup fresh bread crumbs
4 tablespoons unsalted butter
½ cup chopped green onion tops

Dip the unskinned cheese round in egg and then coat both sides with bread crumbs. Heat 2 tablespoons of butter until it starts to brown. Over high heat brown cheese round on both sides. Remove to a heated serving plate and keep warm. Add remaining butter to skillet. When foamy, sauté the onions for 2 minutes. Pour over top of cheese and serve immediately with water biscuits.

The Only Texas Cookbook

Cheese Fingers

3 loaves day-old bread
2 eggs
1½ cups milk

Melted margarine
3 (8-ounce) cans Parmesan cheese

Remove crusts from bread. Combine eggs and milk in a bowl. In a second bowl, place melted margarine; in a third bowl, place cheese. Dip 1 slice bread in egg mixture, and place between 2 slices dry bread. Cut into 4 fingers. Dip each finger in margarine, then in cheese, leaving bottom side clean. Place clean side down on cookie sheet. Bake at 350° for 10 minutes. Allow at least 3 per person. Yields about 80.

Hospitality

Chili Cheese Cubes

8 eggs
½ cup flour
1 teaspoon baking powder
¾ teaspoon salt
3 (12-ounce) cups Monterrey Jack cheese, grated

1½ cups small curd cottage cheese
2 (4-ounce) cans mild green chilies, drained, seeded and chopped

In large mixing bowl, beat eggs until light (4–5 minutes). Stir together flour, baking powder and salt. Add to eggs, and mix well. Fold in cheeses and chilies. Turn into greased 9×9×2-inch baking dish. Bake at 350° for 40 minutes. Remove from oven and let stand for 10 minutes. Cut into small squares, and serve hot. Yields 36–48 appetizers.

Tasteful Traditions

Hot Cheese in a Jar

2 pounds melted Velveeta cheese (do not substitute)
1 medium onion, grated or ground
1 (5.33-ounce) can evaporated milk

1 pint Miracle Whip salad dressing*
1 (8-ounce) can seeded, deveined, jalapeño peppers, chopped fine (cut off stems)

Melt cheese in top of double boiler. Add onion, milk, Miracle Whip and peppers to melted cheese, and mix well. Pour into 6 (8-ounce) jelly jars. Cool, screw on caps, refrigerate. May be used as a cheese spread or let stand about 30 minutes at room temperature and may be used as a dip. Ingredients may be mixed in a blender then added to the melted cheese. Yields 6 jars.

The jars of cheese, tied with a ribbon make nice gifts at Christmas, or at any time when something small would be appreciated, but remember, it must be refrigerated.

*Do not use substitution.

Cowtown Cuisine

Bleu Cheese Tarts

CRUST:
1 (3-ounce) package cream cheese   1 cup flour
1 stick unsalted butter

Mix and roll in small balls. Place a ball into each cup of small muffin tin. Spread with fingers across bottom and up the sides to line the cup.

FILLING:
2 eggs	1 teaspoon flour (instant)
½ teaspoon salt	⅓ cup milk
White pepper	1 (5-ounce) package bleu cheese
1 teaspoon onion juice	

Beat eggs, add salt and pepper, onion juice, flour and milk, add crumbled bleu cheese. Put 2 teaspoons filling into each pastry cup. Bake at 375° for 15–20 minutes or until well browned. Serve hot. Will freeze. Makes three dozen. These tarts can be made in small barquette tins for a more elegant tart.

Entertaining at Aldredge House

Potatoes in Tuxedos

Small new potatoes, cleaned, leaving jackets on	Seasoning salt
	Cayenne pepper
Sour cream	Parsley, finely chopped

Allow 2 potatoes for each person. Select very small, round new potatoes. Boil until just done (do not overcook); chill. Scoop out top portion of the potato; fill with sour cream (approximately 1 tablespoon per potato). Sprinkle with seasoning salt, cayenne pepper, and parsley. Serve chilled. Good pick-up food for a cocktail buffet.

Enjoy!

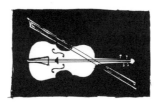

Artichoke Fritata

2 (6-ounce) jars marinated
   artichokes
1 small onion, finely chopped
1 clove garlic, mashed
4 eggs
2 teaspoons minced parsley

¼ cup fine bread crumbs
1 teaspoon pepper or oregano
Few drops of Tabasco
½ pound (2 cups) sharp cheese,
   shredded

Drain marinade from 1 jar of artichokes into a frying pan. Drain off other jar. Chop all artichokes and set aside. Add onions and garlic to frying pan and sauté until limp. In bowl beat eggs and add bread crumbs, salt, and other seasonings. Stir in cheese, parsley, artichokes, onions and garlic. Put mixture into greased 7×11×2-inch baking dish. Bake at 325° for 30 minutes or until set. Cool in pan and cut into 1-inch squares. Serve cold or reheat at 325° for 10 minutes. Freezes well. Delicious!

Cookin' Wise

Curried Moroccan Muffins

6 English muffins, halved
2 cups chopped pitted ripe olives
2 cups grated Cheddar cheese
3 green onions, chopped

1 cup mayonnaise
¾ teaspoon curry powder
Salt and pepper

Mix above ingredients and "pile on" muffins. Cut each muffin half into six wedges (as you would a pie). Freeze on a cookie sheet; then put in a baggie. Bake frozen at 375° until bubbly. Yields 72 appetizers.

Lagniappe

Pico de Gallo

1 bundle green onions and stalks, chopped
1 medium tomato, diced
1 large Anaheim pepper, finely chopped
1 teaspoon salt
2 teaspoons fresh cilantro, chopped
1 can Rotel tomatoes

Mix all ingredients and place in covered bowl in refrigerator for 5–6 hours. Serve on tacos or use as a dip.

"I'm Glad I Ate When I Did, 'Cause I'm Not Hungry Now"

Dallas Dip

2 small cans chopped green chilies
2 small cans chopped ripe olives
4 tomatoes, chopped
1 bunch green onions, chopped
5 tablespoons salad oil
3 tablespoons vinegar
1 teaspoon garlic powder

Mix together the first four ingredients. Add the salad oil, vinegar and garlic powder. Serve with chips.

Through Our Kitchen Door

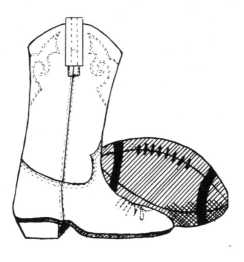

Picadillo

Texans are known for their easy, carefree style of entertaining. The main ingredient that makes this work is the flexibility of the host or hostess. Often friends drop by at the spur of the moment for a short visit which turns into a fun-filled evening. With the right foods on hand, this does not have to mean hours in the kitchen or a full course meal. Picadillo (pee-kah-DEE-yoh) is a hearty, robust meat dip with a wonderful blend of flavors, which can be made ahead and refrigerated for a week or frozen for up to three months, ready and waiting for just such an occasion. Simply heat and serve with tostados or corn chips or spoon into warmed flour tortillas. It is guaranteed to take the edge off the biggest appetite.

1 pound ground beef
1 pound ground pork
4 large tomatoes
4 green onions, finely chopped
1 cup diced pimiento
1 cup slivered almonds
2 cloves garlic, minced

12 ounces tomato paste
4 canned jalapeños, seeded and
  chopped
1 cup raisins
1 teaspoon ground cumin
  (comino)
1 teaspoon oregano

Brown beef and pork in a large pan over high heat, separating with a fork, until cooked through. Lower heat to medium and place whole tomatoes on top of meat. Cover and let simmer 10–15 minutes. Remove tomatoes, peel and dice them, and return to pan with their juice. Stir in remaining ingredients and mix well. Cover and simmer for 20–30 minutes or until the mixture is well blended and the raisins are plump. Yields 12–18 servings.

Cooking Texas Style

Picadillo (pee cah DEE yoh)—A Spanish or Mexican dish of chopped or ground pork and veal cooked together and then mixed with tomatoes, garlic, onion, olives, and other ingredients.

Picadillo

2 pounds lean ground beef or
  venison
4 tablespoons olive oil
2 onions, finely chopped
1 clove garlic, crushed
2 apples, peeled, cored, and
  chopped
1 (14½-ounce) can tomatoes with
  onion and green pepper

3 canned jalapeño chilies,
  chopped
½ cup raisins
Salt and pepper to taste
Pinch of ground cinnamon
Pinch of ground cloves
2 ounces slivered almonds

In a large skillet, brown meat in 3 tablespoons oil. Add onion and garlic and brown. Add remaining ingredients, except the almonds, and simmer for 20 minutes. Sauté almonds in 1 tablespoon oil until golden, add to other ingredients, and cook 2 minutes. Serve with large Fritos as a dip or as a main dish with rice. Serves 6.

Picadillo resulted from the merging of Spanish cookery with Aztec cuisine, and with variations is enjoyed throughout Latin America.

Flavors

Garlic Shrimp

Shrimp, cooked, peeled and
  deveined
8 cloves of garlic
1 teaspoon thyme
1 teaspoon dry mustard

Juice of one dozen lemons
Dash of oregano
Dash of cayenne
Salt and pepper to taste

Pour sauce over shrimp and refrigerate 12–24 hours. Serve as hors d'oeuvres.

Trading Secrets

Cartier Caviar

The gelatin is delectable, yet it maintains the stunning layering.

1 package unflavored gelatin
¼ cup cold water

Line bottom of 1-quart soufflé dish with foil extending 4 inches beyond rim of dish on 2 sides. Oil lightly. Soften gelatin in cold water in measuring cup. Liquefy gelatin by setting cup in pan of hot water, or in microwave oven for about 20 seconds at lowest setting. This gelatin will be divided among the 3 layers.

EGG LAYER:

4 hard-cooked eggs, chopped
½ cup mayonnaise
¼ cup parsley leaves, minced
1 large green onion, minced

¾ teaspoon salt
Dash of hot pepper sauce
Freshly ground white pepper

Combine all ingredients with 1 tablespoon of gelatin. Taste and adjust seasoning. Neatly spread egg mixture into prepared dish with spatula, smoothing top. Wipe any egg mixture from foil with paper towel.

AVOCADO LAYER:

1 medium avocado (9 ounces), puréed just before adding
1 medium avocado (9 ounces), diced just before adding
1 large shallot, minced

2 tablespoons fresh lemon juice
2 tablespoons mayonnaise
½ teaspoon salt
Dash of hot pepper sauce
Freshly ground black pepper

Combine all ingredients with 1 tablespoon dissolved gelatin. Taste and adjust seasoning. Gently spread mixture evenly over egg.

SOUR CREAM AND ONION LAYER:

1 cup sour cream
¼ cup minced onion
1 (3½ or 4-ounce) jar black or red caviar

Fresh lemon juice
Thinly sliced pumpernickel bread

Mix sour cream, onion and remaining 2 tablespoons gelatin. Spread carefully over avocado layer. Cover dish tightly with plastic wrap and refrigerate overnight.

CONTINUED

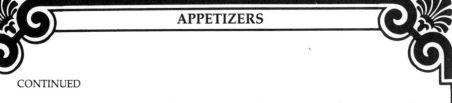

CONTINUED

Just before serving, place caviar in fine sieve and rinse gently under cold running water. Sprinkle with lemon juice. Drain. Lift mold out of dish using foil extensions as "handles." Transfer mold to serving dish using wide spatula. Spread caviar over top. Serve with thin slices of dark pumpernickel bread. Serves 12–16.

Enjoy!

Texas Shrimp Pâté

1 (10-ounce) can tomato soup, undiluted
1 package plain gelatin
3 tablespoons cold water
1 (8-ounce) package cream cheese, softened
¾ cup mayonnaise

1 small onion, grated
1 cup celery, chopped fine
Dash cayenne pepper
1 small can shrimp, drained and chopped or 1 cup cooked shrimp
Parsley sprigs

Heat soup. Remove from heat. Dissolve gelatin in cold water. Add to soup. Stir well. Add all ingredients except parsley and mix well. Spoon into oiled 4 cup mold. I use a Texas-shaped cake pan. Chill. Unmold and garnish with parsley, serve with crackers.

Variations: You may substitute 1 can of mushroom soup for the tomato soup and 1 small can crab meat, flaked, for the shrimp, and spoon into an oiled fish mold.

A Different Taste of Paris

Texas Crab Grass

½ cup butter
½ medium onion, finely chopped
1 package frozen chopped
  spinach, cooked and drained

1 (7-ounce) can crabmeat
¾ cup Parmesan cheese, grated
Melba rounds or crackers

Slowly melt butter in heavy saucepan. Add onion and sauté until soft. Add spinach to onion mixture. Add crabmeat and cheese. Transfer to chafing dish and serve with Melba rounds.

Noted Cookery

Crab Mousse

2 cans white crab meat
2 tablespoons plain gelatin
¼ cup cold water
2 (3-ounce) packages cream
  cheese
1 can mushroom soup

1 cup mayonnaise
1 small onion, grated
1 tablespoon Worcestershire
  sauce
½ teaspoon salt
1 cup chopped celery

Dissolve gelatin in cold water. Put soup, mayonnaise, onion, cream cheese in double boiler. Mix well. Add gelatin mixture. Stir until all is dissolved. Cool. Drain crab; add celery and combine all. Pour into a mold. Chill until firm. Serve with crackers.

Scrumptious

Crab Dip à la Sarah Smith

2 pounds crab meat
1 teaspoon powdered sugar
Lawry's Seasoned Salt, to taste
3 (8-ounce) packages cream
  cheese

½ cup mayonnaise
1 clove garlic, minced
½ cup white wine
2 teaspoons prepared mustard

Combine all ingredients except crab meat, in the top of a double boiler. Heat and stir until smooth. Add crab meat. Serves 50 as a dip.

The Galveston Island Cookbook

Oyster Roll

1 (8-ounce) package cream cheese
1 tablespoon mayonnaise
3½–4 ounces smoked oysters

1 teaspoon lemon juice
Chopped parsley
Paprika

Cream the cheese and mayonnaise, and spread thinly on an 8 × 12-inch piece of waxed paper. Place the cheese mixture on a cookie sheet and refrigerate overnight. Drain the oysters, chop finely and add the lemon juice. Take cheese from the refrigerator for a few minutes, until it just begins to soften. Spread oysters on the cheese and roll the cheese up, using a spatula to get it started, and pulling the paper off as the cheese rolls up. Put the roll on a tray, sprinkle the top with parsley and paprika, and surround the roll with crackers and a butter spreader.

San Angelo Junior League Cookbook

Snail Butter (Escargots)

1 (6-ounce) can snails (escargots)
2 cups Burgundy wine
1 pound butter
10–15 cloves garlic, crushed
   (pressed)

½ large bunch parsley, finely
   chopped
½ cup bread crumbs

Simmer snails in wine 10 or 15 minutes to flavor. Melt butter, add garlic and crumbs. Simmer to blend and develop flavor. To serve, place desired number of snails in a small bowl, cover with snail butter and top with a slice of French bread for "sopping". Number of servings depends on number of snails per serving.

San Antonio Conservation Society Cookbook

Salmon Party Log

1 pound can salmon	1 teaspoon horseradish
1 (8-ounce) package cream cheese	¼ teaspoon liquid smoke
1 tablespoon lemon juice	½ cup chopped pecans
2 teaspoons grated onion	3 tablespoons chopped parsley

Drain and flake salmon removing skin and bones. Combine salmon with next six ingredients. Mix thoroughly and chill several hours. Combine pecans and parsley. Shape salmon mixture into 8 × 2-inch logs and roll in nut mixture.

(Gerald Irons) *The Woodlands Celebrity Cookbook*

Mushroom Croustades

24 slices white bread, very thinly sliced	Soft butter

Cut 24 croustades, using a 3-inch cutter, fluted or plain. Coat each heavily with butter. Fit bread into tiny muffin tins. Bake in a 400° oven for 10 minutes. Do not over brown.

FILLING: MUSHROOM DUXELLES

4 tablespoons butter	½ teaspoon salt
3 tablespoons finely chopped green onions	¼ teaspoon cayenne
½ pound mushrooms, chopped	1 tablespoon finely chopped chives
2 tablespoons flour	½ teaspoon lemon juice
1 cup heavy cream	2 tablespoons Parmesan cheese

Heat butter until foam subsides. Add onions and sauté for 4 minutes. Stir in mushrooms. Sauté until moisture evaporates. Remove from heat. Sprinkle in flour. Stir. Add cream. Bring to a boil and simmer 1 minute. Add salt, cayenne, chives, and lemon juice. Refrigerate. Spoon into croustades. Sprinkle with cheese and dot with butter. Bake in a 350° oven for 10 minutes. Freezes beautifully. Serves 8–12.

Amarillo Junior League Cookbook

Duxelles (dukes ELL)—A combination of mushrooms, chopped shallots, and herbs, simmered in butter. It has the consistency of a hash, and is often used to flavor sauces, soups, and stuffings.

Spicy Stuffed Mushrooms

36 mushrooms (about 1½
   pounds—silver dollar size)
1 stick butter or margarine
1 bunch green onions
8 ounces cream cheese, softened
½ teaspoon garlic powder
1 tablespoon Worcestershire
   sauce

¼ cup nuts (pecans or walnuts),
   finely chopped
½ teaspoon cayenne pepper
   (more or less to taste)
1 tablespoon anchovy paste (or
   mash 3-4 filets)
Parsley sprigs
Paprika

Clean mushrooms with damp cloth. Carefully snip off stems (save for another use). Melt ½ stick butter in large heavy skillet and sauté half of onions about 3 minutes. Add (just one layer at a time) mushrooms and very lightly sauté about 2–3 minutes on each side. Carefully remove and place "cup side up" on large cookie sheet. Repeat process for remainder of mushrooms. Mix softened cream cheese until fluffy. Add remainder of ingredients as well as the sautéed onions from skillet.

Mound filling in cups of mushrooms using teaspoon. Garnish with sprig of parsley and paprika. Broil amount desired until bubbly, about 5 minutes. Yields 36. Freezes.

All of the directions, prior to broiling, may be done in advance of serving time. The mushrooms should then be covered and refrigerated or frozen. Allow them to reach room temperature before broiling. Serve hot, with a napkin!

La Piñata

Barbecued Pecans

2 tablespoons margarine
¼ cup Worcestershire sauce
1 tablespoon ketchup

2 dashes of hot sauce
4 cups pecan halves
Salt

Melt margarine in a large saucepan, add Worcestershire sauce, ketchup and hot sauce. Stir in pecans. Spoon into glass baking dish and spread evenly. Toast at 400° about 20 minutes, stirring frequently. Turn out on absorbent towels and sprinkle with salt.

The Dallas Pecan Cookbook

Deep Fried Mushrooms

1 pound fresh mushrooms	Flour
2 eggs, slightly beaten	Bread crumbs

Wash and clean mushrooms. Cut large ones in half. Dip in flour, eggs and bread crumbs. Deep fry in oil. Serve with mustard dip.

MUSTARD DIP FOR VEGETABLES AND FRIED MUSHROOMS:

1 cup sour cream	1 clove garlic
1 cup Miracle Whip salad dressing	Dash salt
	3 dashes Worcestershire sauce
3 tablespoons Dijon mustard	Paprika
¼ cup chopped onion	

Combine all ingredients. Sprinkle paprika on top. Serve with raw vegetables. Delicious with fried mushrooms.

Hullabaloo in the Kitchen

Waikiki Meatballs

1½ pounds ground beef	2 tablespoons cornstarch
⅔ cup cracker crumbs	½ cup brown sugar
⅓ cup minced onions	1 (13½-ounce) can pineapple
1 egg	tidbits, drain and reserve syrup
1½ teaspoons salt	⅓ cup vinegar
¼ teaspoon ginger	1 tablespoon soy sauce
¼ cup milk	⅓ cup chopped green pepper
1 tablespoon shortening	

Mix thoroughly beef, crumbs, onion, egg, salt, ginger and milk. Shape mixture into ½-inch balls. Melt shortening in large skillet. Brown and cook meatballs, until done. Remove meatballs and keep warm. Pour fat from skillet. Mix cornstarch and sugar. Stir in reserved pineapple syrup, vinegar and soy sauce until smooth. Pour into skillet, cook over medium heat, stirring constantly, until mixture thickens and boils. Add meatballs, pineapple tidbits and green pepper. Heat thoroughly. Can be stored and/or frozen in plastic sealed bags. Serves 6 (main dish); 10–12 (hors d'oeuvres).

Amarillo Junior League Cookbook

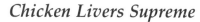

Chicken Livers Supreme

1 pound chicken livers, fresh or frozen
1 (8-ounce) can water chestnuts, sliced ⅛-inch thick
1 pound bacon
5 ounces soy sauce
2 tablespoons honey

2 ounces bourbon
1 teaspoon garlic powder
1 (10-ounce) jar plum jelly
Lemon juice
¼ teaspoon vinegar
¼ teaspoon dry mustard

Slice chicken livers ¼-inch thick. Wrap ½ slice bacon around chicken liver and water chestnut slice, and secure with a toothpick. Marinate the livers in a mixture of the soy sauce, honey, bourbon and garlic powder for five hours, basting often. Drain marinade and bake livers for 45 minutes at 350°. Drain grease from pan twice during baking or cook on a rack. Make a sauce by heating plum jelly and adding lemon juice until it is sour. Mix vinegar and dry mustard into a paste and add to jelly. Serves 15–20.

San Angelo Junior League Cookbook

Mock Pâté

1 pound Braunschweiger, room temperature
1 (8-ounce) carton sour cream
1 (8-ounce) package cream cheese

1 package green onion dip mix
Dill and almonds
Nuts

Mix first four ingredients and season with dill to taste. Chill, mold into ball or log and decorate with nuts.

Tempting Traditions

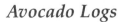

Avocado Logs

1 cup mashed avocado
1½ cups dry-roasted cashew nuts,
   chopped
8 ounces cream cheese, softened
½ cup sharp Cheddar cheese,
   grated
2 teaspoons lime juice

1 garlic clove, crushed and
   minced
½ teaspoon Worcestershire sauce
½ teaspoon salt
Dash Tabasco
Paprika

Combine all ingredients except paprika, and mix well. Cover mixture and refrigerate 30 minutes. Divide mixture in half and shape each into roll. Sprinkle waxed paper with paprika, turning roll to cover with paprika. Wrap each roll in foil and refrigerate until ready to serve. Slice and serve with crackers. May be made up to 2 days ahead of serving. Yields 2 logs.

Of Magnolia and Mesquite

Dream Fruit Dip

12 ounces cream cheese
1 cup confectioners' sugar,
   unsifted
1 (7-ounce) jar marshmallow
   creme
1 cup sour cream

2 teaspoons vanilla extract
2 teaspoons almond extract
2 teaspoons cinnamon
2 tablespoons cognac (optional)

In small bowl of electric mixer cream the cheese until soft and smooth. Add the confectioners' sugar and beat until well blended. Add the sour cream and the rest of the ingredients. Blend just until well combined. Place in a pretty bowl. Cover and chill several hours before serving. Just before serving place in the center of an attractive large platter. Surround bowl with a variety of fresh fruits, bananas, strawberries, cherries, honeydew melon balls, cantaloupe balls, grapes, pineapple chunks and apple slices.

My friends love this dip. It is great for parties.

Sweets. . . . From Marina With Love . . . .

Salads

Bastrop State Park, east of Austin, offers 3,350 acres of "Lost Pines" isolated far from vast piney woods of East Texas.

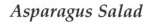

Asparagus Salad

1 tablespoon butter	1 can white asparagus (drain and
2 tablespoons flour	reserve ½ cup of the liquid)
Juice of 1 lemon	4 eggs
Salt and pepper to taste	½ pint heavy cream, whipped
1 envelope unflavored gelatin	

In the top of a double boiler, melt butter and add flour, lemon juice, salt and pepper. Dissolve gelatin in the liquid from the asparagus and add to mixture. Beat the eggs and add. When cool, fold in the cream. Arrange the asparagus in the bottom of a dish. Pour mixture over and refrigerate. To serve, cut into squares and top with homemade mayonnaise. Serves 8.

The Galveston Island Cookbook

Mexican Congealed Salad

2 tablespoons unflavored gelatin	½ cup minced onion
1 cup cold water	2 large avocados
2 (10½-ounce) cans condensed	2 tablespoons lemon juice
tomato soup	1 teaspoon ground cumin
2 tablespoons vinegar	1 teaspoon chili powder
8 drops Tabasco	1 cup mayonnaise
2 tomatoes, peeled and chopped	Lettuce
1 cup finely chopped bell peppers	

Soften gelatin in water; blend in soup, vinegar, 4 dashes of Tabasco. Heat and stir until gelatin dissolves. Chill until slightly firm; fold in tomato, bell pepper, onion; pour into two 3-cup ring molds, or 9 × 13 Pyrex dish; chill until firm. Mash avocado, add lemon juice, cumin, chili powder, 4 dashes Tabasco. Blend and correct seasonings. Stir in mayonnaise. Arrange aspic on lettuce and spread generously with avocado salad. The aspic may be doubled to serve approximately 24. (It is not necessary to double avocados.)

The Cottage Kitchen Cookbook

Cumin (CUHM in) or *comino* (coh MEE noh)—An herb plant whose seeds are used as a flavoring. Cumin is a member of the parsley family.

Molded Gazpacho Salad with Avocado Cream

GAZPACHO SALAD:

2 envelopes gelatin
4½ cups tomato juice, divided
¼ cup wine vinegar
1 clove garlic, crushed
2 teaspoons salt
¼ teaspoon pepper
Dash of cayenne pepper
2 large tomatoes, peeled, chopped, and drained
½ cup finely chopped green onion
¾ cup finely chopped green pepper
¾ cup peeled, finely chopped cucumber, drained
¼ cup finely chopped pimiento
Parsley

Soften gelatin in 1 cup tomato juice for 5 minutes. Heat until mixture simmers and gelatin is dissolved. Remove from heat and add remaining tomato juice, vinegar, garlic, salt, pepper, and cayenne. Chill until mixture begins to set. Fold in tomatoes, onion, green pepper, cucumber, and pimiento. Pour into a greased 6-cup ring mold. Chill about 3 hours or until firm. Unmold salad, garnish with parsley, and serve with Avocado Cream. Serves 6–8.

AVOCADO CREAM:

⅓ cup mashed avocado
½ cup sour cream
½ teaspoon salt
Dash of cayenne pepper

Combine ingredients and blend well.

This recipe is particularly popular with men.

Flavors

Gazpacho (gahz PAH choh)—A cold vegetable soup, one that usually includes onions, garlic, green peppers, tomatoes and cucumbers.

Squash Salad

5 medium squash (yellow, green
  or mixed)
½ cup thinly sliced onion
½ cup chopped celery
½ cup green pepper, chopped
1 clove garlic, crushed (or garlic
  powder)

2 tablespoons wine vinegar
¾ cup sugar (or less)
1 teaspoon salt
½ teaspoon pepper
⅓ cup salad oil
⅔ cup cider vinegar

Combine squash which has been thinly sliced, onion, celery and pepper; toss lightly. Combine all other ingredients; stir well. Spoon over vegetables. Chill 12 hours, stirring occasionally.

Note: Sugar substitute can be used instead of sugar.

The Pride of Texas

Fantastic Cold Green Bean Salad

½ cup olive oil
⅛ cup white wine vinegar
1½ tablespoons lemon juice
¼ teaspoon paprika
¼ teaspoon dry mustard
1½ teaspoons dill weed
2 (1-pound) cans green beans (cut
  or whole)

Salt and pepper to taste
½ cup mayonnaise
4 tablespoons sour cream
¼ cup bleu cheese
2 bunches green onions, chopped
1½–2 cucumbers, sliced

Make a dressing from the olive oil, white wine vinegar, lemon juice, paprika, dry mustard, dill weed, salt and pepper. Add the mayonnaise, sour cream, and bleu cheese to the above mixture. Pour over beans and marinate two hours before serving. Add the green onions and cucumber and toss lightly. Serves 6–8.

Entertaining at Aldredge House

Shoepeg Corn Salad

1 (16-ounce) can French-style
   beans, drained
1 (16-ounce) can shoepeg corn,
   drained
1 (16-ounce) can small peas,
   drained

1 cup celery, chopped
3 or 4 onions, chopped
1 (4-ounce) jar pimientos
1 green pepper, chopped

Combine all vegetables. Pour sauce over vegetables. Refrigerate for 24 hours before serving. "Keeps forever!"

SAUCE:
1 cup sugar
½ cup cooking oil

¾ cup vinegar
Salt and pepper to taste

Mix ingredients. Bring to boil. Cool slightly.

Tasteful Traditions

Stuffed Lettuce Salad

1 firm head of lettuce
½ cup Cheddar cheese, grated
½ cup mayonnaise
¼ teaspoon curry powder

1 cup ham, chopped
⅓ cup celery, chopped
1 pimiento, diced
⅛ cup fresh parsley, snipped

Wash and drain a firm head of lettuce. At the core end cut a circle out. Continue cutting down to within ½ inch of the top of the head. Then hollow out. Blend Cheddar cheese, mayonnaise, curry powder. Stir in ham, celery, pimiento and parsley. Pack mixture solidly into lettuce. Tie a string around lettuce to hold in place. Chill until firm. Serve in slices with French dressing. This recipe is nice for lunch. Serves 4–6.

A Different Taste of Paris

Spinach Salad with Mango Chutney Dressing

2 heads spinach torn in bite-size
  pieces
4 green onions, sliced
½ can ripe olives, halved

Cracked pepper and salt
1 (4-ounce) can mandarin orange
  slices, drained

Combine ingredients and serve with Mango Chutney Salad Dressing.

MANGO CHUTNEY SALAD DRESSING:

17 ounces mango chutney
2 teaspoons minced garlic
1½ tablespoons stone ground
  mustard

1 cup red wine vinegar
1 cup vegetable oil
Raisins (optional)

Chop chutney in blender or food processor. Blend in garlic, mustard and vinegar. Add oil. Let stand overnight. Serve dressing over spinach. Makes 3 cups.

My greatest salvation from entertaining failure came when I was a bride of 3 months and entertaining our first couple who had been married 10 years. I was tossing the salad and the bowl fell to the floor—spilling all of the contents. With horror I looked at my female guest who looked critically at the floor, scooped up the salad and placed it back into the bowl. She responded, 'The floor looks clean and you did say it was a tossed salad.' "

A Doctor's Prescription for Gourmet Cooking

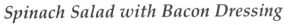

Spinach Salad with Bacon Dressing

1½ pounds fresh spinach leaves, tender, washed, torn

½ cup Bacon Dressing
2 eggs, hard-boiled, shredded

In a salad bowl, toss spinach with Bacon Dressing until leaves are well coated. Divide in salad plates and top each with shredded egg.

BACON DRESSING:

1 slice bacon, very crisp, cooled and blotted
1½ teaspoons red-wine vinegar
½ teaspoon hickory-smoked salt

¼ teaspoon dry mustard
1 tablespoon water
5 tablespoons vegetable oil

Crumble the crisp bacon and add it to the vinegar in a jar with a tight lid. Add the hickory-smoked salt and dry mustard. Mix until the salt is dissolved. Add water and oil. Cover jar tightly and shake vigorously for 30 seconds. Store covered in refrigerator. Makes ¼–½ cup. Yields 4–6 servings.

La Piñata

Rice Salad

1 cup Minute Rice, cooked with ½ cup water and ½ cup Italian dressing
1 (10-ounce) package frozen English peas, cooked and drained
1 small cucumber, grated

1 bunch green onions, chopped
½ cup mayonnaise
1 small jar ripe olives, sliced with small amount of juice
Chopped parsley
1 (2½-ounce) jar sliced mushrooms, drained

Mix all ingredients together; chill.

Note: Best when made early in the day for evening, or night before if served at lunch. Serves 4.

Enjoy!

Right-in-the-Skillet Potato Salad

2 pounds potatoes
6 slices bacon
¼ cup bacon drippings
1½ tablespoons flour
1 cup water
⅓ cup vinegar
1¾ teaspoons salt

⅛ teaspoon pepper
1 tablespoon sugar
1 head romaine, broken
1 cup celery, cut
6 radishes, sliced thin
1 medium onion, chopped
2 teaspoons celery seed

1. Cook potatoes in jackets, peel and slice.
2. Cook bacon, drain, and crumble. Add flour to bacon drippings in skillet, add water, stirring until smooth; add vinegar, salt, pepper, sugar.
3. Cook sauce over low heat until thickened.
4. Add 1 layer each of potato, then celery, romaine, onion, repeating until all are used. Pour on sauce.
5. Toss the salad with spatula taking care not to break potato slices. Sprinkle radishes, bacon, and celery seed over top. Keep warm while serving. Serves 6–8.

Morning, Noon and Night Cookbook

Hominy Bowl Salad

1 (16-ounce) can yellow hominy,
   drained
½ cup corn oil
3 tablespoons red wine vinegar
¼ cup minced onion
1½ teaspoons seasoned salt
⅛ teaspoon pepper

1 cup sliced celery
¼ cup chopped green pepper
¼ cup pimiento
1 head lettuce, torn into chunks
6 slices bacon, cooked and
   crumbled

Drain hominy and combine with oil, vinegar, onion, seasoned salt, and pepper. Chill several hours.

Just before serving, add celery, green pepper, and pimiento. Tear lettuce into chunks and add hominy mixture. Toss lightly. Add bacon and toss again. Yields 6 servings.

Flavor Favorites

Speedy Potato Salad
(Microwave)

1 (2-pound) bag frozen Potatoes
  O'Brien or hash browns
2 eggs
2 ribs celery, chopped
1 dill pickle, chopped
3 tablespoons pickle liquid

1 cup mayonnaise
2–3 tablespoons prepared
  mustard
1 teaspoon salt
½ teaspoon pepper

Make a 1-inch slit in bag of frozen Potatoes O'Brien and place on paper plate. Microwave on HIGH 13–15 minutes, turning bag upside down and redistributing contents every 5 minutes. Let stand 5 minutes.

Break eggs into 2 (6-ounce) custard cups. Pierce yolk twice with fork. Cover each with plastic wrap. Microwave on 50% (MEDIUM) 3 minutes, rotating each cup once. Let stand 5 minutes.

Chop celery, pickles and cooked eggs. Combine in large serving bowl with drained contents of bag and remaining ingredients. Chill 4 hours or more before serving. Serves 10–12. Keeps 3 days in refrigerator.

Microwave Know-How

Pasta Salad

1 box Fettucine Verde or spinach
   noodles (Mennucci)
2 quarts water
2 bouillon cubes
½ box cherry tomatoes, cut in
   halves
½ teaspoon Sugar Twin
¼ teaspoon only Puritan oil
1 tablespoon apple cider vinegar

¼ teaspoon rosemary
¼ teaspoon lemon-pepper
6 raw cauliflower flowerettes,
   sliced thin
6 broccoli flowerettes, sliced thin
1 bunch fresh green onions with
   some green
½ cup chopped parsley

Cook pasta in water with bouillon cubes—do not overcook. While pasta cooks, combine in refrigerator container cherry tomatoes, Sugar Twin, Puritan oil, vinegar, rosemary, lemon-pepper. Cover and let rest in refrigerator for 30 minutes. Prepare other vegetables.

When pasta is cooked, pour into colander, drain quickly and gently rinse with cold water. Drain thoroughly. Pour into serving salad bowl. With fork, separate pasta to prevent pack-sticking and quickly pour the prepared vegetables over pasta, lightly toss, then add tomatoes with seasoned juice. This makes all the dressing necessary. Lift pasta several times with salad fork and spoon to aerate and help mix the vegetables and dressing. Chill until serving.

Serve wheat Parmesan sticks (Creole Cheese Sticks) with this instead of fat slices of bread and butter. With pasta, no bread is needed, but the toasted fingers will satisfy the thought of needing bread.

La Galerie Perroquet Food Fare

Luncheon Salad Supreme

10 ounces chopped, cooked
   chicken (tuna may be
   substituted)
2 cups cooked rice
1 (8½-ounce) can small English
   peas
½ cup chopped onion

1 cup chopped or diced celery
1 teaspoon salt
½ teaspoon pepper
½ cup mayonnaise
8 medium tomatoes
Lettuce

Combine chicken with all ingredients except tomatoes, lettuce and dressing. Chill. Remove stem ends from tomatoes. Cut from top about ¾ of the way down each tomato in about 8 pieces. Spread tomatoes open on shredded lettuce or lettuce leaf. Fill with salad mixture and top with:

AVOCADO DRESSING:

1 avocado (I use two unless they
   are very large)
1 cup mayonnaise
1 cup sour cream
½ teaspoon pepper

½ teaspoon Worcestershire sauce
½ teaspoon onion juice
¼ teaspoon garlic powder
½ teaspoon salt

Place all ingredients in blender container. Blend until smooth. Chill. (If prepared well ahead of serving time, place avocado seed in dressing to prevent turning dark).

A Taste of Victoria

Roquefort Dressing

1 (8-ounce) package cream cheese
¼ cup buttermilk
1 cup sour cream
1 pint Hellman's mayonnaise
1 (3-ounce) Roquefort cheese

3 cloves garlic, pressed
1 tablespoon Worcestershire
   sauce
1 tablespoon minced onion

Mix all ingredients in blender and chill before topping green salad or baked potato. Yields 1 quart.

Trading Secrets

A Truly Different Chicken Salad

8 chicken breast halves, skin removed
1 tablespoon lemon juice
½ teaspoon salt
¾ cup vinaigrette dressing
1 cup mayonnaise

2 teaspoons tarragon, fresh, chopped *or* 1 teaspoon dried
1 lemon rind, grated
1 bunch of lettuce, red-tip, curly leaf, etc.

Put the chicken breasts into a Pyrex dish or pan in a single layer. Mix the lemon juice and salt and pour over the chicken. Cover and bake for 30 minutes at 400°. Cool and cut chicken into small, bite-sized pieces. Marinate it in the vinaigrette dressing for about 3 hours at room temperature. Mix the mayonnaise, tarragon and lemon rind. Combine with the drained chicken pieces. Chill. When ready to serve, put salad on large lettuce leaves. Serves 8.

VINAIGRETTE DRESSING:

½ teaspoon dried parsley
¼ teaspoon basil
¼ teaspoon dried chives
¾ teaspoon salt
½ teaspoon pepper

1 clove garlic, crushed
1 teaspoon dry mustard
¼ cup white wine vinegar
½ cup olive oil
¼ cup salad oil

Mix all of the ingredients by shaking in a jar. Chill. Shake well before serving.

Chicken salad recipes are usually good, but this one is so different from the rest that it is now our favorite.

Of Magnolia and Mesquite

Exotic Symphonic Chicken Salad

3 cups cooked chicken or turkey,
    cut in large chunks
2 teaspoons onion, grated
2 cups celery, diced
1 cup slivered almonds or pecans,
    chopped
2 cups seedless green grapes
2 (6-ounce) cans water chestnuts,
    drained and chopped

2 cups apples, pared and diced
½ cup mayonnaise
⅓ cup wine
1 tablespoon salt
⅛ teaspoon pepper
3 avocados
Lemon juice

Combine chicken, onion, celery, almonds, grapes, water chest-nuts and apples. Mix mayonnaise, wine, salt and pepper; toss with chicken mixture. Refrigerate until served. Cut avocados in half, seed and sprinkle with lemon juice just before serving. Serve salad in avocado halves, topped with a few grapes. Serves 6.

Noted Cookery

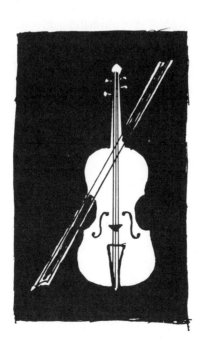

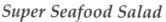

Super Seafood Salad

1½ cups fresh white crabmeat
1½ cups medium shrimp, cooked, shelled, and deveined
1¼ cups 1-inch chunks fresh pineapple
2 tablespoons chutney
1 cup celery, sliced
1¼ cups green onions, sliced (including some tops)

1 cup sliced water chestnuts
½ cup toasted almonds, slivered
1¼ cups good quality mayonnaise (not salad dressing)
½ cup sour cream plus 2 tablespoons
1¼ teaspoons curry powder

1. Using a large bowl, combine crabmeat, shrimp, pineapple, chutney, celery, green onions, water chestnuts, and almonds. Toss together lightly. Cover and refrigerate.

2. In a small bowl, combine mayonnaise, sour cream, and curry. Mix well. Cover and refrigerate for at least 2 hours.

3. An hour before serving, pour dressing over seafood and mix lightly, making sure all ingredients are covered thoroughly. Let set in refrigerator for an hour for flavors to set.

4. Serve in tomato halves, avocado halves, or on a bed of lettuce. Yields 6–8 servings. Preparation time: 45 minutes, plus 1 hour set time.

Rare Collection

Shrimp Filled Avocado Shells

1 avocado, halved and seeded
Fresh lemon or lime juice
½ cup cooked small shrimp
¼ cup minced water chestnuts
2 green onions, minced

2–3 tablespoons mayonnaise
½–1 teaspoon curry powder to taste
Salt and freshly ground pepper
Lettuce leaves

Sprinkle cut edges of avocado with lemon or lime juice. Combine all remaining ingredients *except* lettuce and toss lightly. Mound in avocado halves. Set each on lettuce-lined plate. Cover and chill until ready to serve. Serves 2.

Spindletop International Cooks

Scandinavian Salad

This recipe was found in an old collection of recipes given to my wife Carolyn by her late grandmother. Over 20 years ago Scandinavian Salad was published along with a monthly electric bill to residents in a small West Texas Community, and also was once named prize winner of the *Fort Worth Star-Telegram's* annual recipe contest.

2 cups crab meat	1 tablespoon minced onion
2 hard cooked eggs	½ cup chopped celery
2 diced apples	¼ cup chopped green pepper
2 cups cold diced potatoes	1 cup seedless raisins

Cut all vegetables into cubes and mix with eggs, apples, crab meat and raisins. For a dressing use 1 cup of mayonnaise with ½ cup of whipped cream. Add a dash of pepper and salt to taste; then add a squeeze of lemon juice. Pour dressing over the salad and toss lightly. Serve very cold.

(Tom Hannon) *The Woodlands Celebrity Cookbook*

Taco Salad

1 pound lean ground beef	2 tomatoes, chopped
1 tablespoon chili powder	½ cup onion, chopped
½ teaspoon cumin	1 cup grated sharp cheese
1 clove garlic, pressed	1½ heads iceburg lettuce
½ teaspoon oregano	1½ cups crushed Fritos
¼ teaspoon dry red pepper	2 avocados, peeled and sliced

Sauté the beef with the seasonings until done. Drain very well. Keep at room temperature. Combine and toss all the ingredients with the dressing. Dressing: Mix 2 tablespoons lemon juice and ½ cup of mayonnaise.

A great and relatively thinning luncheon—a nice change from chef salad.

It's a Long Way to Guacamole

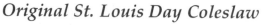

Original St. Louis Day Coleslaw

The beautiful Gothic church in Castroville is the third St. Louis church on this site and is the result of the work of a dedicated priest, Father Peter Richard. On August 25, 1870, special services were celebrated for the first time as the sun streamed through the beautiful stained-glass windows. Each year, on the Sunday closest to August 25, Castrovillians honor this memorable service with a festival that proves how dearly Alsatians love good food and drink. St. Louis Day draws thousands of visitors.

The townsfolk prepare a giant Alsatian sausage and barbecue meal, and family recipes are featured at the numerous food booths scattered throughout Koenig Park. If you can't be in Castroville for this memorable feast, you can share the original coleslaw as prepared by Lora Mae McVay at the Alsatian Restaurant.

1 large head cabbage, shredded very fine	1 green pepper, chopped
1 onion, chopped	20 stuffed olives
	1 cup sugar

Combine first four ingredients and pour sugar over vegetables. Let stand 15 minutes.

DRESSING:

1 cup white vinegar	1 tablespoon salt
1 tablespoon celery seed	1 tablespoon prepared mustard
½ cup salad oil	

Combine ingredients and pour over vegetables. Serves 6–8.
  (The Landmark Inn, Castroville) *Texas Historic Inns Cookbook*

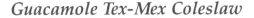

Guacamole Tex-Mex Coleslaw

3 ripe avocados, mashed
2 tablespoons lemon juice
6 cups shredded cabbage
1 cup finely chopped onion
1 cup finely chopped green
  pepper
½ cup mayonnaise or salad
  dressing

1 tablespoon sugar
1 tablespoon tarragon vinegar
½ teaspoon salt
¼ teaspoon garlic powder
¼ teaspoon pepper
Dash of hot sauce
Dash of Worcestershire sauce
¼ teaspoon paprika

Combine in large bowl, mixing well avocados and lemon juice. Add cabbage, onion, and green pepper. Mix well. Combine mayonnaise or salad dressing, sugar, vinegar, salt, garlic powder, pepper, hot sauce and Worcestershire sauce. Stir into mixture. Sprinkle with paprika. Yields 8–10 servings.

Calf Fries to Caviar

 Tex-Mex—The term used to describe Texans' version of Mexican cooking.

Audre's Lime Salad

20 regular size marshmallows
2 cups water
1 small package lime Jello
1 (No. 2) can crushed pineapple

1 cup grated Cheddar cheese
1 cup chopped pecans
½ pint whipped cream

Melt marshmallows in hot water. Add Jello and stir until dissolved. Set in refrigerator until partially set. Add other ingredients, adding whipped cream last. Fold in well. Pour into lightly oiled mold and let set.

A Taste of Victoria

Fruit Salad

Vinaigrette dressings are surprisingly good with many fruits as well as vegetables for an interesting and refreshing salad to accompany both tortilla specialties or grilled entrées. This salad pairs well with brunch dishes from egg-and-bacon tacos to your favorite huevos rancheros.

DRESSING:

3 tablespoons white wine vinegar	1 shallot, finely minced
2 tablespoons fresh orange or grapefruit juice	½ teaspoon salt
½ cup safflower oil	¼ teaspoon dry mustard
	Pinch of white pepper

In a blender or a food processor fitted with a metal blade, combine the dressing ingredients and set aside.

SALAD:

1 head Bibb lettuce	1 cup fresh berries, preferably
2 cups (about 4 grapefruits) pink grapefruit sections	raspberries or thickly sliced strawberries
2 papayas, sliced	2 avocados, sliced

Mist the lettuce to clean and wipe dry. Line 4 cold salad plates with lettuce leaves. Arrange the fruits and avocado sections on the lettuce, with the berries placed at random. Drizzle with dressing just prior to serving. Yields 4 servings.

Storage, Freezing, and Advance Preparation: All the fruits, except the avocados, may be sliced about 2 hours ahead. Do not add the dressing or arrange the salad until serving time, as the fruits will lose their crisp texture and may become mushy.

Creative Mexican Cooking

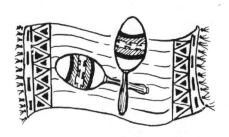

Holiday Cranberry Salad

2 (3-ounce) packages cream
  cheese
2 tablespoons mayonnaise
2 tablespoons sugar
1 cup canned whole cranberry
  sauce

1 cup crushed pineapple
½ cup chopped nuts
1 cup whipping cream, whipped
½ cup confectioners' sugar
1 teaspoon vanilla

Soften cream cheese. Blend with mayonnaise and sugar. Add cranberry sauce, pineapple and nuts. Fold in cream which has been whipped with confectioners' sugar. Add vanilla. Pour into 9 × 13-inch container and freeze 6 hours. Cut into squares. Serves 6–8 people. Triple recipe for 3-quart container. Keeps in freezer. Seal well. This dish does not stay around long.

Beautiful. May be served as a salad or a dessert.

A Doctor's Prescription for Gourmet Cooking

Mango Congealed Salad

1 large can mangoes, juice and all
1 large bar Philadelphia cream
  cheese

½ cup orange juice
2 cups boiling water
2 small packages lemon Jello

Mix Jello with 2 cups boiling water. Place mangoes and cream cheese in blender and blend well. Add Jello and orange juice. Pour into individual molds or perhaps a bundt pan (to be sliced at serving time) and refrigerate until ready to use. Serve on lettuce leaves. (1 tablespoon Knox plain gelatin may be added if served at a buffet and might be standing a while—just to assure firmness.) Garnish with avocado and ruby red grapefruit slices for variety. Serves 12–14.

Spindletop International Cooks

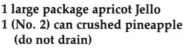

Apricot Mousse
A Tea House Favorite

1 large package apricot Jello
1 (No. 2) can crushed pineapple
  (do not drain)
¾ cup sugar

2 small jars apricot baby food
1 (8-ounce) package cream cheese
1 large can evaporated milk,
  chilled 2 or 3 hours

Mix Jello, pineapple and sugar and cook for about 5 minutes. Add cream cheese, cook until cheese is melted. Add baby food. Cool . . . then whip milk and combine. Pour into 9 × 12-inch Pyrex dish greased with oleo. Refrigerate. When ready to serve, cut into squares and place on a lettuce leaf.

Collectibles II

Paradise Fruit Salad

1 (15½-ounce) can pineapple
  chunks
1 (11-ounce) can mandarin
  oranges

2 kiwi fruits
1 cup strawberries
2 sliced bananas
½ cup coconut, shredded

Drain canned fruit. Wash and slice kiwi fruits and strawberries. Mix all fruits except coconut; sprinkle one tablespoon coconut over each serving. Drizzle dressing over each.

DRESSING:
6 tablespoons coconut milk
2 tablespoons honey
2 tablespoons lime juice

Mix all ingredients for dressing together in a large jar and shake until well blended. Serves 8.

Lagniappe

Bread and Breakfast

Sunrise at resort campground in Big Thicket National Preserve.
North of Beaumont.

Huevos Rancheros
(Eggs Ranch Style)

1 can Rotel tomatoes and green chilies	2 ribs celery, chopped
1 small (14½-ounce) can whole tomatoes	4 slices bacon
1 medium onion, chopped	4 eggs
	Grated Cheddar cheese
	4 corn tortillas

Fry bacon crisp and put aside for later. Sauté onions and celery in 2 tablespoons of bacon drippings. Add both cans of tomatoes to the sautéed mixture. Let simmer till liquid cooks down some. Make a little "well" in the mixture for each egg. (Depending on size of skillet—you may be able to cook only 3 eggs at a time). Place a whole egg in each "well"; cover and let simmer till desired doneness. Serve each egg on a warm tortilla and cover with tomato mixture. Sprinkle grated cheese and crumbled bacon on top of each serving.

A Taste of Victoria

 Huevo (WAY boh)—The Spanish word for egg.

Avocado Omelet

6 farm fresh eggs	½ cup grated raw milk cheese
2 tablespoons water	½ cup chopped avocado
2 tablespoons raw milk butter	¼ cup alfalfa sprouts

Beat eggs; add water. Pour eggs into heated buttered skillet and cook on low-medium heat, gently lifting edges to let liquid run under, until all is set.

Spoon vegetables onto ½ of the omelet, top with cheese, and fold over. Remove to plate and serve. Yields 4 servings.

Nature's Kitchen

Brunch Eggs

1 cup (4-ounces) Canadian bacon, diced
¼ cup green onion, chopped
3 tablespoons butter or margarine
12 beaten eggs
1 (3-ounce) can mushroom pieces, drained
1 recipe Cheese Sauce
4 teaspoons butter or margarine, melted
2¼ cups soft bread crumbs (3 slices)
⅛ teaspoon paprika

In a large skillet, cook Canadian bacon and onion in the 3 tablespoons of butter until onion is tender but not brown. Add eggs and scramble just until set. Fold mushrooms and cooked eggs into cheese sauce. Turn into a 12×7×2-inch baking dish. Combine remaining melted butter, crumbs, and paprika, and sprinkle on top of eggs. Cover and chill until 30 minutes before serving. Bake, uncovered, in 350° oven for 30 minutes. Serves 10.

CHEESE SAUCE:
2 tablespoons butter
2 tablespoons all-purpose flour
½ teaspoon salt
⅛ teaspoon pepper
2 cups milk
1 cup (4-ounces) processed American cheese, shredded

Melt butter and blend in flour, salt and pepper. Slowly pour in milk, cooking and stirring constantly until thickened and smooth. Stir in cheese and stir until melted.

Cookin' Wise

Bad Hombre Eggs

2 tomatoes, sliced thin	Cooking oil
1 avocado, peeled, pitted, and sliced	4 corn tortillas
	Butter or margarine
Juice of half a lime	8 eggs
4 thin slices purple onion	Salt and pepper
1 cup shredded Longhorn cheese	Green chili salsa

Squeeze lime juice over avocado. Have tomatoes, avocado, onion, and cheese ready near the stove along with the salsa and salt and pepper. Warm four ovenproof dishes in the oven.

Heat about 1 tablespoon of oil in a 7-inch skillet. Using kitchen tongs, cook tortillas one at a time, turning once, until lightly brown and crisp. Add oil as needed. Remove to warmed plates. Pour out any remaining oil. Melt butter or margarine in skillet and break eggs into skillet two at a time. Fry them or scramble them, depending on your preference. Place cooked eggs on tortillas, salt and pepper to taste, then add toppings of tomato, avocado, salsa, onion, and finally cheese. Run under the broiler until cheese melts. Serve immediately. Feeds 4 in 20 minutes.

An American Gumbo

 Tortilla (tor TEE yah)—A thin pancake of masa.

Rave Eggs

2 cups butter
4 medium onions, finely chopped
2 cups sliced mushrooms
2 cups flour
16 cups half-and-half
4 cups Swiss cheese, grated
1 cup dry white wine
4 tablespoons Worcestershire
sauce
1 teaspoon salt, more to taste
1 teaspoon white pepper, more to
taste

4 pounds ham, cubed
4 pounds shrimp, cooked and
drained
4 (14-ounce) cans artichoke
hearts, drained and cut into
fourths
4 (8½-ounce) cans English peas,
drained
4 dozen hard-boiled eggs, peeled
and quartered
Paprika
Buttered bread crumbs

In very large saucepan, melt butter, add onions and cook until soft. Stir in mushrooms, sauté. Sprinkle flour over vegetables, stirring in well. Cook over low heat 5–6 minutes, stirring constantly. Slowly add cream, stirring constantly until mixture is smooth. Add cheese, wine, Worcestershire and pepper. Blend well. Correct seasonings. In four greased 13 × 9 inch Pyrex dishes arrange ham, shrimp, artichokes, peas, and eggs. Pour cheese sauce over, cover and bake at 275° for 1 hour. Remove cover, sprinkle with bread crumbs and paprika. Bake at 350° for 10–15 minutes. May be made day ahead. Return to room temperature before baking if made day ahead and refrigerated. Serves 50.

Of Magnolia and Mesquite

Saucy Eggs Mornay

6 thin slices ham
Butter or margarine
3 English muffins, split, buttered
  and toasted

6 eggs, poached
1 tablespoon chopped chives

Lightly brown ham in small amount of butter. Place ham slice on each muffin half and top with poached egg. Keep warm while preparing Mornay Sauce. Pour Mornay Sauce over eggs and sprinkle with chives. Serve immediately. Serves 3–6.

MORNAY SAUCE:
3 tablespoons butter or margarine
3 tablespoons flour
¾ teaspoon salt
¼ teaspoon nutmeg

Dash pepper
1 cup light cream
¼ cup dry white wine
⅓ cup shredded Swiss cheese

Melt butter in saucepan. Blend in flour, salt, nutmeg and pepper. Stir until smooth and bubbly. Add cream all at once and cook quickly, stirring constantly until mixture thickens and bubbles. Stir in wine. Add cheese and stir until melted. Use at once.

Becky's Brunch & Breakfast Book

Breakfast Enchiladas

5 eggs, beaten
2 tablespoons milk
¼ cup diced green chilies
Salt and pepper to taste

2 tablespoons butter or margarine
4 corn tortillas
¾ cup shredded Cheddar cheese

Preheat broiler. Combine eggs, milk, chilies, salt and pepper. In a skillet over medium-low heat, scramble egg mixture in melted butter. Cook until firm as desired. Dip tortillas 1 at a time into hot Enchilada Sauce until soft. Spoon ¼ of the eggs down center of each tortilla. Roll up and place, seam side down, in a single layer in a greased 10 × 6-inch glass baking dish. Bring remaining sauce to boil. Pour evenly over rolled tortillas; sprinkle with cheese. Broil about 4 inches from heat 2–3 minutes or until cheese melts. Serves 2.

CONTINUED

CONTINUED

ENCHILADA SAUCE:
1 small onion, chopped
½ cup chopped green pepper
1½ tablespoons cooking oil

1 (15-ounce) can tomato sauce
1½ teaspoons chili powder

In a small skillet over medium heat, sauté onion and green pepper in oil until onion is limp. Stir in tomato sauce and chili powder. Reduce heat to low and simmer while the eggs are cooking.

Becky's Brunch & Breakfast Book

Enchilada (ain chee LAH dah)—A corn tortilla, filled with cheese and shredded meat. The tortillas for enchiladas are fried lightly in oil so that they remain soft.

Migas

1 package corn tortillas
⅓ cup oil
2 cloves garlic, minced
1 medium onion, chopped
4 tomatoes, diced
¼ cup butter
2 dozen eggs
10 ounces medium sharp
 Cheddar cheese, grated

10 ounces Monterey Jack cheese,
 grated
Salt, pepper, and garlic powder
 to taste
Chorizo sausage (hot Mexican
 sausage)
Flour tortillas
Salsa

1. Fry corn tortillas in oil until crisp.
2. Sauté garlic, onions, and tomatoes in butter until tender.
3. Beat eggs with salt, pepper, and garlic powder to taste. Add egg mixture to tomato mixture.
4. Cook over medium-low heat until soft.
5. Crumble the fried tortilla chips. Add chips and both grated cheeses to egg mixture. Stir until cheeses melt and the chips soften.
6. Serve with Chorizo sausage, flour tortillas, and fresh salsa. Yields 10–12 large servings. Preparation time: 45 minutes.

Rare Collection

Eggs Maxmilian

Cappy's flavorful sauce is prepared without butter or oil, which makes it a low-calorie sauce, perfect for eggs, chicken, fish, or grilled meats. To save preparation time, you may use crisp tortilla shells or toasted English muffins in place of masa cups. If fresh masa is not easy to obtain, use masa harina, adding 1 teaspoon sugar and 1 tablespoon cornmeal to the package directions.

RANCHERO SAUCE:
1 (2½-pound) can whole tomatoes
1 onion, chopped
1 bell pepper, seeded and
  chopped
4 cloves garlic, minced
3 tomatoes, chopped
3–4 serrano chiles, finely minced

Snipped cilantro
1 cup water
4 ounces tomato paste
1½ teaspoons salt or to taste
½ teaspoon black pepper
½ teaspoon leaf oregano
½ teaspoon ground cumin

Drain all the juice from the canned tomatoes into a large saucepan. Roughly chop the tomatoes, combine with all the other vegetables, and bring to a boil.

Add water, tomato paste, and seasonings and return to a boil. Reduce heat and simmer for 20 minutes. Yields 5 cups sauce.

POACHED EGGS:
1 poached egg per serving
Butter

Poach the eggs and hold them at room temperature, brushed with butter, while preparing the masa cups.

FRESH MASA:
Fresh corn masa (about 1 ounce
  per mold)

Peanut oil for frying

Spray 3-inch fluted tin molds with a non-stick vegetable coating. Pinch off a ball of masa and then press into molds. Deep-fry, using tongs, in oil heated to 375°. The molds will sink to the bottom and, as the masa cooks, it will separate from the molds and float. Turn to fry both sides. Take care not to overcook or the masa cups may become tough. Drain on paper towels. Yields 8–10 servings.

Creative Mexican Cooking

Hot Cheese Grits

You simply cannot find a more southern dish than grits. Those Yankees who come down South turn up their noses at one of the best foods that ever originated in America. What would a slice of tender fried ham be without grits and redeye gravy? Some prefer grits with their breakfast eggs, because Mother always served them that way. And there is nothing better than a bowl of grits with melted butter and a touch of salt to start the day. There is quite an art to cooking grits so they aren't too watery and certainly not lumpy. The exact consistency may take a few practice cookings, but once you get the knack, you'll "Kiss My Grits!"

Grits have also become sophisticated. Here is Dorothy's recipe with sherry and green chilies.

2 cups quick grits
8 cups boiling water
1 teaspoon salt
1½ sticks margarine
8 ounces Kraft hot jalapeño
 cheese
16 ounces Kraft garlic cheese

2 eggs, beaten
2 tablespoons sherry
1 teaspoon Lea & Perrins
 Worcestershire sauce
1 teaspoon Tabasco sauce
2 (12-ounce) cans green chilies,
 chopped

Slowly stir grits into boiling water. Turn heat off. Add margarine and cheese to grits mixture. Cool.

Add eggs, sherry, Lea & Perrins, Tabasco, and chilies. Spoon mixture into greased baking dish and bake 1 hour at 300°.

Note: This freezes well. Water will appear on top, but just remix and reheat. Superb with ham or chicken. Serves 30.

(Lamplighter Inn, Floydada) *Texas Historic Inns Cookbook*

Sausage and Egg Brunch Bake

2 cups herb croutons
1 pound bulk sausage, cooked
  and well drained
4 eggs, lightly beaten
2½ cups milk

1 teaspoon dry mustard
1½ cups (6 ounces) shredded
  Cheddar cheese
1 (10¾-ounce) can cream of
  mushroom soup

Line bottom of greased 9×13-inch glass baking dish with croutons. Cover with sausage. Combine eggs, milk, mustard, cheese and soup. Pour over sausage. Run a knife cross-wise through mixture as you would to marble cake batter. Cover and refrigerate overnight. When ready to bake, preheat oven to 325°. Bake uncovered 1 hour and 15 minutes or until firm in center and brown on top. Let stand 5 minutes before cutting into squares. Serves 8.

Becky's Brunch & Breakfast Book

Farmer's Breakfast
Great for a change

6 slices bacon, cut into 2-inch
  pieces
3 medium-size potatoes, cooked,
  peeled, and cubed
¼ cup green bell pepper,
  chopped
¼ cup onion, chopped

1 cup Cheddar cheese, grated
6 raw eggs
1 teaspoon Knorr Swiss Aromat
  Seasoning for Meat
½ teaspoon salt
¼ teaspoon black pepper

1. In a large skillet using low heat, fry bacon until crisp; remove and drain bacon. Leave 3 tablespoons of bacon drippings in the skillet.
2. Add potatoes, peppers, and onions to the skillet and cook about 5 minutes or until potatoes are browned.
3. Sprinkle cheese over potatoes and stir until cheese melts.
4. Break eggs into skillet, add the seasonings, and stirring gently, cook mixture until eggs are done.
5. Sprinkle top with bacon pieces and serve. Serves 6.

Leaving Home

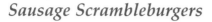

Sausage Scrambleburgers

½ pound bulk sausage
2 tablespoons chopped green pepper
2 tablespoons finely sliced green onion
4 eggs, beaten

4 tablespoons milk or cream
½ teaspoon salt
⅛ teaspoon pepper
2 onion rolls, split, buttered and toasted

Form sausage into 2 patties large enough to cover rolls. Fry in medium skillet until thoroughly cooked. Remove from skillet; drain on paper towels and keep warm. Drain all but 1 tablespoon of the sausage fat. Sauté green pepper and onion in reserved fat until tender, about 5 minutes. Combine eggs, milk or cream, salt and pepper; blend thoroughly. Pour egg mixture over vegetables. Scramble gently to keep well formed. Place sausage patties on bottom half of rolls; top with scrambled eggs and remaining roll halves. Serve immediately. Serves 2.

Variation: Cook the bulk sausage, breaking into small pieces. Proceed as recipe directs, returning sausage to the skillet when the egg mixture is added to the vegetables.

Becky's Brunch & Breakfast Book

Baked Mushroom Delight

½ pound fresh mushrooms, sliced
2 tablespoons butter or margarine
8 strips bacon, fried crisp, drained and crumbled

3 cups (12 ounces) shredded Monterey Jack cheese
8 eggs, beaten
Salt and pepper to taste

Preheat oven to 275°. Sauté mushrooms in butter; place on bottom of a well-greased 8-inch square baking dish. Top with bacon and then the cheese. Combine eggs, salt and pepper; pour over layered ingredients. Bake 45 minutes or until top is golden brown. Do not overcook. Serves 6–8.

To Prepare in Advance: Assemble up to the point of pouring the egg mixture over the layered ingredients. This "Delight" can also be frozen after baking and reheated.

Becky's Brunch & Breakfast Book

Spinach Roll-ups

OMELETS:

4 tablespoons flour	Olive oil
4 large eggs	Melted butter
4 tablespoons milk	Romano cheese
⅜ teaspoon salt	

Put the flour in a medium-sized bowl and add the eggs one by one, beating with a fork until all the eggs are in. Mix the milk, add the salt and beat again for moment.

FILLING:

1 pound fresh Swiss chard or spinach, or 1 (10-ounce) package frozen chopped spinach	4 tablespoons cream cheese
	1 tablespoon milk
	2 or 3 tablespoons unsalted butter, melted

If you use fresh chard or spinach, wash it thoroughly, discard the stems, cook in boiling salted water until tender, drain thoroughly. When the greens are cool enough, squeeze out the last of the water and chop well. If you use frozen spinach, cook it in boiling salted water until tender. Drain and squeeze dry.

Put the cheese in a medium-sized mixing bowl, add the milk and butter and mix well with a fork. Add the minced greens and mix again. Taste for salt and add a pinch if needed.

Heat a seasoned omelet pan, add a film of olive oil, and ladle in about ¼ cup of beaten eggs, or enough to make a very thin omelet. Keep the heat of the pan medium-low so that the omelet cooks slowly on the bottom side. When the top looks almost firm, put 2 or 3 tablespoons of filling in the center of the omelet. Roll the omelet up on itself, cook another ½ minute, and remove to a heated plate. Continue making and filling and rolling the omelets until all are done. Pour the melted butter over and sprinkle with Romano cheese.

(Don Nelson) *Houston Celebrity Cookbook*

Apple Pancakes

5 beaten farm fresh eggs
½ cup stone-ground whole wheat
   pastry flour
¼ cup non-instant milk powder
¾ cup plain raw milk yogurt

1 teaspoon pure vanilla
¼ teaspoon nutmeg
1 large unpeeled chopped apple
   (peel, if waxed)

Combine all ingredients except apple; mix lightly, add apple and spoon onto hot griddle. Bake until golden on both sides.

Serve hot with fruit, pure maple syrup or raw honey. Yields 4 servings.

Nature's Kitchen

Kartoffel Puffer
(Potato Pancakes)

6 medium potatoes, peeled
1 small onion, grated
3 eggs

¾ cup flour
2 teaspoons salt
Enough oil for frying

Grate potatoes coarsely into a bowl filled with cold water. This keeps potatoes from turning dark and removes some of the excess starch, making the potatoes crisper. In another bowl combine the onion, eggs, flour and salt. Drain potatoes, pressing out all liquid. Beat the potatoes into the batter. Heat the oil. Spoon heaping tablespoonfuls of batter into oil, spreading batter with the back of the spoon in 4-inch rounds. Brown on one side, then turn and brown on the other side. Brown potatoes slowly, so potatoes will have a chance to cook through properly. Drain on absorbent paper. Serve hot with applesauce.

Served annually at the New Braunfels Wurstfest by the Bracken Volunteer Fire Department.

Guten Appetit!

Potato Toast

1 cup coarsely grated pre-boiled
  potatoes (2 medium potatoes)
5 slices day-old white bread
2 egg whites, beaten
½ teaspoon salt

2 tablespoons cornstarch
2 tablespoons green onions,
  minced
1 tablespoon milk
1 teaspoon paprika

Boil 2 new potatoes until tender and chill in the refrigerator. After the potatoes are chilled, peel and grate coarsely or cut in very small cubes. Remove crust from bread slices and cut each slice in four pieces. Make paste of all other ingredients except bread. Spread potato paste on bread squares. Put one inch of oil in a frying pan or deep fat fryer. Place each square face down into the fat. As it puffs up and browns, turn it to other side. Drain thoroughly on paper towel, garnish with bits of parsley or chopped ham, and serve while hot. This is the Depression '80s version of Chinese Shrimp Toast.

Mrs. Blackwell's Heart of Texas Cookbook

Stuffed French Toast

1 (8-ounce) package cream
  cheese, softened
¼ cup crushed pineapple
½ cup pecans, chopped
1 (16-ounce) loaf French bread
4 eggs

1 cup whipping cream
½ teaspoon vanilla
1 teaspoon ground nutmeg
1 (12-ounce) jar (1½ cups) apricot
  preserves
½ cup orange juice

Beat cream cheese and pineapple together until fluffy. Stir in nuts; set aside. Cut bread into 10–12 1½-inch slices; cut a pocket in the top of each. Fill each with 1½ tablespoons of the cheese mixture. Beat together eggs, whipping cream, vanilla, and nutmeg. Using tongs, dip the filled bread slices in egg mixture, being careful not to squeeze out the filling. Cook on lightly greased griddle until both sides are golden brown. Meanwhile, heat together preserves and juice. To serve, drizzle apricot mixture over hot French toast. Yields 10–12 slices.

(Annie's Bed and Breakfast, Big Sandy)
Texas Historic Inns Cookbook

French Toast
Santa Fe Railroad Diners' Special

3 slices bread, 1-inch thick   Dash salt
  ("Texas toast")   ½ cup milk
3 eggs   2 cups shortening
Dash nutmeg

Trim crusts from bread slices, round corners and edges, and cut diagonally. Beat eggs, add nutmeg and salt. Add milk and thoroughly beat mixture. Dip bread slices into this batter. Soak bread, then take bread between hands and press batter out of the bread. Soak again to be sure bread is saturated. Stroke each slice lightly reducing the slice to about half its height to remove batter drippings. Fry in moderately hot shortening until golden brown. Drain on paper towel. Place toast on cookie sheet with a paper towel under each slice. Bake 5 to 6 minutes per side at 400°. Dust generously with powdered sugar. Serve hot with jam, marmalade, syrup or honey. Serves 3.

This was a recipe that the Santa Fe Railroad served on its diners in the days when many people rode trains. Of all the items served, the French Toast was the most popular. People would actually get on the Santa Fe in Houston and get off in Rosenberg, or get on in Chicago and get off in Joliet, just so they could have French Toast!

Cook'em Horns

Hot Flitters

5 cups flour
1 teaspoon salt
1 cup shortening
¼ cup sugar
3 teaspoons baking powder

2 cups buttermilk with 1
   teaspoon soda dissolved in it
1 package of yeast or 1
   tablespoon dry yeast

Sift and measure flour. Add sugar, salt and baking powder and sift again. Cut in shortening. Dissolve yeast in 2 tablespoons warm water and add soda-buttermilk mixture. Then add dry ingredients. Put in ice box and cover. When ready to use, roll on floured pastry cloth ¼-inch thick and cut with biscuit cutter. Let rise 1 hour. Bake at 425° for 10–12 minutes. Makes about 60 flitters. Will keep in ice box 4–5 days.

Note: "For years I (Ann Elizabeth) had been making yeast biscuits. But one Thanksgiving, Sam and some of his friends dropped by, and he couldn't believe I called them biscuits. They were little and round and squashed and looked like somebody had stomped on them. Sam took one look at the biscuits and said, 'Mother, these are flat as flitters.' And the name stuck."

"I'm Glad I Ate When I Did, 'Cause I'm Not Hungry Now"

Pull-Apart Coffee Cake

1 (16-ounce) package frozen
   bread rolls, still frozen
1¼ sticks butter
1 (3⅝-ounce) package vanilla
   pudding (dry, *not* instant)

4 teaspoons cinnamon
½ cup brown sugar, packed
½ cup nuts, chopped

Butter a tube pan (or a 9 × 13" pan) heavily. Place rolls in pan. Pull each roll apart. Melt butter. Pour over rolls. Combine and sprinkle over rolls, pudding, cinnamon, brown sugar and nuts.

Let stand, uncovered, on cabinet top overnight. Bake at 375° for 20 minutes. When done, remove from oven and let set 10 minutes. Invert on plate. Yields 8 servings.

Variation: May use 1 cup brown sugar, 1 package butterscotch pudding (use dry, not instant), 1 stick butter and ½ cup chopped nuts.

Calf Fries to Caviar

Sour Cream Coffee Cake

½ cup butter
1 cup sugar
2 eggs
2 cups flour
1 teaspoon baking powder

1 cup sour cream
1 teaspoon baking soda
½ teaspoon salt
1½ teaspoons vanilla

TOPPING:
½ cup powdered sugar
½ cup flour
½ cup sugar

5 tablespoons butter
1 teaspoon vanilla

Mix topping ingredients until crumbly in a small bowl and set aside. Cream butter and sugar well and beat in eggs one at a time. Sift flour, baking powder, salt together. Stir half of flour mixture into creamed butter and sugar. Add soda to sour cream and add to creamed mixture. Stir in remaining flour. Mix until smooth. Add vanilla. Put batter into greased 9 × 13-inch pan and sprinkle on topping. Bake 35 minutes in 350° oven.

Guten Appetit!

Apple Fritters

1 cup flour
⅓ cup milk
1 egg
1½ teaspoons baking powder

½ teaspoon salt
1½ cups fresh apple, grated or 1
    can apple pie filling
Powdered sugar

Beat egg well, then mix with milk. Blend flour, baking powder, and salt into egg mixture. Stir in apples. Drop by tablespoonsful into hot grease. Deep fry at 350° until golden brown. Roll hot fritters in powdered sugar. If you like a sweeter fritter, add ¼ cup sugar and 1 teaspoon cinnamon to batter. Canned chunk pineapple can be used instead of apples.

These are best hot, just out of the fryer, but are pretty good for a couple of hours if they last that long. Yields 3 dozen.

Scrumptious

Schnecken

These are sweet and wonderful. (Apple Schnecken and Sugar Twist recipes follow.)

DOUGH:

1½ cakes compressed yeast or 1½ tablespoons dry yeast
¼ cup warm water
4 tablespoons light brown sugar
¾ cup butter or margarine
1½ teaspoons salt

3½–3¾ cups sifted unbleached white flour
¾ cup sour cream
2 large eggs, well beaten
1½ teaspoons vanilla

Dissolve yeast and 2 tablespoons of sugar in the water, and allow this to become frothy. Mix butter or margarine into the flour and salt until the mixture has a coarse-meal texture. Stir the sour cream, eggs, remaining sugar and vanilla into the yeast, add the flour mixture and mix well for eight minutes. Put the dough in a plastic bag and close with a plastic tie. Refrigerate overnight.

Place the chilled dough in a greased mixing bowl. Lightly grease the top of the dough, and cover with a towel. Allow dough to rise until double in size. (This may take 3 or 4 hours.)

Punch down and turn out dough on a lightly-floured surface. Knead for 2 minutes, until soft and satiny but workable. This dough may be used in several ways.

APPLE SCHNECKEN:

3 large apples, pared, cored and chopped
1 cup brown sugar
¾ cup butter, softened to room temperature

1 teaspoon cinnamon
1 cup walnuts or pecans, chopped

Roll the Schnecken dough into a thin rectangle. Spread the butter over the surface of the dough. Sprinkle with a mixture of brown sugar and cinnamon. Sprinkle the chopped apples and nuts over the sugar mixture. Roll as if for a jellyroll. Cut into 1-inch slices. Place in 3 greased, 13×9-inch oblong cake pans. Cover with a towel and let dough rise until double in size. Bake in a 375° oven for 20–30 minutes. Yields 36 rolls. May be frozen after baking.

CONTINUED

CONTINUED

SUGAR TWISTS:

1 cup granulated sugar
2 teaspoons cinnamon

¾ cup chopped walnuts or
   pecans

Divide Schnecken dough in half. Roll each half into a rectangle 8 × 16 × ⅓-inch thick. Sprinkle each rectangle with ⅛ cup of the sugar-cinnamon mixture.

Fold each piece of dough in half and roll into a rectangular form again. Sprinkle again with the sugar mixture. Continue folding and rolling until all but ⅛ cup of the sugar-cinnamon is used.

Fold rectangles in half. Cut into strips about 1½ inches wide and 6 inches long. Twist ends of strips in opposite directions, stretching dough slightly. Sprinkle the twists with the remaining sugar-cinnamon mixture and the nuts. Place the twists on greased cookie sheets, shaping them in a crescent form. Cover with a towel and let rise until double in size. Bake in a preheated 375° oven for 15 minutes or until browned. Yields 48 twists. May be frozen after baking.

Rolling in Dough

 Schnecken (SHNAY ken)—Fruit-filled or nut-filled sweet rolls, named for the German word for snails because of their shape.

Cherry Nut Muffins

⅛ pound butter (no substitute)
½ cup sugar
½ cup brown sugar
2 egg yolks, beaten well
1 cup cake flour
¼ teaspoon baking powder
2 tablespoons maraschino cherry
   juice

2 egg whites, beaten stiffly
½ cup pecans, ground finely
1 (4-ounce) jar maraschino
   cherries
Powdered sugar

Cream together butter, sugar and brown sugar. Add egg yolks. Mix thoroughly. Add cake flour, baking powder and cherry juice. Fold in egg whites. Butter small muffin tins and sprinkle with pecans. Fill tins with a teaspoon of batter, a cherry, and another teaspoon of batter. Sprinkle top with pecans. Bake at 400° for 8 minutes. Roll in powdered sugar. Flavor improves after storing in tins at least 10 days. Makes 24 small muffins.

Tasteful Traditions

Sweet Potato Rolls
Selected to be in Southern Living *magazine*

3 cups whole wheat flour
3 cups all-purpose flour
2 packages dry yeast
1½ cups warm water (105°–115°)
⅓ cup firmly packed brown sugar
1¼ teaspoons salt

½ cup butter or margarine,
  softened
2 eggs
1 (9-ounce) can sweet potatoes,
  undrained

Combine flour, mixing well. Combine yeast and warm water in container of electric blender; process to dissolve yeast. Add sugar, salt, butter, eggs, sweet potatoes, and 1 cup flour to yeast mixture; blend until smooth. Place remaining flour in large bowl; add yeast mixture; mixing to make a soft dough.

Turn dough out on a lightly floured board; knead about 5 minutes or until smooth and elastic. Place in a greased bowl, turning to grease top. Cover with plastic wrap, and refrigerate 6 hours or overnight.

About 1 hour before baking, divide dough in half. On a lightly floured surface, roll out each half into a 16-inch circle about ¼-inch thick. Cut each circle into 16 wedges; roll up each wedge, beginning at widest edge.

Place wedges on greased baking sheets with the point on bottom. Cover and let rise in a warm place about 30 minutes or until light. Bake at 350° for 15 minutes. Yields 32 rolls.

Flavor Favorites

Cream Cheese Braids

1 cup sour cream	2 packages of yeast
½ cup sugar	½ cup warm water
1 teaspoon salt	2 eggs, beaten
½ cup melted butter or margarine	4 cups flour

Heat sour cream over low heat. Stir in sugar, salt and butter. Cool to lukewarm. Sprinkle yeast over warm water in a large mixing bowl, stirring until yeast dissolves. Add sour cream mixture, eggs and flour. Mix well. Cover tightly. Refrigerate overnight. Next day, divide dough into 4 equal parts. Roll out each part on a well-floured board into a 12×8-inch rectangle. Spread one-fourth of the cream cheese filling on each rectangle. Roll up jellyroll fashion, beginning at long sides. Pinch edges together and fold ends under slightly. Place the rolls seam-side down on greased baking sheets. Slit each roll at 2-inch intervals about two-thirds of the way through the dough to resemble a braid. Cover and let rise in a warm place, free from drafts until doubled in bulk, about 1 hour. Bake at 375° for 15–20 minutes. Spread with glaze while warm. These freeze nicely. Yields four 12-inch loaves.

CREAM CHEESE FILLING:

2 (8-ounce) packages cream cheese, softened	1 egg, beaten
¾ cup sugar	⅛ teaspoon salt
	2 teaspoons vanilla

This filling can be made in the food processor. Or, combine cream cheese and sugar in a small mixing bowl. Add egg, salt and vanilla. Mix well. Yields about 2 cups.

GLAZE:
2 cups powdered sugar
4 tablespoons milk
2 teaspoons vanilla

Combine powdered sugar, milk, and vanilla in a small bowl or food processor and mix. Yields 1 cup.

Entertaining in Texas

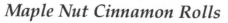

Maple Nut Cinnamon Rolls

1 packet dry yeast	½ cup shortening
¼ cup warm water	⅓ cup brown sugar
2 eggs	1½ teaspoons salt
1 cup quick-cooking oats	3½–4 cups flour
¾ cup milk, scalded	

Proof yeast in warm water. Add unbeaten eggs. Combine oats, milk, shortening, brown sugar and salt. Add yeast mixture. Beat well. Gradually add enough flour to form a stiff dough. Beat well. Cover and let rise in warm place until double, about 1½ hours.

TOPPING:

½ cup maple syrup	1 tablespoon water
¼ cup brown sugar	¼ teaspoon maple flavoring
½ stick butter	⅔ cup nuts

Combine in a 9 × 13-inch pan the syrup, brown sugar, butter, water, flavoring and nuts. Heat mixture until butter melts. Knead dough 3–5 minutes on floured surface. Roll out to a 12 × 24-inch rectangle.

FILLING:

¼ cup butter, softened	1 tablespoon grated orange rind
⅔ cup brown sugar	1 teaspoon cinnamon

Spread dough with softened butter. Combine remaining ingredients and sprinkle across buttered dough. Roll up dough from the 24-inch side. Cut into 1-inch slices. Place in pan on topping mixture. Let rise until light and double in bulk. Bake 30–35 minutes at 350°. Cool 1 minute. Invert immediately. May be frozen and reheated. Yields 24.

Tempting Traditions

Sunflower Seed Bread

The deliciously moist, nutty flavor makes this unusual.

1½ tablespoons dry yeast	½ cup hulled and cleaned
3 tablespoons light brown sugar	sunflower seeds
¼ cup lukewarm water	¼ cup unprocessed bran flakes,
1 cup low-fat milk, scalded	optional
1 egg, beaten	3½ cups unbleached white flour,
¼ cup margarine	approximately
2½ teaspoons salt	¾ cup whole wheat flour

Mix yeast with warm water and 2 tablespoons of sugar. Scald milk, remove from heat and add salt, margarine, remaining sugar and beaten egg. Add yeast to milk when the latter has cooled to room temperature.

Add 3 cups of flour, bran flakes and sunflower seeds, the whole wheat flour and beat well. Add the remaining flour slowly and mix well. The dough will be rather sticky. Grease the top of the dough, cover with a towel and allow dough to rise until double in bulk.

Beat down, then form into a loaf and place in a well-greased pan. Cover and allow to double again.

Place in a cool oven. Turn oven to 325° and bake about 45 minutes. Remove bread from the pan and cool on a rack. Yields one loaf. May be frozen after baking.

Rolling in Dough

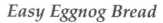

Easy Eggnog Bread

3 cups flour
¾ cup sugar
1 tablespoon baking powder
1 teaspoon salt
½ teaspoon nutmeg
1 egg, beaten

¼ cup butter, melted
1½ cups eggnog
¾ cup chopped walnuts or
  pecans
¾ cup candied fruits

In large mixing bowl, sift together flour, sugar, baking powder, salt and nutmeg. Combine egg, butter and eggnog. Add to dry ingredients, stir until thoroughly mixed. Add nuts and fruits. Bake in loaf pan 60–70 minutes at 350°. Cool on wire rack. Yields 1 loaf.

This bread is wonderful with Swiss, Cheddar, or brick cheeses and cold meats . . . especially for a quick supper during the Christmas season.

Cook 'em Horns

Lemon and Lime Bread with Cashews

1 cup sugar
½ cup butter
2 eggs, lightly beaten
1¼ cups sifted flour
1 teaspoon baking powder
½ cup milk
¾ cup salted, toasted chopped
  cashews

Zest of 1 lemon, grated
Zest of 1 lime, grated
3 tablespoons fresh lemon juice
3 tablespoons fresh lime juice
7 tablespoons sugar

Preheat oven to 350°. Cream sugar and butter; add eggs. Combine flour, baking powder, and salt; sift together. Alternately add dry ingredients and milk to the creamed mixture, stirring well after each addition. Stir in nuts, lemon, and lime zest. Pour into a greased and floured loaf pan and bake 1 hour. Remove bread from pan. Make small holes in bread with toothpick. Mix lemon and lime juice with sugar; pour over bread while hot. Yields 1 loaf.

The Dallas Symphony Cookbook

Monkey Bread

1 envelope yeast
¼ cup warm water
¾ cup butter, softened
½ cup sugar
3 cups flour

1 cup milk
2 eggs
1 teaspoon salt
Melted butter

Dissolve yeast in warm water. Cream butter and sugar together. Add 1½ cups flour, yeast mixture, milk, eggs, and salt and beat well. Let mixture rise one hour. Add other 1½ cups flour. Refrigerate overnight, covered with a damp cloth. When it is time to assemble bread, more flour may be added to dough if it is too sticky; dough, however, should be soft. Make small balls with the dough. Dip the balls in butter and arrange in a bundt pan or a ring mold. Fill mold one-half full. Let bread rise 45 minutes in a warm place. Cook 30 minutes in a 325° oven. Raise temperature to 350° and cook 15 minutes.

San Angelo Junior League Cookbook

Annette's Cheesebread

2½ cups margarine or butter
½ teaspoon poppy seed
1 teaspoon dry mustard
1 teaspoon oregano
1 teaspoon basil

1 pound Kraft Swiss cheese
  slices, long (each slice
  quartered)
1 loaf French bread
Parmesan cheese

Slice bread. Melt butter and add seasonings. Paint each side all through loaf with mixture. Place 2 slices of cheese between each slice of bread. Paint top with remaining butter. Sprinkle with Parmesan cheese. Wrap in heavy duty foil and bake for 30–40 minutes at 350°.

Cuckoo Too

Mushroom Bread

1 package hot roll mix
1 egg
¾ cup water
2 tablespoons parsley
1 pound mushrooms, finely
  chopped
1 large clove garlic, minced

¾ stick margarine
¼ cup dry sherry
¼ teaspoon salt
⅛ teaspoon pepper
2 tablespoons fresh or dried
  chives, chopped
½ cup dairy sour cream

Mix hot roll mix as directed on package, using one egg and ¾ cup of water. Let rest 30 minutes. Sauté next 3 ingredients in margarine. Add sherry, salt and pepper. Continue to sauté until liquid evaporates. Add chives and sour cream. Roll dough flat and thin (like pizza dough), and spread mushroom mixture over entire loaf. Roll up jelly-roll style. Let rise until double in bulk on cookie sheet. Bake at 375° for 18 minutes.

Cookin' Wise

Creole Cheese Sticks

1 loaf Pepperidge Farm wheat
  bread, sliced extra thin
2 tablespoons unsalted oleo
¾ cup water
1 packet Butter Buds
1 small can Parmesan cheese

1 teaspoon Tony's Creole
  Seasoning (or ¼ each thyme,
  celery seed, marjoram, and
  white pepper if Tony's not
  available)

In boiler, melt oleo with water, Butter Buds and seasoning. Keep warm 5 minutes before brushing each slice of bread, both sides, with mixture. Slice each slice into 3 fingers.

In a flat pan, put Parmesan cheese. Press to coat each bread finger on both sides. Bake in preheated 350° oven only until lightly brown and crunchy.

La Galerie Perroquet Food Fare

Popovers

1 cup sifted flour
¼ teaspoon salt
2 eggs, beaten

1 cup milk
2 tablespoons shortening, melted

Sift flour and salt together. Combine eggs, milk, and shortening; gradually add to flour mixture, beating approximately 1 minute or until batter is smooth. Fill greased, sizzling hot pans ¾ full; bake at 450° approximately 20 minutes. Reduce heat to 350° and continue baking for 15–20 minutes.

"This is one of our favorite 'house dishes'—our friends know they're sure to have Popovers for one meal during a house party."

(Lady Bird Johnson) *Enjoy!*

Bread

1 package dry yeast	⅓ cup sugar
¼ cup warm water	1 teaspoon salt
½ cup melted butter	2 eggs, well beaten
1 cup scalded milk	5–5½ cups flour

Soften yeast in warm water. Scald milk; add butter, sugar, and salt. Cool to lukewarm. Stir in eggs and yeast mixture. Stir in flour, one cup at a time, to form a fairly stiff dough. (You should never add more flour than the dough can absorb. This is one cause for tough bread. If the dough is too sticky, correct by adding more flour as you are kneading.) Turn out onto a lightly floured surface and knead until dough is smooth. Place in greased bowl and turn to grease top. Cover and let rise in warm place until doubled in bulk, about 1 hour. Punch down dough and divide in half. Shape into two loaves, place in greased loaf pans, cover and let rise again until almost doubled, about 30–45 minutes. Bake 30 minutes at 350°. Remove from oven; brush tops with additional melted butter.

This bread freezes well and is also excellent toasted. I have used this bread recipe more than any other and it is always dependable.

CHEESE-FILLED BREAD:

1 recipe of Bread dough	1 small can chopped ripe olives,
Melted butter	well drained
¼ cup mayonnaise	1 small can chopped green
2 cups grated cheese: Cheddar,	chilies, well drained
Monterey Jack, or combination	1 small clove garlic, minced
both	About 1 cup additional cheese,
½ cup green onion, tops and	same choices as above,
bottoms, chopped	reserved

Make bread as directed, allow to rise in bowl, punch down and divide dough in half. Working with one half at a time, roll out into rectangle, about 12×8. Brush with melted butter. Mix remaining ingredients and spread half of mixture over dough, leaving a clear border all around. Starting with one of the short sides, roll up tightly and tuck in ends, forming a nicely shaped loaf. Place loaf in well-greased loaf pan (9×5×3 inches). With a sharp knife,

CONTINUED

CONTINUED

make a deep slit down center of loaf. Stuff ½ of the additional cheese in slit. Cover and allow to rise 30 minutes. Bake 30–35 minutes at 350° (repeat with remaining dough). Remove loaves from oven, brush with melted butter.

This is the bread that started the cookbook! When the Corders moved to Plainview, I took a loaf of Cheese-Filled Bread to them. Suzanne called the next day for the recipe and we have been trading recipes ever since. You may not end up writing a cook-book but we promise that you will love this bread!!

Of Magnolia and Mesquite

Jean's Garlic Bread

1 loaf Italian bread, halved
1 bowl whipped margarine
2 teaspoons garlic powder
8 ounces Mozzarella cheese,
  grated

2 small red onions, sliced in rings
1 can ripe olives, sliced
⅛ cup parsley

Mix garlic powder and whipped margarine. Let sit for at least 30 minutes. Spread on bread. Add Mozzarella cheese, onion, ripe olives and parsley. Heat in 350° oven for 10 minutes. Serves 10–12.

A Doctor's Prescription for Gourmet Cooking

Very Special Southern Batter Bread

This recipe, in Rachel Allen's handwriting, noted that it was dictated to her by Judge James Christopher Paul, who founded the first commercial bank on the Plains of Texas and whose home was the Square House.

1 pint milk, scalded	3 egg yolks, well beaten
½ teaspoon baking powder	3 egg whites, beaten well
1 teaspoon sugar	7 heaping tablespoons flour
1 teaspoon salt	4 heaping tablespoons white
1 scant tablespoon butter	cornmeal

Add butter to scalded milk. Whip yolks until light and add dry ingredients, alternating with hot milk. Fold in beaten whites. Butter a baking dish and place bread in 350° oven 30 minutes or longer until browned on top and sides. Be sure it is completely done. It will be a velvety texture. Serve hot. It is delicious for breakfast with maple syrup.

Square House Museum Cookbook

Cornbread Muffins

1¼ cups cornmeal	¾ cup flour
1 teaspoon salt	½ tablespoon sugar
2 tablespoons baking powder	2 small eggs
2 cups milk	2 tablespoons shortening

Sift dry ingredients. Beat dry ingredients. Beat eggs well. Add a little more than half of the milk to the eggs and beat well. Add egg mixture to flour mixture and beat well. Stir in rest of milk and melted shortening. Fill hot, well-greased muffin tins about half full. Bake at 500° for about 15–18 minutes. Makes 12 muffins.

(Tom Landry) *Texas Celebrity Cookbook*

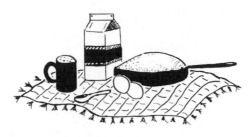

Betty Ewing's Jalapeño Corn Bread

1 cup corn meal
1 tablespoon sugar
½ tablespoon baking powder
1 teaspoon salt
2 eggs, beaten
½ cup bacon drippings
1 (No. 2) can cream style corn
1 large onion, diced

½ to ¾ pounds Cheddar cheese, grated
¼ cup jalapeño pepper, seeds removed
⅛ cup pimento
1 pod garlic, squeezed thru press
1 tablespoon Pace's hot sauce

Mix above ingredients in order of succession. Pour into well greased casserole. Bake at 400° for 35 minutes.

March of Dimes Gourmet Gala Cookbook

Mexican Cornbread

1 cup yellow cornmeal
½ teaspoon baking soda
2 teaspoons baking powder
1 cup milk
2 eggs
1 (17-ounce) can cream style corn

4 jalapeño peppers, chopped fine
1 large onion, chopped
½ pound rat cheese, grated
½ pound ground meat, cooked (or use sausage)
½ cup bacon drippings

Mix all of the ingredients together. Pour into a 9 × 9-inch greased pan. Bake at 350° for 40–45 minutes.

Trading Secrets

Jalapeño Cornbread

1 cup yellow cornmeal
1 tablespoon baking powder
1 (8-ounce) can yellow creamed corn
⅔ cup Mazola
2 eggs

½ pint sour cream
½ teaspoon salt
1 cup grated rat cheese
1 small onion, grated
4 jalapeño peppers, seeded and chopped

Preheat oven to 400°. Combine all ingredients. Pour into well-greased baking pan (12 × 8 × 2). Bake 20–25 minutes. This is good with ½ cup chopped bacon added.

Cuckoo Too

Sausage-Spinach Sandwich Loaf

1 (1-pound) loaf frozen bread
  dough
¾–1 pound sausage
1 large onion, chopped
1 (10-ounce) package frozen
  chopped spinach, thawed

1 (2¼-ounce) can sliced ripe
  olives, drained
¼ teaspoon crushed red pepper
⅔ cup grated Parmesan cheese
Melted butter

1. Thaw bread as directed on package. 2. Meanwhile, crumble sausage into frying pan with onion. 3. Cook until meat is browned and onion is limp; discard fat. 4. Drain spinach and add spinach and pepper to meat mixture. 5. On floured board, roll dough into an 11 × 15-inch rectangle. Scatter meat mixture onto dough to within 1 inch of edges. 6. Sprinkle with olives and cheese. 7. Starting with long side, roll up tightly; pinch ends and seams. 8. Place loaf seam-side down on greased baking sheet; tuck ends under. 9. Brush with melted butter and slash top. 10. Bake at 350° until golden, about 35 minutes. 11. Cut into thick slices. This is good hot or cold. Serves 6.

Easy Does It Cookbook

Ribbon Sandwich Loaf

1 loaf thin-sliced bread
(preferably sliced lengthwise
by your bakery)
Salad dressing
¼–½ cup green or ripe olives

Salad dressing to bind
½ pound Velveeta cheese, grated
Pimientos, mashed
Reserved pimiento juice

Remove crust from bread. Spread each slice with a very thin layer of salad dressing so spreads will go on easily.

FILLINGS:
1 (3-ounce) package spiced ham
luncheon meat, ground
2 tablespoons sweet pickle relish

½ cup (or more) salad dressing
3 or 4 hard boiled eggs

Make three fillings by combining the luncheon meat, pickle relish and salad dressing in one bowl; the eggs, olives and salad dressing in another bowl; and the Velveeta cheese and pimientos with a little juice in a third bowl. Alternate layers of sliced bread with three fillings. Makes about 6 or 7 layers.

ICING:
1 (8-ounce) package cream cheese   Salad dressing

Combine cream cheese with salad dressing until it will spread easily and ice the finished loaf top and sides. Chill and cover with wax paper until ready to serve. It will keep for several days. This is a very rich sandwich and one thick slice is a nice serving.

Scrumptious

 Pimento or *pimiento* (pee MAIN toh)—A sweet Spanish pepper.

Golden Sandwiches

8 slices bread	4 slices ham
4 slices Swiss cheese	4 slices turkey
4 slices American cheese	4 slices chicken breast

Make 4 sandwiches using bread, cheese, ham, chicken and turkey. Cut into fourths and secure with toothpicks. Dip into batter. Fry in deep hot oil until golden brown. Drain on paper towels. Serves 8.

BATTER:

1¼ cups ice water	Dash salt
1 egg yolk, beaten	1 egg white, beaten until stiff
1½ cups self-rising flour	Oil for frying

Add half of water to egg yolk. Stir in flour, salt, and add remaining water. Then fold in beaten egg white. A pretty fruit cup would be a nice accompaniment.

Hullabaloo in the Kitchen

Soups

Showplace dining room in historic Ashton Villa reflects opulence of its era. Galveston.

Gazpacho

1 clove garlic	⅓ cup olive oil
3 pounds tomatoes	3 tablespoons vinegar
2 cucumbers	Salt and freshly ground pepper
½ cup minced green pepper	¼ teaspoon Tabasco
½ cup minced onion	Avocado slices
2 cups iced tomato juice	

Chop garlic very fine, add to a large bowl with peeled, seeded and chopped tomatoes. (Try to save as much of the juice as you can.) Peel and seed the cucumbers and add to the bowl with the pepper, onion, and tomato juice. Add the olive oil and seasonings, cover and chill thoroughly. Taste for seasoning (more garlic is usually complimentary). Serve in chilled bowls with ice cube of frozen tomato juice and an avocado slice.

(Dr. Denton A. Cooley) *Texas Celebrity Cookbook*

White Gazpacho

3 large cucumbers, peeled, sliced lengthwise, seeds removed, coarsely chopped	1 cup plain yogurt
	2 cups (1 pint) sour cream
	3 tablespoons white vinegar
1 cup seedless grapes	2 teaspoons salt
1 avocado, diced	2–3 drops Tabasco sauce
2 large cloves garlic	
3 cups chicken stock or 2 (13¾-ounce) cans chicken broth	

ACCOMPANIMENTS:

2 tomatoes, peeled, juiced, seeded, chopped	1 cup almonds, slivered, toasted
	½ cup parsley, finely chopped
½ cup scallions, finely chopped	1 cup garlic croutons
1 green pepper, seeded, finely chopped	

Place cucumbers, grapes, avocado, and garlic in blender or food processor and pureé. Add chicken stock, yogurt, sour cream, vinegar, salt, and Tabasco sauce. Process until smooth. Cover, refrigerate until thoroughly chilled, at least 1 hour. Before serving, whisk to blend, taste for seasoning. More salt or Tabasco sauce may be added. Serve in chilled soup bowls. Pass accompaniments in separate bowls. Serves 20–22.

San Antonio Conservation Society Cookbook

Avocado Soup

4 fully ripe California avocados
2 cups chicken broth
2 teaspoons lime juice
½ teaspoon salt
⅛ teaspoon garlic powder
2 cups heavy cream

Halve avocados lengthwise, twisting gently to separate halves. Whack a sharp knife directly into seeds and twist to lift out. Peel avocado halves; then purée in electric blender with broth, lime juice, salt and garlic powder. Stir in cream. Chill thoroughly. Garnish with lemon slices or with heavy cream, whipped with a dash of garlic powder.

Square House Museum Cookbook

Cream of Squash Soup

FOR PURÉE:
1 pound summer squash (yellow, zucchini or white)
1 medium onion, chopped coarse
2 tablespoons butter
1 tablespoon water
Salt to taste
Pepper to taste

Wash squash well and trim, but do not peel; cut in small cubes. Cook squash and onions in butter until golden and limp. Add water if necessary. Purée squash a little at a time in blender or food processor.

FOR SOUP:
2 tablespoons butter
¼ teaspoon crumbled rosemary or dill weed
3 tablespoons flour
Salt to taste
Pepper to taste
2 cups chicken broth
1 cup milk
2 cups (approximately) squash purée
1 cup light cream

Melt butter in large heavy saucepan over moderate heat; add rosemary or dill weed. Cook and stir about 1 minute to develop the herb flavor. Blend the flour, salt and pepper; then slowly stir in chicken broth and milk. Heat until thickened and smooth. Add squash purée and heat 3–4 minutes longer. Add cream; heat to good serving temperature. Serves 4–6.

Repast

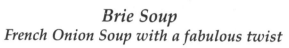

Brie Soup
French Onion Soup with a fabulous twist

4 large onions, thinly sliced
3 tablespoons butter, melted
½ teaspoon salt

4 cups beef broth or consommé
⅓ cup dry Madeira
4 ounces Brie cheese

Sauté onions in butter. Add salt and cover tightly. Cook over low heat until tender, approximately 15 minutes; do not brown. Add broth and simmer 20 minutes. Add Madeira. Strain, if desired. Dice cheese in bottom of soup cups and cover with hot soup. Stir and serve. Serves 6.

This is a recipe of Miss Helen Corbitt.

The Dallas Symphony Cookbook

Garlic Soup

20 pods of garlic, peeled and
    sliced
4 tablespoons butter
2 fresh tomatoes, peeled, seeded
    and diced
½ cup carrots, scraped and sliced

¼ cup celery, sliced
¼ cup onion, diced
4 cups chicken broth
1 egg, separated
½ tablespoon cider vinegar
Salt and pepper to taste

In a large saucepan, sauté the garlic in butter until very soft. Stir in the tomatoes and cook briefly. Add carrots, celery and onion and cook until onion is soft. Stir in broth and simmer, uncovered, until vegetables are cooked through. Remove from heat. In a separate bowl, combine egg yolk and vinegar and beat slightly. Carefully stir in 2 or 3 ladlesful of the soup mixture. Stir slowly back into soup a little at a time. Without beating beforehand, whisk egg white into soup mixture. Season to taste with salt and pepper. Reheat, if necessary, but do not allow to boil. Serves 4.

Note: Don't be put off by the title. This is an aromatic, beautiful and delicious soup. When the garlic is boiled, it loses the familiar pungency and instead flavors the soup subtly and almost indefinably.

Galley Buffet Soup Cookbook

Onion Soup Gratinée

5 cups thinly sliced onions
5 tablespoons butter
1 tablespoon oil
1 teaspoon flour
1 teaspoon salt
1 teaspoon Dijon-style mustard

Pepper to taste
6 cups brown stock or beef broth
1 cup dry sherry
⅓ cup Parmesan cheese
⅓ cup grated Cheddar or Gruyère
    cheese

In a deep, heavy skillet, sauté the onions in the combined butter and oil for 30–40 minutes, or until well-browned. Stir in flour, salt, mustard and pepper. Cook an additional 2 minutes. Heat stock or broth and add to onions. Add sherry and cook over low heat, stirring well, until mixture comes to a boil. Simmer for 30 minutes. Transfer soup to an earthenware casserole and sprinkle with cheeses. Place casserole under pre-heated broiler for 3–4 minutes, until brown and bubbly. To serve, place one slice of Cheese Toast in each of six heated bowls. Divide soup among them.

CHEESE TOAST:
6 (½-inch) slices French bread
Softened butter
6 tablespoons grated Parmesan
    cheese

Spread each slice of bread with butter and sprinkle with 1 tablespoon of cheese. Toast at 325° until brown. Serves 6.

The Galveston Island Cookbook

Gratinée (grah tee NAY)—A dish that has been sprinkled with cheese or bread crumbs, then replaced in the oven until the top becomes crisp and golden.

Potage Velouté Aux Champignons
Cream of Mushroom Soup

¼ cup minced onions	⅓ bay leaf
5 tablespoons butter	⅛ teaspoon thyme
5 tablespoons flour	Salt and pepper to taste
6 cups chicken stock	Chopped stems from 1 pound
2 parsley sprigs	fresh mushrooms

Sauté the yellow onions until tender, add the flour, stir in the hot stock, parsley, bay leaf, thyme and salt and pepper to taste. Add stems of mushrooms. Simmer partially covered for 20 minutes or more, skimming occasionally. Strain, pressing juices out of stems. Return soup to pan.

2 tablespoons butter	Thinly sliced mushroom caps
1 teaspoon lemon juice	Salt

Melt butter. Add mushrooms, lemon juice and salt. Cover and cook slowly for about 5 minutes. Add to soup base. Simmer for 10 minutes.

2 egg yolks	1–3 tablespoons butter
½–¾ cup whipping cream	

To enrich the sauce, beat the egg yolks and cream together. Add some soup to egg and cream mixture. Gradually add to soup base. Correct seasoning. Add butter. Decorate with fluted mushrooms (cooked in butter and lemon juice) and/or minced chervil or parsley. Serve hot.

Hullabaloo in the Kitchen

Corn Chowder in a Flash

1 medium onion, chopped and	Add:
sautéed in	1 (10½-ounce) can potato soup
3 tablespoons of butter or	¾ soup can of milk or light cream
Chiffon margarine	1 can cream style corn
	Salt and white pepper to taste

Heat until hot . . . do not boil. Serves 2.

Serve with a good green salad and/or a fried cheese sandwich. Makes for a good supper or lunch.

Collectibles II

Tortilla Soup

1 small onion, chopped
2 garlic cloves, mashed
1 (4-ounce) can green chiles, diced
2 tablespoons oil
1 (8-ounce) can stewed tomatoes
2 cups chicken broth
1 cup beef bouillon
1 teaspoon ground cumin
1 teaspoon chili powder
1 teaspoon salt
¼ teaspoon pepper
2 teaspoons Worcestershire sauce
1 cup Monterrey Jack or Cheddar cheese, grated
4 corn tortillas
Oil for frying tortillas

Using a medium saucepan, sauté onion, garlic and green chiles in oil until soft. Add tomatoes, chicken broth and beef bouillon. Mix in spices and simmer for 1 hour.

Cut tortillas into quarters, then into ½-inch strips. Fry strips in hot oil until crisp and drain.

Add fried tortilla strips to soup and simmer 10 minutes. Ladle into bowls and top with shredded cheese.

Variation: If you are using ovenproof bowls for soup, place bowls under broiler for 4–5 minutes to melt cheese. Serves 4.

Taste & Tales From Texas . . . With Love

 Sopa (SOH pah)—The Spanish word for soup.

Sopa de Tortilla

2 (10¾-ounce) cans Campbell's chicken broth, diluted according to instructions
½ cup chopped celery
1 teaspoon chili powder
1 small tomato, peeled, seeded, and chopped
1 teaspoon chopped onion
3 small cloves garlic, minced
1 teaspoon chopped parsley
1 tablespoon olive oil
1 medium package (6¾-ounce) Doritos, regular flavor
1 cup grated sharp Cheddar cheese

Boil broth, celery, and chili powder until celery is tender. Fry tomatoes, onion, garlic, and parsley in oil until onion is soft. Add tomato mixture to broth. Break the Doritos into medium pieces and add to soup, boiling briefly until the Doritos are soft. Add cheese just before serving.

Flavors

Broccoli-Cheese Soup

4 tablespoons butter, melted	1 cup Cheese Whiz
3 tablespoons flour	Salt & pepper
1 quart milk or cream	1 (10-ounce) package chopped,
2 tablespoons dry onion soup mix	frozen broccoli

1. Cook frozen broccoli according to package directions. 2. Cool and blend in blender with part of milk until creamy. 3. Melt butter and add flour to make smooth paste. 4. Add milk and cheese. Cook, stirring constantly until cheese melts. 5. Add broccoli. Heat thoroughly. Serves 4–5. Great!

Easy Does It Cookbook

Chipped Beef Cheese Soup
(Microwave)

3 teaspoons chicken-flavored bouillon granules	¼ teaspoon onion powder
1½ cups water	¼ teaspoon salt
2 tablespoons margarine	⅛ teaspoon white pepper
3 tablespoons flour	1 (8-ounce) package process
2 cups milk	cheese spread (shredded)
	1 (2½-ounce) jar sliced dried beef

Mix bouillon granules and water in 2-cup microwave-safe measure. Microwave on FULL (100%) POWER 1–2 minutes to dissolve granules. Microwave margarine in 4-quart microwave-safe container on FULL (100%) POWER 30 seconds to melt margarine. Blend flour into margarine. Add milk gradually, stirring to blend. Add chicken bouillon mixture, onion powder, salt, and white pepper. Microwave on MEDIUM (50%) POWER 15–18 minutes, or until thickened to soup consistency. Blend cheese into hot mixture. Rinse and drain beef to soften for easier chopping. Dice beef into very fine pieces. Stir beef into soup mixture. Microwave on LOW (30%) POWER 5 minutes to blend flavors. Yields 3½ cups.

The Texas Microwave Cookbook

Cheese Soup

4½ quarts rich chicken stock
¾ pound diced carrots
1 medium celery stalk, diced
2 medium onions, chopped
3 bay leaves
½ tablespoon white pepper
1 teaspoon granulated garlic
2 teaspoons celery salt
Yellow egg food coloring

1 pound Velveeta cheese
½ pound Parmesan cheese
1 can beer
½ pound flour
½ pound margarine
1 quart milk
1 pint light cream (half and half)
Chicken base

Step 1. Boil vegetables in 4 quarts of stock with spices until tender (about 45 minutes). Strain off vegetables. Keep stock hot and add enough extra stock to bring total up to 4 quarts.

Step 2. Make a roux by melting margarine and adding flour. Use wire whip to blend into a paste. Cook for about 5–6 minutes over medium heat. Stir occasionally. Do not brown.

Step 3. Heat milk and cream when roux is about ready to add to stock. Add some chicken base to hot milk, so as not to dilute stock.

Step 4. If at this point the roux did not blend totally then strain. With enough mixing with the wire whip, you should be able to have a smooth texture. Add roux to stock, stirring well.

Step 5. Add milk and cream mixture to stock. Continue mixing. Add Parmesan. Whip or stir to blend in Parmesan. Then add the Velveeta, which has been softened. After the cheeses have been blended into the stock, you may want to add a few drops of food coloring.

Step 6. Stir in the beer and add the vegetables back.

Step 7. Serve or cool fast to store. Yields 1¾ gallons.

This is a recipe from The Windows Restaurant.

Entertaining in Texas

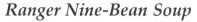

Ranger Nine-Bean Soup

The Texas Ranger chapter of Texas history is filled with more drama and braver heroes than a top fiction writer could invent. Formed in 1835 by Stephen F. Austin, the Rangers were charged with the protection of west and south Texas settlers from hostile Indians. Later they took on Mexican bandits, fence-cutting ranchers and countless outlaws. Their territory was vast, their job dangerous and their pay low, yet this small band of men did their job with courage, steadiness and confidence. Their legend is brought to life in the Texas Ranger Museum and Hall of Fame located at Fort Fisher in Waco.

Parcels of mixed pinto, black, northern, red and tiny lima beans with split peas are available at many food stores. The interesting combination of flavors makes a good soup.

1 pound mixed beans	1 teaspoon chili powder
2 quarts water	1 (28-ounce) can tomatoes
Ham hocks or ham bone	Juice of 1 lemon
1 large onion	Salt and pepper
1 clove garlic, mashed	

Wash beans thoroughly and place in large kettle. Cover with water and soak overnight. Drain. Add water, ham hocks or ham bone and onion. Simmer 2 hours. Remove meat from bones and return to beans. Add spices, tomatoes and lemon juice. Simmer another hour to blend flavors. Salt and pepper to taste. Serve with cornbread. Serves 6–8.

Tastes & Tales From Texas . . . With Love

Potato Soup

1 quart water	1 teaspoon salt
1 quart milk	2 tablespoons butter
5 medium potatoes, cut up	½ cup light cream
3 large onions, chopped	¼ cup chopped parsley
½ cup celery, chopped	¼ teaspoon ground dill seed or
¼ teaspoon coarse pepper	dill weed

Add potatoes in water and milk. Brown onions in butter (optional). Add other seasoning. Boil together until potatoes fall apart. Add cream. Serve with Parmesan cheese sprinkled on top.

Guten Appetit!

Old Fashioned Cabbage and Potato Soup

1 medium onion, minced
2 tablespoons butter or oleo
3 cups shredded cabbage
¼ cup chopped cabbage
3 cups water
1 teaspoon salt

2 cups diced potato
1 (14½-ounce) can evaporated
   milk
Minced parsley
Dash of paprika

Cook onion slowly in the butter until golden. Add cabbage to the onion with the water, salt and potato. Cook until tender, 15–20 minutes. Add milk and reheat, but do not boil. Serve sprinkled with minced parsley and a dash of paprika. Makes 6 servings.

Trading Secrets

Reducing Soup

2 quarts water
1 head shredded cabbage
4 large onions, chopped
5 ribs celery, chopped
1 large bell pepper, chopped
4 garlic buds, pressed
1 package dry onion soup mix

1 fifth Bloody Mary mix
1 can beef broth
1 can chicken broth
¼ teaspoon cayenne pepper
2 zucchini, diced
2 yellow squash, diced
1 cup broccoli florets

Use a 2-gallon pot. Mix all ingredients, *except* squash and broccoli. Bring to a boil; simmer 1 hour or so. Add squash and broccoli; simmer 15 minutes. (You can eat all you want because it is made with "free vegetables." Curb your appetite by eating this during the day if dining out at night. Remember, it takes more calories to digest than the soup contains; therefore, negative calories. So, the more you eat, the more you lose!) Can be made ahead and frozen. Makes 1½ gallons.

Spindletop International Cooks

Meatball Minestrone

Spinach meatballs (directions
  follow)
1 large onion, chopped
7 cups water
7 beef bouillon cubes
1 can stewed tomatoes (about 1
  pound)
1 (1 pound) can kidney beans

½ teaspoon dry oregano
½ teaspoon basil leaves
1 cup sliced carrots
1 cup sliced celery
1 cup elbow or bow-shaped
  macaroni (uncooked)

In a Dutch oven, brown meatballs over medium heat; remove from pan as browned.

Add the onion and sauté until limp. Stir in water, bouillon cubes, tomatoes, beans and their liquid, oregano, and basil; cover and simmer 10 minutes. Add carrots and celery; cover and simmer 10 minutes. Stir in macaroni; cover and simmer until tender, about 10 minutes. Return meatballs to soup and heat through; skim fat. Serves 6.

SPINACH MEATBALLS:
1 (10-ounce) package frozen
  chopped spinach, thawed
1½ pounds lean ground beef
⅓ cup fine dry bread crumbs

1 egg
1 teaspoon salt
¼ teaspoon pepper

Squeeze liquid from thawed spinach; mix with ground beef, bread crumbs, egg, salt, and pepper. Shape into 1-inch balls.

(Albert L. Rosen) *Houston Celebrity Cookbook*

Sunday Night Fireside Soup

1 pound sausage meat
4 cups water
2 (15¼-ounce) cans red kidney
  beans, drained
1 (1-pound 13-ounce) can
  tomatoes
1 onion, chopped
1 large bay leaf
½ clove garlic, minced

2 teaspoons salt
⅛ teaspoon black pepper
½ teaspoon thyme
⅛ teaspoon caraway seed
A pinch of crushed red pepper
1 cup raw potatoes, peeled and
  diced
1 small green pepper, with seeds
  removed, chopped

Brown sausage meat in a skillet. Drain the sausage and crumble it. In a kettle combine the sausage meat with the water, red kidney beans, tomatoes, onion, bay leaf, garlic, salt and black pepper, thyme, caraway seed and red pepper. Simmer the mixture for 1 hour. Add the potatoes and green pepper. Simmer, covered, for another 20 minutes. Adjust seasonings and serve. Serves 8.

Gallery Buffet Soup Cookbook

Pistou Country French Vegetable Soup

1½ quarts water
1 cup dry white beans
2 potatoes, pared and diced
½ pound fresh green beans
¼ cup dried basil
5 cloves garlic, crushed
2 onions, sliced
¼ cup olive oil
3 tomatoes, peeled, or 1
  (16-ounce) can tomatoes

1 (8-ounce) can tomato sauce, *if*
  using *fresh* tomatoes (If using
  canned tomatoes, omit)
2 zucchini
2 tablespoons salt, or less (to
  taste)
1 teaspoon pepper
¼ cup parsley, chopped

In large kettle, bring water to boil. Add white beans; boil 2 minutes. Reduce heat and simmer, covered, 1½ hours. Add potatoes, snapped green beans, basil and garlic; simmer 15 minutes. Sauté onions in olive oil until golden; add to soup with tomatoes, tomato sauce (if using fresh tomatoes), zucchini, salt and pepper. Simmer, covered, 15 minutes. Just before serving, sprinkle top with parsley. Serves 6.

Repast

Pistou (pehs TOO)—A kind of soup, with Italian origins, made with string beans, tomatoes, potatoes, and a variety of seasonings.

Mulligatawny Soup

½ cup onion, finely chopped
3 tablespoons butter
2½ tablespoons flour
2 teaspoons curry powder
1 quart chicken broth, heated
1 pint half and half cream
Salt and white pepper

1 cup cooked chicken, cut up in
  thin slices
1 raw tart apple, peeled, cored
  and finely chopped
1 tablespoon fresh parsley,
  chopped

In a large saucepan, sauté onion in butter until soft. Stir in flour and curry powder and cook about 2 minutes. Gradually stir in heated broth. Stir constantly until mixture thickens and is smooth. Stir in half and half cream. Season to taste with salt and white pepper. Add chicken slices and apple 10 minutes before serving. Adjust seasonings, if necessary. Garnish each serving with chopped parsley. Serves 6–8.

Note: Mulligatawny is a compatible first course with almost any lamb dish. It originally came from India and is at once both exotic and subtle, as well as beautiful. Have fun with your guests and see who can identify the surprise ingredient (apple)!

Gallery Buffet Soup Cookbook

Bongo Bongo

¼ cup onion, finely chopped
1 clove garlic, minced
4 tablespoons butter
1 pint fresh oysters, chopped
4 tablespoons flour
3 cups light cream

1 cup chicken broth
¾ cup spinach purée (puréed in
  blender from fresh or frozen
  spinach)
Salt and pepper to taste

In a medium-size saucepan, sauté the onion and garlic in butter until soft. Add oysters and cook until they curl. With a slotted spoon, carefully remove oysters from mixture and set aside. Add flour to mixture and cook until foamy. Add cream and cook, stirring, until soup is thickened. Return oysters to mixture. Stir in chicken broth and spinach. Bring to boil. Remove from heat. Season to taste with salt and pepper. Serves 4–6.

Gallery Buffet Soup Cookbook

Cold Peach Soup
With Fresh Blueberry Garnish

1½ cups water
4 cloves
¾ cup sugar
1 cinnamon stick, broken into
  pieces
2 tablespoons cornstarch mixed
  with ¼ cup cold water

1½ cups dry white wine
3 pounds ripe peaches
1 cup fresh blueberries
1 cup heavy cream

Pour water into a small saucepan. Add the cloves, sugar and cinnamon. Bring to a boil. Reduce heat and simmer for 10 minutes. Add the diluted cornstarch, whipping it into the syrup with a wire whisk. Bring the syrup to a boil again. Remove from stove, stir in the wine and refrigerate. Wash and peel the peaches. Split lengthwise and remove the seeds. Slice enough of the best peaches to make about 2 cups. Remove the cloves and cinnamon from the syrup. Add the sliced peaches to the syrup. Chop the remainder and purée in the blender. Add to the syrup mixture. Chill thoroughly. To serve, ladle into chilled bowls, sprinkle with blueberries and garnish with a generous dollop of whipped cream. Serves 6–8.

Gallery Buffet Soup Cookbook

Fresh Strawberry Soup

1½ cups water
¾ cup Taylor Lake Country red
   wine
¼ cup sugar
2 tablespoons fresh lemon juice
1 quart strawberries, hulled and
   puréed

1 (3-inch) cinnamon stick
½ cup heavy cream, whipped
¼ cup sugar
1 lime, thinly sliced (optional)

1. In a large saucepan, bring water, wine, ½ cup sugar, lemon juice, and cinnamon stick to a boil.

2. Boil gently for 15 minutes, stirring often. Add strawberry purée and simmer for 10 minutes. Discard cinnamon stick and chill soup for a minimum of 4 hours.

3. When ready to serve, whip cream and ½ cup sugar until stiff.

4. Fold whipped cream into soup mixture and serve in individual bowls or cups.

5. Garnish with a slice of lime, if desired. Yields 4 servings. Preparation time: 30 minutes.

Rare Collection

 Puréed (pure RAID)—Put through a sieve or blender and made into a pulp-like consistency.

Seafood Gumbo

Almeta Scott has cooked for many Houston families. I feel fortunate that she has shared with us some of her famous recipes, of which gumbo is #1. Vera Harris (Bebe), the Bruce's family cook for many years, made her gumbo a little different—but with much the same results. Try it both ways!

ALMETA'S GUMBO:

Bacon grease or other grease
2 tablespoons flour
1 pound okra
1 large can tomatoes
1 tomato can of water
1 cup chopped celery
1 cup chopped onion
¼ cup chopped bell pepper
Salt and pepper to taste
1 teaspoon gumbo filé
1 can white crab
1 can dark crab
1 pound cleaned shrimp (1½ pounds uncleaned)

Add 2 tablespoons flour to grease in a large pot. Brown this very well. Add onions, celery, and bell pepper. Stir while cooking a few minutes. Add tomatoes, water, okra, salt and pepper. Cook slowly one hour or until the vegetables are well done. Add shrimp and crab plus gumbo filé. I often add a few shakes of Tabasco. Serve over rice. Serves 8.

Variation: Substitute goose or duck for the seafood. Boil until tender. Skin and tear into bite-size pieces. Substitute broth for water.

BEBE'S GUMBO:
Bebe sautés 2 onions, 1 green pepper, and 1 pod of garlic in the grease from 4 slices of bacon. Then she adds a pound of okra and a large can of tomatoes, salt and pepper and gumbo filé and cooks 1½–2 hours slowly. She adds crabmeat and crumbled bacon at the end.

Cuckoo Too

Shrimp and Chicken Gumbo

1 (2 to 3-pound) chicken, cooked,
  reserving stock (about 3 quarts)

ROUX:

5 tablespoons oil or bacon   1 tablespoon Kitchen Bouquet
  drippings
4 tablespoons flour

Stirring constantly, cook oil and flour until dark golden. Add Kitchen Bouquet to make it darker.

6 small green onions with tops,   Dash of pepper
  chopped   Dash of Tabasco
1 medium onion, chopped   4 or 5 dashes of Worcestershire
1 small green pepper, chopped   2 pounds shrimp, cooked and
4 stalks celery, chopped   deveined
5 cups cut okra, fresh or frozen   ½ pound crabmeat, optional
2 tablespoons salt, more or less   Filé to taste
½–¾ teaspoon garlic powder or 2
  cloves garlic, pressed

Add vegetables to roux and stir and cook until wilted. Add this to chicken stock, bring to a boil, and add chicken which has been boned and cut into pieces. Add okra and season with salt, garlic, pepper, Tabasco, and Worcestershire. Simmer for a few minutes. Add shrimp. Serve over rice and add filé to taste. *Sausage may be used instead of seafood.* Serves 10–12.

Hospitality

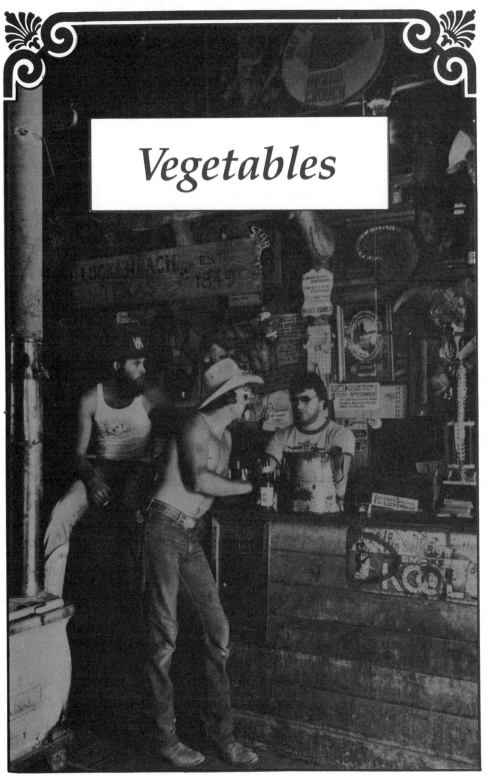

Vegetables

Backroom saloon behind Luckenback's general store which also serves as post office, dance hall, blacksmith shop. West of Austin near Fredericksburg.

Asparagus Casserole

48 ounces canned asparagus, whole or cut style
1–2 tomatoes
3 slices red onion

8 slices (or more) crisp bacon, crumbled
1 cup grated Cheddar cheese

Place drained asparagus in an 8×8-inch buttered casserole dish. Place enough sliced tomato on top of asparagus to cover. Next layer onion slices, crumbled bacon, and cheese. Bake in 325° oven for 20 minutes or until hot. This casserole is also good served cold. Serves 6.

San Angelo Junior League Cookbook

Sweet-Sour Bean Casserole

8 slices bacon
1 onion, chopped
½ cup brown sugar
½ cup catsup
¼ cup vinegar
½ teaspoon salt

½ teaspoon dry mustard
½ teaspoon Worcestershire sauce
1 (1-pound) can pork and beans
1 can green lima beans, drained
1 can kidney beans, drained

Fry bacon till crisp, then crumble. Pour off most of fat. Sauté onions in remaining fat till tender. Add other sauce ingredients; simmer 5 minutes. Add beans. Bake in 1½-quart casserole for 1 hour at 350°. May add:

1 can yellow wax beans, drained
1 can green beans, drained

1 can dry lima beans, drained

Then, double amounts of onion and spices and use a 3-quart casserole. Yields 6–8 servings using 3 kinds of beans, 12–16 with 6 kinds.

Great for barbecues, picnics or buffets. Men love it.

Keepers

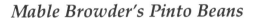
Mable Browder's Pinto Beans

4 cups #2 pinto beans
3 quarts water
1 cup chopped bell pepper
2 cups chopped onions
4 cloves garlic
2 bay leaves
1 pound bacon chopped and fried
  or ¼ cup bacon grease

4 cups canned tomatoes or 2
  (8-ounce) cans tomato sauce
4 teaspoons salt
2 tablespoons chili powder
1 teaspoon dry mustard
1 teaspoon oregano

Soak beans overnight (or boil rapidly two minutes only; cover, allow to stand one hour). In heavy pot bring beans, water, and salt to boil; simmer, covered, one hour. Add all other ingredients and simmer another hour, or longer if desired. Serves 12 generously.

Through Our Kitchen Door

Frijoles Mexicana
(Mexican Refried Beans)

Make day prior to serving.

2 cups frijoles (Mexican beans, or
  use pinto beans)
5 cups water
4 tablespoons lard

1 tablespoon chopped onion
½ cup tomato purée
Chili powder (optional)

Soak beans overnight and cook, covered, in five cups of water for 1½ hours, or until very tender. Drain (and save liquid). Heat 2 tablespoons of the lard in frying pan, add beans and fry over low heat about 10 minutes, mashing them with a fork. Add water in which the beans were cooked a little at a time, stirring constantly. Keep over low flame until the water has evaporated. Cool and place in a refrigerator until the following day.

Melt the other 2 tablespoons of lard in a large skillet. Fry onion for a few minutes, add tomato purée and chili powder if desired. When onion is tender, add fried beans and cook until beans are very hot. Serves 6.

From My Apron Pocket

Frijoles

There probably are as many ways of cooking this all-time Texas favorite staple as there are recipes for chili. Endless discussions take place among cooks as the best way to prepare pintos. The basic ingredient, of course, is dried beans. However, if you are lucky enough to be at a farmers' market in a big city in the spring, these wonderful beans can be obtained fresh in the shell. And fresh-cooked pinto beans are absolutely magnificent, no matter what seasoning you use. Alas, the season is short, and Texans must have their frijoles all year, so here is how Mr. Flores of the Kincaid serves his customers.

3 cups dried pinto beans   1 cup salt pork, diced
4 quarts water   Salt
1 clove garlic, peeled

Wash beans well and remove "rocks." Cover with water and soak overnight. Drain. Cover with fresh water, add garlic and salt pork, but not salt. Cover pot tightly and bring to a boil. Reduce heat and simmer for 1½ hours or until beans are tender but not mushy. Add boiling water during cooking if necessary and stir occasionally. When beans are done, remove lid, turn up heat, and cook until all liquid has been absorbed. Add salt to taste. Serves 8.

(Kincaid Hotel, Uvalde) *Texas Historic Inns Cookbook*

Frijoles (free HOH lays)—Beans.
Frijoles refritas (ray FREE tahs)—Refried beans, a favorite Tex-Mex dish. Beans are first cooked with tomatoes, onions, chili peppers and other seasonings, then mashed and fried.

Navy Beans for Writers

You get you two sacks of dried Navy beans and put 'em in the biggest pot you can find and run hot water on 'em till they drowned. Cover 'em with pepper till they about half-choked. Cut up garlic and onions and add more pepper. Many people don't add enough black pepper. Then find you a hambone or at least a pound of bacon and cook it till it's greasier than your hair and then dump the whole @!#¢@! in the pot, grease and all, and add more pepper.

Smoke some cigarettes while you bring all this to a boil, then turn the stove down low and let them sumbitches cook for about two or three hours, after which you got you some Navy beans for writers what you can eat on for two or three days while you write your books. A man who can cook his own beans don't hardly need to ask anybody anything about nothing.

(Dan Jenkins) *Texas Celebrity Cookbook*

Broccoli Supreme Casserole

2 packages frozen broccoli spears
½ stick oleo
½ cup onions, chopped
1 can cream of mushroom soup
½ stick garlic cheese

½ cup sour cream
½ cup bread crumbs
¼ cup slivered almonds
Salt and pepper to taste

Cook broccoli spears and drain. Put in casserole dish; sauté onions in oleo. Add soup, cheese and sour cream; stir until melted and smooth. Pour over broccoli. Top with bread crumbs and almonds. Bake at 350° for 30 minutes or until brown. (A small can of mushrooms may be added.) Serves 8.

The Pride of Texas

Barbecue Beans

1 can dark red kidney beans
1 can baked beans
1 garlic clove, mashed
1 medium onion, chopped
3 tablespoons bacon drippings

½ cup catsup
1 tablespoon dark brown sugar
1 tablespoon dry mustard
Salt and pepper to taste

Mix all ingredients and bake in 350° oven for 1 hour.

San Antonio Cookbook II

Copper-Penny Carrots
(Microwave)

1 pound fresh carrots, sliced	2 tablespoons red wine vinegar
2 tablespoons water	2 tablespoons sugar
1 medium onion, sliced into rings	2 tablespoons Worcestershire
1 (10.7-ounce) can tomato soup	sauce

Microwave carrots and water in covered 1½-quart microwave-safe casserole on FULL (100%) POWER 5 minutes.

Microwave onion slices in 4-cup microwave-safe measure on FULL (100%) POWER 1 minute. Add tomato soup, vinegar, sugar, and Worcestershire sauce to softened onion. Microwave soup mixture on FULL (100%) POWER 1 minute. Stir well. Pour hot mixture over carrots. Mix well. Cover casserole. Marinate in refrigerator 8 hours. Serve chilled, or reheat to serve hot. Serves 5–6.

The Texas Microwave Cookbook

Neighborhood Favorite Hot Carrots
Great with outdoor barbecues

1 tablespoon salt	½ large onion, sliced into rings
½ teaspoon sugar	1 pound carrots, peeled and
½ teaspoon red pepper	sliced
1 teaspoon dill seed	½ cup vinegar
1 large clove garlic	½ cup water

Combine first 6 ingredients in a pint jar. Pack carrot strips into jar. Combine vinegar and water; bring to a boil. Pour over carrots. Seal jar. Turn jar upside-down; cool. Chill thoroughly. Store indefinitely in refrigerator. Yields 1 pint.

Flavor Favorites

Tangy Carrots

12 carrots
1 onion, chopped
5 tablespoons horseradish
1 cup Hellman's mayonnaise
Salt and pepper to taste

Juice of ½ lemon
½ cup seasoned bread crumbs
3 tablespoons butter
½ cup carrot liquid

Slice carrots in approximately ¾-inch pieces. Cook until barely tender. Reserve ½ cup liquid. Place carrots 1-layer deep in a shallow casserole. Mix all other ingredients except the bread crumbs and butter and pour over the carrots. Cover with bread crumbs and dot with butter. Bake at 375° for 20 minutes.

Comment: Grand with roast beef, steak, grilled calves' liver, etc.

A Different Taste of Paris

Apricot Glazed Carrots

2 pounds carrots cut on the
  diagonal
3 tablespoons butter
⅓ cup apricot preserves
¼ teaspoon ground nutmeg

¼ teaspoon salt
1 teaspoon fresh orange peel,
  grated
2 teaspoons fresh lemon juice
Parsley for garnish

Cook carrots in salt water until tender. Drain. Melt butter, stir in apricot preserves until well blended. Add nutmeg, salt, orange peel and lemon juice. Toss the carrots with the apricot mixture until well coated. Sprinkle with chopped parsley. Serves 6–8.

Entertaining at Aldredge House

Carrot Soufflé

1½ cups puréed carrots
Pinch of cloves
2 tablespoons honey
1 teaspoon salt
½ cup butter

6 tablespoons flour
1½ cups cream
6 egg yolks
8 egg whites, stiffly beaten

Season carrots with cloves, honey and salt. Butter soufflé dish with some of the butter. Melt remaining butter; add flour and cook 1 minute. Add cream and cook until thick. Add egg yolks and carrots. Cool. Fold in egg whites. Bake at 350° for 35 minutes.

Noted Cookery

Sweet-Sour Cabbage
(From Mother's Apron Pocket)

1 large cabbage head, shredded (5
  cups)
3 or 4 slices of bacon, fried
2 tablespoons brown sugar
2 tablespoons flour

½ cup water
⅓ cup vinegar
Salt and pepper to taste
1 small onion, minced (optional)

Cook cabbage in a quart of water for 5 minutes. Fry bacon, crumble and set aside. Add sugar and flour to the bacon drippings; blend. Add water, vinegar and seasonings to taste. Cook until thickened. Add the cooked and drained cabbage to the sweet-sour sauce. Toss with bacon and onion. Heat thoroughly and serve. Serves 6.

From My Apron Pocket

Cauliflower Special
(Microwave)

1 medium head cauliflower (1
  pound)
2 tablespoons water
1 teaspoon salt
½ cup mayonnaise

¼ cup onion, minced
½ teaspoon prepared mustard
½ cup or more grated Cheddar
  cheese

Dissolve salt in water and pour over cauliflower which has been placed in 2-quart casserole. Place cauliflower bottom down and cover. Microwave on High for 7 minutes. Mix mayonnaise, onion and mustard. Spread mayonnaise mixture on cooked cauliflower; sprinkle with cheese. Heat on Medium for 1½ minutes. Let stand 2 minutes before serving.

The Pride of Texas

Corn Casserole

1 (17-ounce) can creamed corn
1 (17-ounce) can whole kernel
  corn, drained
1 cup grated sharp Cheddar
  cheese
1 cup cracker crumbs
½ cup grated onion
1 (2-ounce) jar pimiento
1 egg

⅔ cup evaporated milk
½ cup butter or margarine,
  melted
1 teaspoon salt
1½ teaspoons pepper
1 tablespoon sugar
½ teaspoon cayenne
½ cup chopped bell pepper
Paprika

Mix all ingredients together, except paprika, in order given, stirring well. Pour into slightly oiled casserole, sprinkle with paprika and bake at 400° approximately 1 hour. Serves 12.

Ready to Serve

Baked Corn

2 (12-ounce) cans shoe peg corn
6 ounces Philadelphia cream
  cheese
¼ pound butter

¼ cup sweet milk
Dash of garlic salt
2 seeded jalapeño peppers

Drains cans of corn. (If smaller Green Giant Shoe Peg is used, use 3 cans.) Make a sauce of cream cheese, butter, milk and garlic salt. Heat slowly so that it will not stick. Combine with drained corn. Mince seeded peppers and add. Season to taste and place in buttered baking dish. Bake at 350° or until lightly browned (about 30 minutes).

Square House Museum Cookbook

Jalapeño (hah lah PAIN yoh)—A kind of chile pepper that is frequently used in Tex-Mex recipes. Jalapeños are dark green peppers, with flavor from medium hot to extremely hot.

Stuffed Eggplant

1 (1-pound) eggplant
¼ cup (½ stick) butter
1 (4-ounce) can mushroom stems
   and pieces, drained
⅓ cup fresh tomato, chopped
¼ cup onion, chopped
¼ cup canned bread crumbs
¼ cup green bell pepper,
   chopped
1 teaspoon parsley flakes

½ teaspoon salt
½ teaspoon Knorr Swiss Aromat
   Seasoning for Meat
½ teaspoon sweet basil
½ teaspoon oregano
¼ teaspoon black pepper
¼ teaspoon garlic powder
¼ teaspoon celery salt
⅓ cup grated Parmesan cheese

1. Wash eggplant, dry, and cut off the stem ends as close to the stem as possible.

2. Lay eggplant on its side and cut lengthwise across the top as to create a top side. You don't have to cut off more than ½ inch in depth. Slice just enough off the bottom side to make the eggplant sit level in the baking dish.

3. Using a sharp knife, cut around the entire edge to create a cavity.

4. Using a spoon dig out the insides (pulp) of the eggplant. Chop up the insides.

5. Melt the butter in a skillet and add all the ingredients, except the Parmesan cheese.

6. Cook over medium heat until onions are tender (about 10 minutes). Remove from the heat, stir in the Parmesan, and immediately pile this mixture into the cavity of the eggplant.

7. Bake in a preheated 350° oven for 30 minutes. Makes 2 cups of stuffing.

Leaving Home

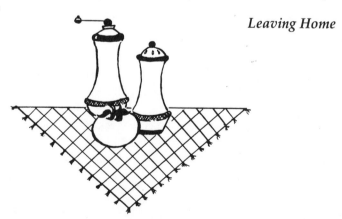

Unbelievably Eggplant
(Microwave)

Even eggplant haters love it this way.

1 (1½-pound) eggplant, peeled
   and cut into ½-inch cubes
⅓ cup chopped onion
Margarine
3 tablespoons flour
1½ cups milk
1 cup shredded sharp Cheddar
   cheese (4 ounces)

¼ teaspoon pepper
1 (2¼-ounce) can sliced ripe
   olives, drained
1 cup dry herb stuffing mix (such
   as Pepperidge Farm)

Place eggplant and onion in a 2-quart glass batter bowl. Cover and Microwave on HIGH 8 minutes, stirring after 4 minutes. Drain. Transfer to a 1½-quart round casserole.

Place 3 tablespoons margarine in same glass bowl. Microwave on HIGH 30 seconds, or until melted. Blend in flour using a wire whisk. Whisk in milk. Microwave on HIGH 2 minutes; stir with whisk. Microwave on HIGH 2 minutes, or until mixture begins to boil; whisk. Stir in cheese until melted. Add pepper.

Stir in reserved eggplant and onions, and half the can of olives. Pour half of eggplant mixture into casserole. Sprinkle with half of stuffing. Add remaining eggplant mixture and top with remainder of stuffing. Garnish with remaining olives and dot with margarine. Microwave on 70% (MEDIUM-HIGH) 6 minutes, or until heated through. Makes 4–6 servings.

Micro Quick!

Mexican Eggplant

1 eggplant, peeled, sliced
   ¼-inch thick
2 cloves garlic, chopped fine
1 large green pepper, chopped
   fine
2–4 green chile peppers, chopped

1 can tomato paste
1 can of water
2 eggs, beaten
Grated yellow cheese
Salt and pepper
Olive oil

Sauté garlic, green pepper and green chile peppers until soft in olive oil. Add tomato paste, water, salt and pepper to taste and simmer until sauce thickens. Dip eggplant into the eggs and sauté until golden brown in olive oil. Place eggplant slices in a baking dish and cover with the sauce and grated yellow cheese. Bake at 350° for 30 minutes. Serves 6.

San Antonio Cookbook II

Frosted Green Beans

2 pounds canned green beans,
  whole or cut, drained
6 tablespoons white vinegar
¾ cup salad or olive oil
1 large onion, minced
8 hard-boiled eggs, chopped

6 tablespoons mayonnaise
4 teaspoons vinegar
2 teaspoons prepared mustard
Salt and pepper to taste
8 slices bacon, cooked and
  crumbled

Make a marinade of 6 tablespoons vinegar, oil, salt and pepper. Add drained beans and onions. Marinate several hours or several days in refrigerator. In a bowl combine eggs, mayonnaise, 4 teaspoons vinegar, mustard and salt and pepper to taste. Refrigerate and allow flavor to develop. To serve, drain beans and onions. Place on chilled platter. Top with egg salad. Sprinkle bacon over all.

Comment: This is a wonderful addition to a special meal.

A Different Taste of Paris

Mushrooms with Spinach

2 pounds mushrooms, washed
  and chopped
1 teaspoon caraway seeds
1 tablespoon minced parsley
1 slice bread, cubed

¾ pound spinach
1 onion, chopped
1 tablespoon vegetable oil
½ cup sour cream
Salt to taste

Simmer mushrooms in a small amount of water with caraway seeds, parsley and bread for 5 minutes. Chop spinach and add to mixture. Continue cooking until liquid is almost evaporated. Fry onion in oil. Add mushroom and spinach mixture to onion, stir and add sour cream. Should be juicy, but not too soupy. Makes 4–6 servings.

The Melting Pot

Champignons Farci
(Cheese-Stuffed Mushrooms)

12 fresh mushroom caps, 2–3 inches in diameter
7 tablespoons butter, melted
Salt and pepper to taste
3 tablespoons onion, finely minced
1 tablespoon oil
3 tablespoons shallots, minced
¼ cup Rainwater Madeira
3 tablespoons fine dry bread crumbs

½ cup natural Swiss cheese, grated
¼ cup grated Parmesan cheese
4 tablespoons fresh parsley, minced
½ teaspoon dried tarragon
3 tablespoons heavy whipping cream

Remove stems from caps. Brush caps with 3 tablespoons butter. Place them, hollow side up, in a shallow, large oven-to-table dish. Sprinkle lightly with salt and pepper.

Sauté onion in 2 tablespoons butter and oil for 3–4 minutes without browning over moderate heat in a large skillet. Mince mushroom stems finely and squeeze through a towel to extract juices. Add the shallots and the stems to the butter and onions. Sauté over low heat, stirring, for 6–8 minutes, or until the mushroom pieces begin to separate from each other and brown lightly. Add the Madeira and boil it down until it has almost entirely evaporated. Remove from heat; mix in the bread crumbs, ¼ cup Swiss cheese, ¼ cup Parmesan cheese, parsley, tarragon, and salt and pepper to taste. Blend in cream to moisten, but keep the mixture sufficiently stiff to hold its shape.

Fill the caps with stuffing. Top each with a pinch of Swiss cheese and drops of butter, using 4 tablespoons grated Swiss cheese and 2 tablespoons butter in all. They may be done ahead to this point.

Bake in upper third of 375° oven, 15–20 minutes, or until stuffing has browned lightly. These mushrooms make wonderful hot hors d'oeuvres or garnish for a meat platter. Serves 6–8.

Noted Cookery

 Madeira (mah DEER ah)—A Portugese wine. Rainwater Madeira has a light straw color, but a relatively full flavor and bouquet.

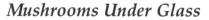

Mushrooms Under Glass

1 pound medium-sized fresh
  mushrooms
12 slices French bread, thinly
  sliced, toasted or 6–8 slices
  sandwich bread, cut in half,
  toasted
¾ cup dry white wine

2 tablespoons minced scallions
  (or onions)
1 teaspoon salt
½ teaspoon white pepper
1½ cups cream or half and half
  cream
Parsley

Carefully rinse, pat dry, trim ends of mushrooms. Set aside.
Generously butter a shallow 10-inch baking dish. Arrange toasted
bread in dish. Pour wine over toasts and pile mushrooms on top
of toasts. Sprinkle scallions, salt and pepper over mushrooms.
Pour ½ cup cream over all. Cover with glass bell or a Pyrex mixing
bowl or place baking dish in center of aluminum foil square. Seal
opposite edges of foil together to form a dome to prevent steam
from escaping during baking. Bake for 15 minutes at 350°. Remove bell, pour in the remaining 1 cup cream over mushrooms.
Cover, seal, bake 15–20 minutes longer. Serve hot. Garnish with
parsley sprigs. Serves 6.

San Antonio Conservation Society Cookbook

Sula's Stir-Fry Okra
Tender, crisp, delicious—the only way to cook okra

2 cups thinly sliced fresh okra
1 tomato, peeled
¼ cup sliced green onion
1 teaspoon fresh lemon juice
¼ teaspoon thyme leaves,
  crushed

1 teaspoon salt
Dash pepper
1 tablespoon salad oil
2 tablespoons butter

Trim stem ends of okra and slice as thinly as possible. Quarter
tomato, then slice quarters lengthwise into thin wedges. Thinly
slice onion, using both white and green parts. Squeeze lemon
juice to measure. Combine seasonings and add to lemon juice.
  Note: All ingredients must be prepared before beginning to
cook. In wok or large skillet, heat oil and butter. Add all ingredients, tossing and stirring constantly over high heat. Cook 3–5
minutes if using wok, or cook 5–8 minutes in skillet. Serve immediately. Serves 4.

Cook 'Em Horns

Pot-Luck Peas

½ pound bacon
2 cups finely chopped celery
2 cups finely chopped onion
2 cups finely chopped bell pepper
1 (16-ounce) can stewed tomatoes, undrained

1 (16-ounce) can tomatoes, undrained
3–4 (16-ounce) cans Ranch Style black-eyed peas, drained
Salt and pepper, to taste

Fry bacon in skillet; remove, drain, crumble and set aside. In a small amount of the bacon grease sauté celery, onion and bell pepper until tender. Add all tomatoes and cook together 15–20 minutes on low heat. Add drained peas, salt and pepper. Cook 10 more minutes on low heat. Add crumbled bacon just before serving.

Cornbread is a must with Pot-Luck Peas!!

Ready to Serve

Texas Caviar
Pickled Black-Eyed Peas

4 cups cooked, dried black-eyed peas
1 cup salad oil
¼ cup wine vinegar
1 clove garlic

½ cup onion, diced
½ teaspoon salt
Freshly ground black pepper to taste

Drain liquid from peas. Mix together thoroughly all other ingredients and add peas. Store in covered container in refrigerator, removing garlic clove after 1 day. Wait 3 days before serving peas, chilled and arranged in attractive bowl for buffet supper.

Noted Cookery

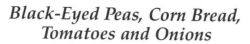

Black-Eyed Peas, Corn Bread, Tomatoes and Onions

"When I was growing up on our Little River Stock Farm in central Texas in the 1930's (says Marion Travis) a smart alecky cousin from Dallas told me, 'Northerners don't eat black-eyed peas. They call them cow feed.'

I was incredulous. Fresh black-eyed peas, with hot corn bread, fresh garden tomatoes and fresh onions were among my favorite foods—in the same class with my Grandmother Brewer's crisply fried chicken and Blue Bird vanilla ice cream from the Palace of Sweets in Cameron.

Properly selected, prepared and served they are uninterrupted joy—the kind that clings in memory from Texan childhood throughout adulthood.

First is the matter of selection. Warnings follow:

Avoid: Dried black-eyed peas (1) sold in bulk or in plastic or cellophane bags, and (2) cans labeled 'cooked, dried' black-eyes.

Be Careful: One step toward proper texture and flavor is canned fresh black-eyes.

These are Better: Frozen, fresh peas.

This is it!: Fresh black-eyed peas. They will poppedy-pop-pop from their long greenish-purple pods into the pan in your lap as you shell them. Each pea is plump and a delicate green with a purplish-black eye. Snap a few young pods into the shelled peas. If you pick them yourself, a full-packed gallon bucket (in the hull) will serve four."

1 quart fresh shelled black-eyed peas	Pan of hot corn bread
1 teaspoon salt	4 large, firm, ripe tomatoes
1 tablespoon fresh bacon drippings or two slices of uncooked, cured bacon	4 onions, approximately 1-inch in diameter
	Salt and pepper to taste

Wash shelled peas thoroughly in a colander or a pan. There will be some delicate pea skins remaining, which is good. Pour all into a large saucepan and cover with water. This becomes the pot liquor. Add salt and ease in fresh bacon drippings or bacon. Do not use margarine, butter, salt pork, ham or other oily ingredients. Cook on high heat until they reach a rolling boil. Turn the heat down to a slow boil for 20 minutes or until tender. The pot liquor will be dark. The peas will be darkish green.

CONTINUED

130

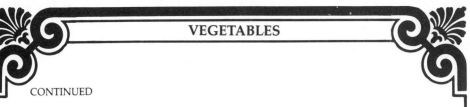
CONTINUED

While the peas are cooking, make your best recipe of corn bread. Perfect this in advance. Good corn bread is essential to the quality of the meal.

Slice tomatoes on a plate with onions. The onions should have green tops but do not have to be the tiny, mild onions often used in salads.

The layered feast should be arranged as follows: mound several spoonfuls of hot black-eyed peas into the center of your plate. Take a large piece of warm corn bread and crumble it quickly over the peas. It should have its stove heat when you begin eating. Do not butter your corn bread. Place cool tomato slices to taste on top of the corn bread and slices of crisp, cool onion to taste on top of tomatoes. Immediately ladle out several spoonfuls of warm pot liquor onto the plate. Not too many. You are not making soup, just a good eating consistency. Take knife in one hand, fork in the other and cut—over and over. This cuts up the tomatoes and onions, completes the corn bread crumbling and mixes the whole culinary marvel together. Dissimilarity in food textures, vegetable and bread temperatures and flavors makes this combination surpassingly delicious.

The Melting Pot

Baked Zucchini and Tomatoes

2 medium zucchini	Pepper to taste
2 medium tomatoes	Butter
1 medium onion, peeled	1 cup Ritz crackers, crushed
Salt to taste	(optional)

Wash zucchini and tomatoes. Slice all vegetables into thin, crosswise slices. In a greased 2-quart baking dish make alternate layers of zucchini, tomatoes and onions, sprinkling each layer with salt and pepper and dotting with butter. Cover top with cracker crumbs. Bake at 350° until vegetables are tender (about 30 minutes). Serves 8.

Repast

Hot Potato Mold

3 pounds potatoes, boiled, peeled and diced
3 eggs, beaten
1¼ cups milk
½ cup butter or margarine, melted
3 tablespoons chopped parsley
½ cup grated Parmesan cheese
8 ounces Mozzarella cheese, grated
Garlic salt to taste (optional)
Bread crumbs, about 3 tablespoons
Paprika

Preheat oven to 350°. Mix all ingredients together except crumbs and paprika. Oil a 3-quart round casserole. Sprinkle sides and bottom with bread crumbs and paprika. Pack potato mixture into casserole. Bake 1 hour. Unmold on serving dish and serve hot. Serves 12.

Variation: Equivalent amount of frozen hash brown potatoes may be used in place of boiled ones; let thaw until they can be well-mixed with other ingredients.

A Texas Hill Country Cookbook

Boxty

Boxty is a traditional potato dish served in Ireland on Halloween. Boxty resembles griddle cakes or potato pancakes.

1 pound potatoes
2 cups cooked mashed potatoes
4 cups flour
Salt and pepper
1 teaspoon baking soda
½ cup melted butter (1 stick)
Enough milk to make batter

Peel the raw potatoes and grate. Squeeze in a clean tea towel and keep the liquid. Mix liquid with mashed potatoes. Add grated potatoes. Add flour, salt, pepper, soda, butter, and enough milk and potato water to make a batter. Grease a skillet and cook pancakes over moderate heat. Boxty is served with butter and sometimes sprinkled with sugar.

The Melting Pot

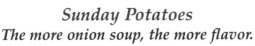
Sunday Potatoes
The more onion soup, the more flavor.

3 potatoes, sliced
Salt and pepper

2 tablespoons onion soup, dry
1 stick butter

Butter a medium casserole and layer potatoes. Sprinkle with salt and pepper and onion soup. Slice on top 1 stick butter. Cover and bake in 325° oven for 1 hour. Yields 4 servings.

Calf Fries to Caviar

Potato Bake

2 (12-ounce) packages Ore-Ida shredded hash-brown potatoes, thawed
1 pint sour cream
1 (10-ounce) can cream of chicken soup

1½–2 cups shredded mild Cheddar cheese
¼–½ cup finely chopped onions
½ cup cornflake crumbs
Salt and pepper to taste

Combine all ingredients and pour into two well-buttered 9-inch pie tins. Top with cornflake crumbs and dot with butter. Bake at 350° to 375° for 30–40 minutes.

Cookin' Wise

Bubble and Squeak

2 pounds potatoes, peeled
1 pound cabbage

2 tablespoons cooking fat

Boil the potatoes. Wash and cook cabbage 15 minutes. Strain and mash the potatoes. Strain and chop the cabbage. Mix potatoes and cabbage together well. Fry in hot fat on medium heat, turning often, until crisp on both sides. Serve with leftover cold roast beef or poultry. Makes 6–8 servings.

The Melting Pot

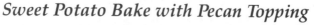

Sweet Potato Bake with Pecan Topping

The pecan tree was so loved by Texas Governor James Hogg that his last request was that a pecan tree be planted at the head of his grave and a walnut tree at the foot, and that when these trees bore, the nuts be given to the people of Texas to plant to make "Texas a land of trees." A few years later, the State Legislature voted to make the beautiful pecan the state tree.

3 cups sweet potatoes, cooked and mashed	**1 teaspoon vanilla**
	2 eggs, beaten
¼ cup milk	**½ teaspoon salt**
⅓ cup butter, melted	

Mix mashed sweet potatoes, milk, butter, vanilla, eggs and salt. Spoon into a 1½-quart oiled casserole.

TOPPING:

1 cup pecans, chopped	**⅓ cup butter, melted**
1 cup brown sugar	**1 cup coconut, optional**
3 tablespoons flour	

Combine topping ingredients and sprinkle over sweet potatoes. Bake at 375° for 25 minutes. Serves 6.

Tastes & Tales From Texas . . . With Love

Artichokes and Spinach Casserole

1 (6-ounce) jar marinated
  artichoke hearts
2 (10-ounce) packages frozen
  spinach, thawed
2 (3-ounce) packages cream
  cheese, softened

2 tablespoons butter
4 tablespoons milk
½ cup freshly grated Parmesan
  cheese
Pepper

Place artichokes in 2-quart casserole. Squeeze spinach dry and place on top of artichokes. Beat cream cheese and butter until smooth; add milk. Spread over spinach. Top with Parmesan and a grind of pepper. Cover. Refrigerate up to 24 hours. Bake at 350° 40 minutes, covered the first 30 minutes, then uncovered 10 minutes. Yields 6–8 servings.

Keepers

Jalapeño Spinach

4 packages frozen chopped
  spinach
8 tablespoons butter
4 tablespoons flour
1 small finely chopped onion
1 cup evaporated milk
1 cup vegetable liquor
1 teaspoon pepper

Dash cayenne
2 teaspoons celery salt
2 teaspoons garlic salt
1 teaspoon salt
2 (6-ounce) rolls jalapeño cheese
2 teaspoons Worcestershire
2 tablespoons lemon juice

Cook spinach. Drain well and reserve liquor. Melt butter, add onions and sauté until tender. Add flour and mix until smooth. Add liquid slowly, stirring constantly to avoid lumping. Cook until it thickens. Add seasonings and cheese. Stir until it is melted. Combine with spinach and place in casserole.. Top with buttered bread crumbs. Before serving, heat until bubbly. This is better if made the day before. It also freezes beautifully.

Cuckoo Too

Texican Squash
(Microwave)

2 pounds squash (yellow and/or zucchini)
1 onion, chopped
1 (4-ounce) can chopped green chilies
2 chopped, seeded jalapeños (optional)

8 ounces shredded Monterey cheese (2 cups)
1 cup dairy sour cream
1½ cups crushed flavored tortilla chips
Paprika

Slice squash ¼-inch thick. Place squash and onions in a 3-quart casserole. Cover and Microwave on HIGH 9–10 minutes, stirring once. Add chilies (including liquid), cheese and sour cream; toss gently so squash will not be mashed. Spread half of crushed chips on bottom of a 2-quart rectangular dish. Pour squash mixture in dish and sprinkle with remaining chips. Dust with paprika. Microwave on 70% (MEDIUM-HIGH) 10 minutes, or until heated through, rotating dish once. Serves 8. Recipe may be halved.

Microwave Know-How

Royal Squash

2 pounds yellow squash
1 large onion, diced
1 can cream of chicken soup
1 small carton sour cream
1 carrot, grated

Dash of garlic salt
1 stick margarine
1 package Pepperidge Farm Herb Dressing

Boil the squash and onion together until tender. Drain well and combine with the soup, sour cream, carrot and garlic salt. Set aside. Melt the margarine and add the dressing; mix well. Spread half of the mixture over the bottom of a casserole. Cover with the squash. Spread on the other half of the dressing. Bake at 350° for about 30 minutes until bubbly. Serves 10–12.

The Galveston Island Cookbook

Baked Acorn Squash

4 medium acorn squash
2 tablespoons butter
Salt and pepper to taste
½ teaspoon ginger
2–3 cups chicken stock

½ cup brown sugar
¼ cup Cointreau (optional)
¼ cup black walnuts, finely
chopped

1. Preheat oven to 350°.
2. Wash squash but do not peel. Split in half and remove seeds. Coat the insides thickly with butter and sprinkle with salt and pepper and ginger.
3. Place squash upright in shallow baking pan with about one inch of warm chicken stock in the bottom. Bake for 45 minutes.
4. Combine sugar, Cointreau, and nuts. Sprinkle mixture over squash and return to oven for 25–30 minutes or until squash is brown and very tender. Serve hot. Serves 8.

Variation:

DATE GLAZE:
1 cup dates, finely chopped
2 cups brown sugar
¼ cup water

¼ cup butter, melted
½ teaspoon nutmeg

1. Combine ingredients in saucepan. Cook until thickened—about 10 minutes.
2. Spread over squash and slip under broiler until bubbly.
3. Serve immediately.

Morning, Noon and Night Cookbook

Marlene's Squash

8 small yellow crookneck squash
3 scallions, chopped, green and
white parts
About 1 cup water

2 bacon slices
¼ cup sugar
Salt and pepper to taste

Boil squash and onions in water until tender. Meanwhile, fry bacon until crisp, and drain. Pour off all but 1 tablespoon of the drippings. Mash squash; place in skillet with drippings, sugar, salt and pepper. Cook until all water is gone and squash begins to brown and caramelize. Serves 4.

Noted Cookery

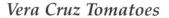

Vera Cruz Tomatoes

3 strips bacon
¼ cup chopped onion
8 ounces fresh spinach, snipped
½ cup dairy sour cream

Dash bottled hot pepper sauce
4 medium tomatoes
½ cup (2 ounces) shredded
Mozzarella cheese

Cook bacon until crisp; drain, reserving 2 tablespoons drippings. Crumble bacon and set aside. Cook onion in reserved drippings till tender. Stir in spinach. Cook, covered, till tender, 3–5 minutes. Remove from heat. Stir in sour cream, bacon and pepper sauce. Cut tops from tomatoes. Remove centers, leaving thick shells. Salt shells; fill with spinach mixture. Place in 8 × 8 × 2-inch baking dish. Bake in 375° oven for 20–25 minutes. Top with shredded cheese; bake 2–3 minutes more or till melted. Makes 4 servings.

Square House Museum Cookbook

Tomatoes Piquant

6 ripe tomatoes, peeled and
    quartered
⅔ cup salad oil
¼ cup tarragon vinegar
¼ cup snipped parsley
¼ cup sliced green onions
1 clove garlic, minced

2 teaspoons snipped fresh thyme
    or marjoram leaves or use ½
    teaspoon of the dried
1 teaspoon salt
¼ teaspoon freshly ground
    pepper

Place tomatoes in deep bowl. In jar combine remaining ingredients. Shake well; pour over tomatoes. Cover and chill at least several hours or overnight, spooning dressing over occasionally. At serving time, drain off dressing. Snip more parsley over tomatoes. Serves 6.

Scrumptious

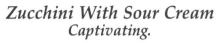

Zucchini With Sour Cream
Captivating.

3 medium zucchini
½ cup sour cream or more
2 tablespoons butter
2 tablespoons grated cheese
Salt and pepper

Paprika
1 tablespoon chopped chives
¼ cup buttered bread crumbs
Additional grated cheese

Slice washed, unpeeled zucchini into thin rounds; simmer, covered, in a small amount of water for 6–8 minutes, shaking the pan frequently. Drain. Combine sour cream, butter, 2 tablespoons grated cheese, salt, pepper and paprika; stir over low heat to melt cheese. Remove from heat and mix in chives; toss lightly with zucchini. Place in a buttered 1½-quart flat baking dish; top with crumbs and sprinkle with additional cheese. Bake in a preheated 375° oven for about 10 minutes. Can be prepared ahead and refrigerated, but increase the baking time to 30 minutes. Serves 6.

Crème of the Crop

Zucchini and Cheese Casserole

3 cups zucchini, grated
1 cup cracker crumbs
1 cup grated Cheddar cheese
2 eggs, beaten

2 tablespoons chopped onion
3 tablespoons margarine, melted
½ teaspoon Lawry's seasoning
Pepper

Combine all ingredients and put into a well-buttered 2-quart casserole. Bake for 1 hour at 350°. Serves 6.

Tempting Traditions

Quick Pizza Treats

12 whole wheat tortillas
1 cup pizza sauce (homemade or
  natural)
½ of a bell pepper, chopped
12 mushrooms, sliced

1 zucchini, sliced
2 green onions, sliced
Oregano
2 cups grated raw milk Cheddar
  cheese

Divide sauce among the tortillas and spread evenly. Sprinkle oregano lightly over sauce. Spread vegetables on top of sauce and layer cheese over vegetables. Broil until cheese melts and edges of tortillas are crisp. Yields 12 servings.

Nature's Kitchen

Vegetable Casserole

3 (16-ounce) cans vertically
  packed whole straight green
  beans
2 (16-ounce) cans whole baby
  Belgian carrots
2 (4½-ounce) jars whole button
  mushrooms
¾ cup margarine

¼ teaspoon lemon pepper
¼ teaspoon Worcestershire sauce
⅛ teaspoon garlic salt
⅛ teaspoon seasoned salt
4 tablespoons dried onion
1 tablespoon dried parsley,
  shredded

Drain green beans and arrange in two long rows in a 3-quart rectangular baking dish. Drain carrots and arrange in rows on top of green beans. Drain and sauté mushrooms in margarine. Add seasonings and onion to margarine and mushrooms. Pour this over the beans and carrots. Sprinkle with parsley. Cover with foil tightly and place in refrigerator to marinate overnight. Leaving foil on, heat thoroughly before serving (approximately 45 minutes at 325°.) Serves 10–15.

This is patterned after a modern Swiss recipe. It is such an attractive dish that guests always want the recipe, and it's so simple to make.

Repast

Vegetable Chalupa

Zucchini, sliced in rounds
Onion, chopped coarse
Mushrooms, cut lengthwise
Celery, cut crosswise
Olive oil
Corn tortillas

Sour cream
Fresh ripe tomatoes, chopped
Very ripe avocado, sliced
Cheddar cheese, grated
Picante sauce

Braise equal amounts zucchini, onion, mushrooms, and celery in small amount of olive oil until onion is clear. Brown tortillas in a dry skillet for about 15 seconds on a side. Put each tortilla on a dinner plate. Pile on the braised vegetables. Top with a dollop of sour cream, tomatoes, avocado, cheese. Run under the broiler until bubbly. Serve with picante sauce.

The Only Texas Cookbook

 Chalupa (chah LOO pah)—Tortilla dough shaped into an oval or boat, filled with shredded meat and other ingredients.

Casseroles

Some of the best ropers in the country compete for big prizes at the annual San Angelo Fall Roping Festival.

Herb Rice
Garlic, bay, marjoram, basil, thyme

3 tablespoons minced onion	1 teaspoon fresh marjoram
1 tablespoon minced fresh garlic	½ teaspoon fresh basil
4 tablespoons butter, melted	1 teaspoon fresh thyme
2 cups uncooked rice	4 cups chicken broth
2 bay leaves	

Sauté onions and garlic in butter, but do not brown. Add rice, bay leaves, marjoram, basil and thyme; cook until translucent. Pour in hot broth and simmer 25 minutes. Serves 10.

Absolutely wonderful!

The Dallas Symphony Cookbook

Rice-Green Chilies Casserole

1 cup raw rice	1 cup shredded Cheddar cheese
1 tablespoon margarine	1 (4-ounce) can chopped green
Salt and pepper to taste	chilies
1½ cups sour cream	

Cook rice according to package directions. Add butter and seasonings. Set aside. Fold sour cream and chilies together. In buttered casserole place a layer of rice and a layer of chilies-sour cream mixture. Cover with half of cheese. Repeat layers, topping with cheese. Bake 350° for 20–25 minutes till heated through. Yields 6–8 servings.

Running late and in a big hurry? Combine cooked rice, one 10¾-ounce can of Cheddar cheese soup, 1 cup sour cream and one 4-ounce can chopped green chilies. It's almost as good, and much faster.

Keepers

 Chile (CHEE lay)—A pepper. The flavor of chiles ranges from mild to very hot. The American spelling is chili.

Green Rice

1 cup uncooked rice
2 cups chicken broth
2 medium bell peppers, chopped
2 green poblanos chilies, sliced
1 medium onion, chopped
1 stick margarine

1 (16-ounce) carton sour cream
½ teaspoon garlic powder
Salt and pepper to taste
1 (12-ounce) package Monterey
   Jack cheese, grated

Cook rice in broth until tender, about 20 minutes. Meanwhile, sauté peppers, chilies, and onion in margarine. Put through the blender with sour cream to make a purée. Add garlic powder and salt and pepper to taste. Spread the cooked rice in a layer over the bottom of a 9 × 12-inch baking dish. Pour sauce over rice and top with grated cheese. Bake at 350° until bubbly.

Our Favorite Recipes

Poblanos (poh BLAH nohs)—Mild to hot, bright green chiles also called green chiles. They are sometimes stuffed and served like bell peppers.

Three Rivers Rice
A delicious choice.

1 huge onion, minced
¼ pound butter
2 cups rice
½ pound sharp cheese, grated
2 (10½-ounce) cans beef
   consommé

1 (8-ounce) can small
   mushrooms, with liquid
1 cup slivered almonds, toasted

Sauté onion in butter; add uncooked rice and simmer 5 minutes. Add remaining ingredients, reserving almonds; pour into a 2½-quart casserole. Cover and bake 1 hour at 325°. Stir in almonds before serving. Can be prepared ahead. Serves 8.

Crème of the Crop

Rice Pilaf

2 cups raw long grain rice	¾ cup chopped celery
⅓ cup butter	¾ cup chopped parsley
4 cups chicken broth	½ cup chopped green onion
¾ cup chopped carrots	1 cup slivered almonds

In a large skillet, stir rice in melted butter until a little brown. Have 3-quart casserole very hot and broth boiling; add the rice. Cook, covered, approximately 20 minutes in 350° oven. Add vegetables and almonds to rice and toss lightly. Return to oven for 15–20 minutes. Serves 12–15.

Lagniappe

Chicken Rice Casserole
(Commonly called Plopped Chicken)

1 cup rice	1 package Lipton's onion soup
1 (2½–3 pound) chicken, cut-up	2 (soup) cans water
1 (10-ounce) can mushroom soup	

Put uncooked rice in bottom of baking dish; place chicken pieces on top. Sprinkle with onion soup. Top with mixed soup and water. Bake 20 minutes at 400°, lower temperature to 350° for 1 hour longer.

Variation: Substitute ¼ cup white wine for water.

Trading Secrets

Sherry Beef and Rice à la Highlands

1 pound chuck or lean hamburger	1 (4-ounce) can mushrooms with
½ cup sliced onion	liquid
1 (16-ounce) can tomatoes	1 cup raw rice
⅔ cup pimiento-stuffed green	½ cup sherry
olives, sliced (or ripe olives)	1 cup shredded Cheddar cheese

Preheat oven to 375°. Brown meat and onion in skillet. Add tomatoes, olives, mushrooms with liquid, rice and sherry. Bring to a slow boil. Pour into a 2½-quart casserole. Cover and bake for 30 minutes. Remove cover and top with cheese. Return to oven and bake uncovered for 15 minutes. Serves 6.

With green salad and garlic bread, it is a fine repast.

A Texas Hill Country Cookbook

Green Enchiladas with Spicy Sauce

ENCHILADAS:
1 dozen corn tortillas
½ cup oil
2 cups shredded Monterey Jack
   cheese
¾ cup chopped onion
¼ cup butter or margarine

¼ cup flour
2 cups chicken broth
1 cup sour cream
1 (4-ounce) can jalapeño peppers,
   seeded and chopped

Cook tortillas, one at a time, in hot oil in skillet for 15 seconds on each side. (Do not overcook or tortillas will not roll.) Place 2 tablespoons of the cheese and 1 tablespoon of the onion on each tortilla; roll up. Place seam side down in baking dish. Melt butter or margarine in another saucepan; blend in flour. Add chicken broth; cook, stirring constantly, until mixture thickens and bubbles. Stir in sour cream and peppers; cook until heated through, but do not boil. Pour over tortillas. Bake at 425° for 20 minutes. Sprinkle remaining cheese on top; return to oven for 5 minutes or until cheese melts. Serve with Spicy Sauce. Serves 6.

SPICY SAUCE:
1 medium tomato, finely chopped
½ cup finely chopped onion
2 jalapeño peppers with seeds,
   finely chopped

¼ cup tomato juice
½ teaspoon salt

Combine all ingredients.

Enjoy!

Cheese Enchiladas, Pronto!
(Microwave)

1 dozen corn tortillas	½ cup chopped onion
1 pound shredded Cheddar cheese (4 cups)	1 (10-ounce) can enchilada sauce or chili hot dog sauce

Wrap 6 tortillas in a damp paper towel. Sandwich between two salad plates and Microwave on HIGH 45 seconds. Place ⅓ cup cheese and a sprinkle of onions on each tortilla and roll up. Place seam-side down in a 2-quart rectangular dish. Repeat for remaining tortillas. Pour enchilada sauce over all. (If using chili hot dog sauce, Microwave on HIGH 3 minutes so it will pour over enchiladas.) Sprinkle with any remaining cheese and onions. Cover and Microwave on 70% (MEDIUM-HIGH) 5–6 minutes. Serves 4–6.

Note: If making half of a recipe, Microwave on 70% 3 minutes.

Microwave Know-How

Chilaquiles

1 dozen tortillas, quartered and softened in hot oil	2 cans stewed tomatoes
2 medium onions, chopped	2 stalks fresh celery, chopped
1 clove garlic, minced finely	Fresh cilantro sprig (optional)
2 cans mild, chopped green chili peppers	2 pounds grated Monterrey Jack cheese
	3 cups sour cream

Simmer all ingredients *except* tortillas and cheese. Salt and pepper to taste. Heat oil; dip pieces of quartered tortilla in hot oil until softened. Layer tortillas, sauce, and cheese to top of a large casserole dish, 13 × 9 inch. Place in oven at 350° for 15–20 minutes to heat thoroughly and melt cheese. Cut through like a cobbler and serve with sour cream on top. A wonderful brunch dish! (Can be prepared ahead of time and refrigerated up to 2 days. Heat at 350° for 1 hour to serve.) Serves 10–12.

Spindletop International Cooks

Chili Relleno

1 (4-ounce) can whole chilies,
halved and seeded
1 (8-ounce) package Monterey
Jack cheese
2 eggs, beaten

1 (5.33-ounce) can evaporated
milk
1 (8-ounce) can tomato sauce
½ cup sherry
¼ stick margarine or butter

Line baking dish with chili peppers, cover with sliced Jack cheese. Beat eggs and add to milk. Pour this over the mixture of cheese and chilies. Bake ½ hour at 350°. Add tomato sauce, mixed with margarine and sherry. Pour over and bake for another ½ hour. Let stand for 15 minutes before serving, so that it will set.

Cowtown Cuisine

Chili Rellenos Quiche

Add Egg Topping for puffy effect for a special "Fiesta."

1 (9-inch) pastry shell
2 cups grated Monterey Jack
cheese
1 (4-ounce) can chilies

4 eggs
1 cup half-and-half
¼ teaspoon pepper
Taco sauce

Bake frozen or prepared pastry shell at 475° for 5 minutes. Sprinkle in partially baked crust 1 cup Monterey Jack cheese. Layer with half of chilies. Sprinkle with remaining 1 cup Monterey Jack cheese. Add rest of chilies, more if you like it hot. Mix together and pour over mixture in crust eggs, half-and-half, and pepper. Bake in a preheated 375° oven for 30 minutes. Serve with taco sauce. Or, add Egg Topping, bake and serve. Yields 6 servings.

EGG TOPPING:
In small bowl, beat until very stiff 2 egg whites. Fold in, just until blended, 2 egg yolks, slightly beaten.

Spoon over baked quiche. Be sure to seal to edge of crust. Return to oven and bake at 375° for 15 minutes or until golden brown.

Calf Fries to Caviar

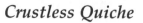

Crustless Quiche

8–10 slices bacon, crisply cooked
  and crumbled
1 cup Swiss cheese, grated
¼ cup onion, minced
4 eggs
13–14 ounces small curd cottage
  cheese
1 package frozen chopped
  spinach, cooked with 1
  teaspoon salt, then drained
½ teaspoon salt
½ teaspoon pepper
1 teaspoon Worcestershire sauce
3 dashes Tabasco sauce

Sprinkle cheese, bacon, and onion in that order in a 10-inch greased pie plate. Beat remaining ingredients until well blended. Pour over bacon mixture. Bake at 350° for 35–40 minutes. Let stand 10–15 minutes before cutting. (This recipe may be baked in miniature muffin tins for 42 individual servings; bake for approximately 20 minutes. Regular muffin tins will yield 14 servings; bake for approximately 25 minutes.)

This is a favorite for our Y bridge luncheons.

Cookin' Wise

Shrimp and Avocado Quiche
(Microwave)

In honor of our *Sacramento Bee.*

1 cup shredded Mozzarella
  cheese (4 ounces)
1 (9-inch) pie shell, baked
1 ripe avocado, sliced
2 teaspoons lemon juice
1 cup cooked or canned shrimp
3 eggs
⅔ cup light cream
2 tablespoons chili sauce
⅛ teaspoon cayenne pepper
⅛ teaspoon basil
1 green onion with top, thinly
  sliced

Place half of cheese in bottom of pie shell. Toss avocado with lemon juice to prevent darkening. Distribute over cheese. Add shrimp and remaining cheese. In a small bowl, beat together eggs, cream, chili sauce, cayenne pepper and basil. Pour over mixture in pie shell. Sprinkle green onions over top. Microwave on 70% (MEDIUM-HIGH) 10–12 minutes, rotating dish once midway through cooking. Let stand 10 minutes before cutting. Makes 6 servings.

Micro Quick!

Yucatán Quiche

CRUST:
¾–1 cup safflower oil
7–8 corn tortillas

In a medium-size skillet, heat the safflower oil. Dip each torilla briefly to soften and seal and then press between paper towels.

Spray a 9-inch pie pan with a non-stick vegetable coating and then line with the prepared tortillas, overlapping them, extending about ½ inch over the pan edge.

FILLING:

2 eggs	1 cup refried beans
2 cups half-and-half or cream	½ pound sausage, cooked and
½ teaspoon salt	drained
2 cups (about 8 ounces) shredded	2 tablespoons mild green chiles,
Monterey Jack cheese	diced

In a small bowl, combine the eggs, half-and-half or cream, and salt. Set aside.

Sprinkle half the cheese over the tortillas, followed by the beans, sausage, chiles, and then the egg mixture. Evenly distribute the remaining cheese over the top. Bake in a preheated 350° oven for 30 minutes or until firm. Yields 6 servings.

PRESENTATION:
1 avocado, sliced
1 tomato, sliced
Snipped cilantro leaves

Garnish the baked quiche with avocado and tomato slices. Place cilantro leaves over the top. Serve warm.

Storage, Freezing, and Advance Preparation: This is as good at room temperature as it is hot, but it does not freeze very well.

Creative Mexican Cooking

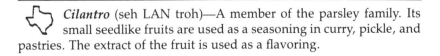

Cilantro (seh LAN troh)—A member of the parsley family. Its small seedlike fruits are used as a seasoning in curry, pickle, and pastries. The extract of the fruit is used as a flavoring.

Onion Pie
"Out of this world!"

2 cups chopped onion
1 cup butter
2 eggs, yolks and whites, beaten separately
½ cup cream or Milnot

Salt and cayenne pepper to taste
1 cup dry white wine
2 (9-inch) prepared pastry shells

Sauté onions in butter until limp, but not browned. Cool. Preheat oven to 350°. Stir egg yolks, cream, salt, cayenne and wine into onions. Fold beaten egg whites into onion mixture. Fill pie shells and bake 30 minutes. Serves 12 generously or serve 6 and freeze one. Serve as a starch with steaks or roast beef. Serve hot or cold as a luncheon dish.

I also like to precondition the crust by brushing with egg white and baking for 8–10 minutes in a 400° oven. Crust should be cool before mixture is poured in and baked.

Collectibles II

Spinach Noodles

4 tablespoons butter
½ clove garlic, minced
5 tablespoons lemon juice (divided)
¼ teaspoon basil
1 (12-ounce) package spinach noodles

½ pound small cooked shrimp
Dash of Tabasco
3 tablespoons sour cream
Chopped parsley

Simmer butter, garlic, 3 tablespoons lemon juice and basil, but do not allow to brown. Cook noodles according to directions on package. Drain. Mix shrimp with 2 tablespoons lemon juice and Tabasco. Add butter mixture and shrimp to noodles. Heat in double boiler. Just before serving, add sour cream and sprinkle with chopped parsley. Increase the amount of shrimp if this is to be used as a main dish. Serves 6–8.

Bravo, Chef!

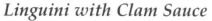

Linguini with Clam Sauce

4 (6½-ounce) cans minced clams
2 sticks butter
5 cloves garlic, crushed
Lawry's garlic salt to taste
1 tablespoon lemon juice
Parmesan cheese for garnish
1 tablespoon grated onion

3 tablespoons fresh parsley,
    chopped
White pepper to taste
½ pint heavy cream
2 tablespoons cornstarch
1 pound linguini

Empty clams, juice and all, into saucepan. Melt butter, add all ingredients and simmer 15 minutes. Add heavy cream with the cornstarch. It will thicken just enough to make it adhere to the linguini. It should not be too thick. Cook one pound linguini with a little oil and serve sauce over it. Top with freshly grated Parmesan cheese. Serves 6. Will serve 12 as an appetizer.

Entertaining at Aldredge House

Mexican Corn Pudding

1 (16-ounce) can creamed corn
2 eggs, beaten
1 can tamales, shucked and cut
    up
2 tablespoons butter

1 (4-ounce) can chopped ripe
    olives
½ cup (or more) grated Cheddar
    cheese

Combine corn, eggs, and tamales; dot with butter. Mix gently; put in greased casserole. Bake at 350° for approximately 45 minutes. Remove from oven; add olives and sprinkle cheese on top. Return to oven until cheese melts. Serve while hot. Makes a nice supper dish with a salad. Serves 4.

Enjoy!

Mary Beth's Lasagne
(Microwave)
The fastest lasagne in the West!

1 pound sweet Italian sausage,
  casings removed
1 (32-ounce) jar prepared
  spaghetti sauce
½ cup dry red wine
¼ teaspoon garlic powder
½ teaspoon dried basil
16 ounces ricotta or cottage
  cheese

⅓ cup Parmesan cheese
1 tablespoon chopped parsley
1 egg, slightly beaten
¼ teaspoon pepper
8 uncooked lasagne noodles
8 ounces Mozzarella cheese,
  sliced

Break up sausage into a hard-plastic colander. Set colander over a 2-quart glass batter bowl and cover with a paper towel. Microwave on HIGH 5 minutes. Drain off fat and place meat in same bowl, breaking up with a fork. Add spaghetti sauce, wine, garlic powder and basil. Stir and Microwave on HIGH 7–8 minutes, or until bubbly.

In a mixing bowl, combine the cheeses, parsley, egg and pepper. Spoon the meat sauce to cover the bottom of a 10 × 10-inch dish. Arrange 4 noodles on the sauce. Spread half the cheese mixture and then half the Mozzarella cheese. Repeat, with sauce as the final layer.

Cover with a glass lid or plastic wrap. Microwave on HIGH 6 minutes; then Microwave on 70% power (MEDIUM-HIGH) 20 minutes. Let rest, covered, 12–15 minutes before serving. Standing time is crucial to the success of this recipe. Do not serve before letting stand! Serves 6–8.

Note: Mary Beth's Lasagne is fantastic! It was developed by Mary Beth Cyvas, Houston home economist who invented the Micro Weigh™ scale. We especially like the Italian sweet sausage used in her recipe.

Microwave Know-How

Veggie Lasagna

2 cups chopped fresh tomatoes	1 teaspoon oregano
2 cups chopped fresh mushrooms	1 teaspoon basil
1 chopped onion	8–10 ounces whole wheat lasagna
1 chopped bell pepper	2 cups tofu or homemade cottage
3 chopped cloves garlic	cheese
1 tablespoon unrefined olive oil	1 pound grated raw milk cheese
¾ cup homemade tomato paste or	
natural bottled pizza sauce	

Steam onions, mushrooms, bell peppers, and garlic. Pour olive oil over mixture and set aside. Put tomatoes and tomato paste in saucepan. Add spices and simmer until flavors are blended. Cook noodles.

In 11 × 13 × 2-inch glass baking dish layer ⅓ of the noodles, ⅓ of the vegetable mixture, ⅓ of the sauce, ⅓ of the tofu, and ⅓ of the cheese. Repeat twice. Top with the cheese. Bake at 350° for 30–45 minutes. Yields 10–12 servings.

Nature's Kitchen

Eggplant Dressing

1 large eggplant	1 pod garlic
1 pound chicken giblets	1–1½ cups rice
1 large onion	Cooking oil
1 green pepper	Salt
½ stalk celery	Pepper

Peel, dice and salt eggplant. Set aside for one hour (until brown water has accumulated at bottom of bowl). Chop all seasoning and sauté in cooking oil (cover bottom of pot with oil). When seasoning is tender, add boiled, chopped chicken giblets. Sauté for 10 minutes more. Then add drained eggplant, salt and pepper to taste; cover and lower flame. Stir occasionally. When eggplant is done (almost puréed), add cooked rice (more if you like dressing dry, less if you prefer it moist). Cover and cook 10 minutes. Do not add rice until serving time. Great with beef, fowl or wild game. Serves 4–6.

(Joyce Gay) *The Woodlands Celebrity Cookbook*

East Texas Turkey Dressing

1 (12-serving size) cornbread
  (made according to recipe of
  choice)
6 slices stale bread ends,
  crumbled
1 cup chopped onion
1 tablespoon sage

1 teaspoon salt
2 eggs, not beaten
½ teaspoon pepper
2 cups chicken or turkey broth
4 teaspoons bacon drippings,
  melted
1 cup drained oysters (optional)

Prepare cornbread to serve 12. Set aside. Combine bread, cornbread, onion, sage, salt, pepper, eggs, stock and bacon drippings. Add oysters if desired. Stir ingredients lightly and stuff into fowl (or bake separately at 350° for 30 minutes). Makes about 3 quarts.

This recipe (Susan Cooper's) can be traced to my great-grandmother. It is likely that it has been served on every Thanksgiving since 1883 by some descendant. My ancestors came from Shelby County near Timpson, and many still remember the thrill of occasionally having fresh oysters in the tiniest town in East Texas.

Through Our Kitchen Door

Corn Bread Dressing

5 or 6 cups chicken or turkey
  broth
1 pan of corn bread
7 or 8 biscuits
2 or 3 eggs, hard-boiled

1 medium size onion, chopped
⅔ cup chopped celery
½ teaspoon salt
½ teaspoon sage
¼ teaspoon black pepper

Cook onion and celery in broth for about five minutes. Crumble corn bread and biscuit with pepper and sage. Add to mixture, stirring until all bread is moist and soft. Add chopped boiled eggs. Beat by hand for one or two minutes. Dressing should be rather soft. Pepper and sage can be increased according to taste. Pour in a 2-quart baking dish and cook in oven at 400° for 45–50 minutes, or stuff inside the holiday bird.

Mrs. Blackwell's Heart of Texas Cookbook

Seafood

One hundred and ten mile long Padre Island offers one of the last natural seashores in the nation. South of Corpus Christi.

Crab Lasagna

1 (8-ounce) package lasagna
  noodles
1 tablespoon oil
4 quarts water
2 cans cream of shrimp soup
14 ounces king crab
2 cups cottage cheese
8 ounces cream cheese
1 egg
1 cup chopped onion
2 teaspoons basil
1 teaspoon salt
¼ teaspoon pepper
1 cup Cheddar cheese, shredded
4 medium tomatoes, peeled and
  sliced
2 teaspoons sugar
2 tablespoons Parmesan cheese

Boil noodles in oil and water about 15 minutes. Drain. Combine soup and crab in medium saucepan and heat until bubbly. Combine next seven ingredients. In baking dish, layer ⅓ of the noodles, ½ of the cheese mixture, ⅓ of the Cheddar cheese, ⅓ of the noodles, all of the crab sauce, ⅓ Cheddar cheese, ⅓ noodles, ½ cheese mixture and ⅓ Cheddar cheese. Top with tomatoes and sprinkle with sugar. Cook 15 minutes in 350° oven. Sprinkle with Parmesan cheese. Bake for an additional 45 minutes. Let stand 15 minutes before serving. The flavors have a chance to blend and its even better if it's made the day before serving. Serves 6–8.

Amarillo Junior League Cookbook

Crabmeat Sharman

2 (8-ounce) packages cream
  cheese
2 tablespoons mayonnaise
4 tablespoons grated onion
1 tablespoon cream style
  horseradish
2 tablespoons milk
13 ounces crabmeat (fresh)
Juice of 1 lemon
Lea & Perrins Worcestershire
  sauce

Mix all ingredients together until smooth. Add a dash of Lea & Perrins Worcestershire sauce and juice of lemon. Bake in 10-ounce buttered pie plate for 30 minutes at 350°. Cover with a sprinkle of paprika. Delicious! This dish makes a fabulous main dish or hot dip. Serve with sesame or rye Old London Melba rounds and toast. This and a good salad are quite a meal! Serves 6 or 20 as a dip.

Cuckoo Too

Crabby Cheese
Much better than it sounds

½ pound fresh mushrooms, sliced
2 tablespoons butter
2 tablespoons flour
1 (10¾-ounce) can chicken broth
1 (10¾-ounce) can cream of mushroom soup
1 (8-ounce) package Old English cheese slices
1 (6-ounce) package Wakefield crabmeat, thawed
2 ounces dry sherry
English muffins or pastry shells

Sauté mushrooms in butter. Remove mushrooms and add flour to butter and juice to make a thick roux. Slowly add chicken broth and allow to thicken. Add cream of mushroom soup and bring to very slow boil. Reduce heat and add Old English cheese slices. Allow these to melt completely. Add crabmeat and mushrooms. Just before serving, stir in sherry. Serve over toasted English muffins or in pastry shells. Serves 4–6. Good for brunch or luncheon.

Hullabaloo in the Kitchen

Crabmeat Casserole

1 cup thick cream sauce
3 tablespoons chopped celery
1 tablespoon butter
1 (4-ounce) can sliced mushrooms, drained
1 pound lump crabmeat
Salt, pepper, paprika
2 tablespoons grated cheese
1 tablespoon sherry
Bread crumbs
Parmesan cheese

Make a thick cream sauce. Sauté celery in butter until tender. Add celery, mushrooms and crabmeat to cream sauce. Stir in salt, pepper, paprika, grated cheese and sherry. Pour into buttered casserole or individual crab shells. Brown bread crumbs in a little melted butter, mix with Parmesan cheese and sprinkle over casserole. Bake in 400° oven for 15 minutes or until thoroughly heated. Yields 4–6 servings.

Keepers

Crabmeat à la Lulu
What else can I say!

¼ cup or (½ stick) butter
1 cup fresh mushrooms, thinly sliced
1 cup milk
1 egg yolk
2 tablespoons lemon juice
1½ tablespoons flour
1 tablespoon green onion, finely chopped

1 teaspoon parsley flakes
¼ teaspoon salt
⅛ teaspoon cayenne pepper
⅛ teaspoon Tabasco sauce
6 ounces cooked crabmeat, if frozen, thaw
½ cup Swiss cheese, grated

1. Preheat oven at 350°.

2. In a small skillet, melt the butter and cook the mushrooms for 10 minutes. Remove from heat.

3. In a blender, combine the milk, egg yolk, lemon juice, flour, onions, parsley flakes, salt, cayenne, Tabasco, and blend briefly.

4. Pour blender mixture into a bowl, add mushrooms and butter, crabmeat, and cheese. Mix well.

5. Pour into baking dish and bake at 350° for 30 minutes.

6. Serve over cooked rice or noodles. Serves 3.

Leaving Home

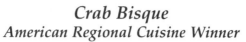

Crab Bisque
American Regional Cuisine Winner

4 shallots, diced
1 clove garlic, minced
8 tablespoons butter
⅛ teaspoon thyme
6 tablespoons flour
2 cups cream
4 cups chicken stock

¼ teaspoon Dijon mustard
¼ teaspoon Worcestershire
1 pound crabmeat, picked over
  for shells
Salt and pepper, to taste
6 tablespoons chopped parsley

Sauté shallots and garlic in 2 tablespoons butter, until fragrant. Add thyme and remaining butter and blend. Add flour and cook the roux over moderate heat until very slightly colored.

Combine cream, stock, mustard and Worcestershire and add in a stream to roux stirring constantly. Add crabmeat. Bring to a simmer and cook for 7–8 minutes. Add salt, pepper, parsley and stir to blend.

Margaret Hughes and Harry Corless were American Regional Cuisine Winners with this recipe.

March of Dimes Gourmet Gala Cookbook

 Bisque (BISK)—A kind of creamy soup made with a purée of seafood, meat, and/or vegetables.

Baked Seafood Casserole

1 pound cooked crabmeat, flaked
2 (4½-ounce) cans shrimp,
  drained
1 cup mayonnaise
1 cup chopped onion
1 cup sliced mushrooms
2 teaspoons Worcestershire sauce
1 teaspoon salt

½ teaspoon paprika
1 (8½-ounce) can water chestnuts,
  drained, sliced
2 cups diced celery
1 cup chopped green pepper
1 cup chopped pecans, toasted
2 cups buttered croutons
2 cups shredded Cheddar cheese

Heat oven to 375°. Combine first 12 ingredients in large bowl. Arrange 1 cup croutons in greased 13 × 9-inch baking dish. Top with half of seafood mixture, 1 cup of cheese, ½ cup pecans and remaining croutons. Repeat layering with remaining seafood mixture, cheese and pecans. Bake at 375° for 30 minutes. Serves 10.

The Dallas Pecan Cookbook

Marinated Shrimp

2 pounds shrimp, cooked and
drained
¼ cup pimiento-stuffed olives
1 pound fresh mushrooms,
quartered
1 cup water
¼ cup low-calorie Italian
dressing

2 tablespoons lemon juice
2 cloves garlic, halved
1¼ teaspoons salt
½ teaspoon thyme leaves
1 teaspoon nutmeg
2 bay leaves
Peppercorns

Combine shrimp and olives in large bowl. Combine remaining ingredients in large saucepan. Bring to a boil: simmer for 5 minutes. Pour over shrimp mixture. Toss lightly to mix, cool. Refrigerate, covered for 6–8 hours or overnight. Pile generous amounts of shrimp mixture with some of the marinade onto crisp salad greens to serve. Serves 6.

A Taste of Victoria

Shrimp Creole

⅓ cup shortening
¼ cup flour
1 cup hot water
1 (8-ounce) can tomato sauce
1 pound medium shrimp, cleaned
and deveined
½ cup green onions and tops,
chopped
4 cloves garlic, pressed
½ cup fresh parsley, chopped

¼ cup green pepper, chopped
1½ teaspoons salt
2 whole bay leaves
½ teaspoon crushed thyme
1 lemon slice
Cayenne pepper
2–3 cups cooked rice (prepared
according to package
directions)

1. In a large skillet, melt shortening. Blend in flour, stirring constantly until mixture is brown (about 5–10 minutes). Add water and cook until thick, stirring constantly.

2. Add tomato sauce and mix thoroughly.

3. Add remaining ingredients, using cayenne pepper to personal taste. Serve over rice. Yields 4 servings. Preparation time: 30 minutes.

Rare Collection

Sweet and Sour Butterfly Shrimp

INGREDIENTS:

24–28 large shrimp (about 1 pound)
1 cup frozen carrots and peas
½ cup diced yellow onion
2 garlic cloves, chopped
2–3 cups oil for frying

BATTER:

1 egg
1 cup all-purpose flour
¼ cup cornstarch
½ cup + 2 tablespoons very cold water
1 teaspoon baking powder
½ teaspoon salt
6 tablespoons cooking oil
Dash of pepper

FOR MARINATING SHRIMP:

1 egg white
1 teaspoon salt
1½ tablespoons cornstarch
2 tablespoons cream sherry

SAUCE: (Double sauce when serving with rice.)

¾ cup water
¼ cup pineapple juice
5 tablespoons sugar
3½ tablespoons white vinegar
1 tablespoon soy sauce
1 tablespoon ketchup
1½ tablespoons cornstarch mixed with 2 tablespoons water
1 tablespoon apricot preserves

TO PREPARE:

1. Shell and devein shrimp. Split each shrimp lengthwise into one big piece from back down (but don't cut all the way through). Rinse and pat dry. Place in a bowl. Marinate with seasonings for about 20–30 minutes.

2. Combine batter ingredients. Beat gently for a few minutes.

TO COOK:

1. Heat 1 tablespoon oil and sauté garlic. Add carrots, peas, and yellow onions. Stir-fry for 30 seconds. Remove.

2. Make sauce by adding pineapple juice, apricot preserves, sugar, soy sauce, ketchup, and vinegar into water in that order. Heat sauce to a boiling point; add cornstarch paste; stir until thickened. Let sauce cool a little. Return vegetables to the sauce.

3. Dip shrimp in batter and fry until golden brown and crisp. Keep warm until serving time.

4. Pour the sauce over fried shrimp. Serve immediately. Serves 6.

Chinese Cooking the American Way

Shrimp Harpin

2½ pounds large raw shrimp,
shelled and deveined
1 tablespoon fresh or frozen
lemon juice
3 tablespoons salad oil
¾ cup raw regular rice
2 tablespoons butter
¼ cup minced green pepper
¼ cup minced onion

1 teaspoon salt
⅛ teaspoon pepper
⅛ teaspoon mace
Dash cayenne pepper
1 can tomato soup, undiluted
1 cup heavy cream
½ cup dry sherry
¾ cup slivered, blanched
almonds

Cook shrimp in boiling, salted water for 5 minutes; drain. Place in a 2-quart casserole; sprinkle with lemon juice and salad oil. Meanwhile, cook rice as label directs; drain.

About 1 hour and 10 minutes before serving: start heating oven to 350°. Set aside about 8 shapely shrimp for garnish. In a skillet, sauté green pepper and onion in butter for 5 minutes. Mix with rice, salt, pepper, mace, cayenne pepper, soup, cream, sherry and ½ cup almonds. Pour over shrimp in casserole. Toss well. Bake at 350° uncovered for 35 minutes. Then top with the reserved shrimp and the remaining ¼ cup almonds. Bake 20 minutes longer or until mixture is bubbly and shrimp are slightly browned. Serves 8.

This recipe can easily be tripled, using a 5-quart casserole and topping with 1 dozen shrimp and ½ cup almonds. Bake as directed, increasing second baking to 35 minutes. Makes 24 generous servings.

Scrumptious

Scampi à la Domingo

SAUCE:

1 (14½-ounce) can Italian
   tomatoes
4 tablespoons olive oil

2 basil leaves
1 large garlic clove, minced
Pinch of red pepper

Combine all ingredients in a saucepan and simmer for 10–15 minutes while preparing scampi.

7 scampi
Olive oil
Salt and pepper
3 tablespoons butter

1 garlic clove, chopped
¼ cup dry white wine
Chopped parsley

Shell and devein scampi leaving the tail attached. Rinse and pat dry. Coat with olive oil, dust with salt and pepper and bake in a 350° oven for 4–5 minutes. Remove from oven, sauté in a skillet with the butter, garlic and wine. Add tomato sauce and simmer for 5–10 minutes, stirring occasionally. Sprinkle with chopped parsley before serving. May be served over spaghetti or linguini.

(Placido Domingo) *Bravo, Chef!*

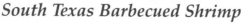
South Texas Barbecued Shrimp

6 uncooked boneless chicken
  breasts
9 slices thinly sliced bacon

1 pound uncooked medium
  shrimp pieces
Your favorite teriyaki sauce

Cut chicken breasts into 1×3-inch strips. Flatten each strip with side of cleaver. Put one-half slice bacon on each strip. Then place a shrimp at one end of the strip, roll up and secure with a tooth-pick. Marinate in teriyaki sauce for 2 hours or more in refrigerator. May be frozen until ready to use. Cook on brazier for approximately 15 minutes. Serves 8.

Entertaining in Texas

My Barbequed Shrimp
Bring on the cold beer

1 pound (18–21 count) raw
  shrimp in shells
½ cup salad oil
¼ cup butter, no substitute,
  please
2 tablespoons fresh lemon juice
2 tablespoons dry white wine
1 tablespoon Worcestershire
  sauce
1 tablespoon parsley flakes

1 teaspoon cracked black pepper
1 teaspoon fresh garlic, pressed
  or finely chopped
½ teaspoon salt
½ teaspoon Knorr Swiss Aromat
  Seasoning for Meat
½ teaspoon Lawry's lemon
  pepper
2 shakes Tabasco sauce

1. Rinse and drain shrimp and place in the bottom of a baking dish.
2. In a small bowl, combine and mix together all the remaining ingredients.
3. Pour sauce over shrimp.
4. Bake in preheated 400° oven for about 20 minutes, stirring once or twice. When cooked, the shells will turn a red color.
5. Serve with crusty French bread, for dipping in sauce. Serves 4 people 5 shrimp each.

Leaving Home

Barbecued Shrimp

4 pounds raw jumbo shrimp,
   peeled and deveined
1 large bottle of Wishbone Italian
   dressing
Garlic powder
1 lemon

3–4 teaspoons melted butter
Lemon pepper
Coarse ground black pepper

Coat shrimp in Italian dressing. Add a sprinkle of garlic powder and juice of ½ lemon. Marinate in refrigerator for 30 minutes. Remove shrimp from marinade (reserving any marinade left in dish). If you use a charcoal grill, place shrimp in a hinged wire grill, and cook 3–4 inches above burned-down coals. If you have a gas grill, you can place the shrimp directly on medium heated grill. For both methods cook shrimp 3–4 minutes per side or until meat turns opaquely white. Don't overcook or shrimp will be tough.

Baste freely with the remaining marinade and sprinkle with lemon pepper and black pepper. When the shrimp are almost done, encourage the grill to flame up and char the shrimp by basting with the melted butter. Remove from heat and squeeze the remaining ½ lemon over top. Serve with coleslaw and garlic bread.

(Z Z Top) *Houston Celebrity Cookbook*

Oysters Rockefeller

1 cup sour cream	1 (10-ounce) package frozen
½ teaspoon salt	chopped spinach, cooked and
½ teaspoon garlic powder	drained
½ teaspoon white pepper	Parmesan cheese
2 teaspoons Worcestershire sauce	Bread crumbs
Oyster shells	Butter, very cold
Rock salt	
1 pint oysters	

Combine sour cream, salt, garlic powder, pepper and Worcestershire sauce. The secret is to mix sour cream and spices to your taste. Use red pepper if a hotter flavor is desired. Place empty oyster shells on a bed of rock salt. Using about one-half of the sour cream mixture, place a spoonful in each shell. Place oyster (two, if small) on top of sour cream. Mix spinach and 1 tablespoon Parmesan cheese with remaining sour cream. Mound this mixture on top of each oyster. Sprinkle top with Parmesan cheese and bread crumbs and dot with butter. Bake for 10 minutes at 400°. Place under broiler 3 inches from heat. Broil 5 minutes or until crumbs are light brown. Serves 2–3 as a main course.

San Angelo Junior League Cookbook

Oysters Erminie

1 quart oysters, semi-defrosted	1 package Pepperidge Farm herb
6 green onions	dressing mix
1 white onion	Salt and pepper
4 stalks celery	1 clove garlic
Butter	Parsley

Chop oysters fine while semi-defrosted. Brown green onions, white onion, and celery in butter. Add most of the package of Pepperidge Farm herb dressing mix, plus a little water if necessary. Add salt, pepper and garlic. Place in shells and sprinkle chopped parsley on top. Bake in 350° oven about 30 minutes. Serves 8.

Cuckoo Too

King Arthur's Oysters
There is never enough.

2 tablespoons butter, melted	3 tablespoons water
¼ cup lemon juice	2 dozen oysters
½ cup dry sherry	Salt
1 cup A-1 steak sauce	Pepper
2 tablespoons flour	

1. In medium size saucepan, combine butter, lemon juice, sherry, and steak sauce. Cook over low heat.

2. Blend flour and water together. Slowly stir into sauce being careful not to let boil.

3. Add oysters to sauce and heat for 1 minute. Adjust seasonings to taste with salt and pepper.

4. Transfer to chafing dish to keep warm. If oysters are to be eaten immediately, they can be placed in a shallow baking dish or serving dish. Yields 6 servings (4 each). Preparation time: 30 minutes.

Rare Collection

Ceviche II

1 pound fresh, sweet white fish (snapper, redfish, etc.)	3 serrano peppers (packed in vinegar), cut up
Juice of 3 limes or enough to cover fish	Juice of 1 orange
1 teaspoon salt	2 tablespoons olive oil
1 tablespoon fresh cilantro, chopped	1 large onion, finely chopped
	2 fresh tomatoes, peeled and chopped

Cut fish into thin bite-sized pieces. Combine lime juice, salt, and cilantro. Pour over fish. Be sure there is enough juice to cover fish. Marinate in refrigerator 4 hours. Add orange juice, oil and tomatoes. Serve in cups with juice and saltine crackers. Serves 6.

San Antonio Conservation Society Cookbook

 Ceviche (say VEESH)—A dish or appetizer made essentially of fish marinated in lime or lemon juice.

Seafood Ballottine

Seafood Ballottine, with its exotic ingredients, typifies the elegance of the French Room.

1 (3-pound) side of salmon, pounded flat	1 small eel, smoked
⅔ cup scallops with roe	3 leaves dry seaweed
⅔ cup lobster meat	1 ounce cognac
2 ounces sea urchins	1 recipe lobster mousse
	1 recipe scallop mousse

LOBSTER MOUSSE:

1 pound lobster	¼ cup reduced fish stock
1 egg	Salt, pepper
1 quart cream	

SCALLOP MOUSSE:

½ pound scallops	¼ cup reduced fish stock
1 egg	Salt, pepper
1 pint cream	

Prepare lobster and scallop mousses separately for rolled ballottine. Grind the lobster and scallops for the mousses the day before and keep refrigerated; meat must be very cold before blending in the food processor. To each, add eggs, salt and pepper and blend to a paste. Add cream slowly and mix to the thickness of heavy cream. Correct seasonings and set each mousse aside.

Mix the lobster mousse with scallops, lobster meat, sea urchins, chives and cognac. Flatten salmon slice and spread with ¼-inch thickness of scallop mousse, then a layer of seaweed leaves. Cover the leaves with lobster mousse and stretch the eel across the center. Roll up carefully. Wrap tightly in buttered aluminum foil. Bake in *bain marie* at 275° for 45 minutes. Remove from foil. Cool and slice for serving. Serves 10–12.

Serve with a medium-bodied white Graves, a California Chardonnay, or, possibly, a Meursault.

The Adolphus Cookbook

Bain marie (ban mah REE)—A French phrase which describes a steam table which has openings for several pots or pans so that their contents can be warmed by hot water or steam circulating around them.

168

Charcoaled Baked Redfish

Build hot fire in covered barbecue grill, placing rack 4–6 inches above coals.

3 pounds redfish, filleted	2 small cloves garlic, pressed
10 tablespoons lemon or lime juice	5 scallions, finely chopped
	¾ teaspoon salt
6 tablespoons butter, softened	½ teaspoon cracked pepper

Place fish in pan in single layer or make pan out of aluminum foil, rolling up edges to hold juices. Pour lemon or lime juice over fish. Let stand 30 minutes, turning frequently.

Meanwhile, mix butter and garlic until blended. Sprinkle scallions on fish. Add salt and pepper. Spread garlic butter over fillets.

Place fish on rack in grill; cover and bake 20 minutes. Test fish to see if it flakes. If not, cook a few minutes more. Serve immediately, pouring pan juices over fish. It will not be browned, but juices will be golden. Serves 6.

Houston Fine Arts Cookbook

Elegant Baked Fish

1½ cups Hellmann's mayonnaise	2 teaspoons garlic powder
1 tablespoon creole mustard	¾ teaspoon curry powder
1 tablespoon lemon juice	Ritz crackers
1 tablespoon Tabasco	
1 tablespoon Worcestershire sauce	

Mix well and spread over eight fish fillets. Sprinkle with crumbled Ritz crackers and bake at 400° for about 20 minutes uncovered. Fish is done when it flakes easily with a fork.

Everyone loves fish cooked this way. We thank Becky McLeary for this recipe!

Of Magnolia and Mesquite

Ballottine (bah leh TEEN)—A French dish of meat, fish, or fowl which has been boned and stuffed with a combination of meats, vegetables, and herbs, then rolled and tied in a bundle shape and cooked in rich stock. Although ballottine can be served cold, it is generally a hot dish.

Stuffed Baked Fish
(From Suzanne's Apron Pocket)

STUFFING:

1 cup bread crumbs	½ teaspoon salt
1 tablespoon grated onion	4 tablespoons melted butter
½ cup chopped celery	Dash cayenne pepper

Melt the butter in a skillet, then mix all ingredients for stuffing together. Try adding a cup of chopped fresh mushrooms, a cup of lump crabmeat, a few raw chopped oysters, a cup of raw shrimp (put into skillet with butter and a tablespoon or so of lemon juice).

1 whole (3–5 pound cleaned weight) red snapper, trout, or whitefish	¼ cup sherry
	2 tablespoons lemon or lime juice
	1 teaspoon seafood seasoning
⅛ stick of butter	Salt and pepper

Dry fish thoroughly and rub inside and out with seasoning. Melt the butter, add sherry and lemon or lime juice. Fill the fish with stuffing; skewer opening. Bake in a very hot oven (450°) for 10 minutes or until brown—½ of the butter and sherry mixture is poured on the fish to start, the other half is added when you reduce the heat to 350° and bake approximately 12 minutes per pound, or until done. Serves 6–8.

Fish 'n tips: Place fish on heavy brown paper on a greased baking sheet for baking. When the fish is done, you can grasp edges of the paper and lift from baking pan, then let slide, unbroken, to platter. Garnish platter with watercress or parsley and lemon wedges.

From My Apron Pocket

Trout Almondine

6 large trout or redfish fillets
Juice of 2 lemons, divided
24 saltine crackers, crushed
2 sticks butter, divided
Garlic salt to taste

Pepper to taste
¾ cup sliced almonds
1 (4-ounce) can mushrooms,
  drained

Marinate fish in the juice of 1 lemon for 5 minutes. Coat fish with crackers and sauté in 1 stick butter for 3–5 minutes on each side. Place fish in a baking pan, sprinkle lightly with garlic salt and pepper, and top with remaining lemon juice. Sauté almonds and mushrooms in remaining butter and pour over fish. Bake at 300° for 20 minutes. Serve immediately. Serves 6.

Flavors

Baked Flounder Fillets

1 pound frozen flounder fillets
¼ cup sour cream
¼ cup mayonnaise
1 tablespoon dried onion flakes
1 tablespoon lemon juice

1 tablespoon butter or margarine
Paprika
Fresh parsley, chopped
Lemon wedges (optional)

Place fish fillets skin down in a greased glass baking dish. Mix sour cream, mayonnaise, onion flakes and lemon juice. Spread on top of fish. Dot with butter, and sprinkle lightly with paprika. Bake, uncovered, 20–25 minutes at 350°. Sprinkle with chopped parsley and, if desired, serve with lemon wedges. Serves 4.

San Angelo Junior League Cookbook

Fish-n-Fowl Sauce

½ cup lemon juice
½ cup salad oil
2 tablespoons grated lemon rind

2 teaspoons dried tarragon leaves
1 teaspoon salt
½ teaspoon pepper

Combine ingredients and use for basting poultry and fish. Yields about 1¼ cups.

Wild-n-Tame Fish-n-Game

Fish-Asparagus Roll-Ups

2 packages frozen filet of
  flounder or sole
Lemon juice
Frozen asparagus (3 spears per
  person)
1 quart water
1 bouillon cube
¼ teaspoon pepper
Few grains sea salt
Asparagus
Oregano

2 cups BCB (basic chicken broth)
1 cup chopped ripe olives
3 thin slices pepperoni, cut finely
1 clove minced garlic
1 finely chopped white onion
½ cup dry white wine
½ teaspoon dried or fresh mint,
  minced
½ teaspoon basil, crushed
½ teaspoon salt substitute
½ teaspoon fresh ground pepper

Rinse fish with cold water to separate filets. Select the most uniform sized filets, squeeze lemon juice over them, let thaw. Put other smaller filets and pieces in airtight Ziploc baggie, return to freezer for other recipes.

While filets thaw, prepare frozen asparagus, allowing 3 spears per person. In a boiler bring to simmer, water, bouillon cube and asparagus. Cover to steam. Do not overcook; 5 minutes should be sufficient.

When filets have thawed, brush each one on both sides with 1 cup BCB, pepper and sea salt. Place flat to roll, fill center with asparagus, roll up fish, secure with toothpicks. Spray large heavy skillet with Pam and place roll-ups seam side down. Sprinkle lightly with oregano.

Place remaining ingredients in a bowl with remaining cup BCB. Stir well to blend and pour evenly over the roll-ups. Cover, steam simmer only as long as it takes fish to flake. The inside rolled part of filet will take a bit longer than outside, but not much longer.

The above is the Italian version. For a French version, substitute 1 cup sliced mushrooms for olives; ½ teaspoon thyme for mint; ½ teaspoon white pepper for black. Add 1 small jar of chopped pimento.

La Galerie Perroquet Food Fare

Trophy Bass Fillets

This one is for fishermen who are tired of fried fish and broiled fish and aren't sensitive to a little excitement in food.

3 pounds bass fillets
1 large lemon, juiced
1 stick oleo, melted
Salt and pepper
½ teaspoon oregano
2 bay leaves
1 large potato, sliced thin

1 dozen green chili peppers and juice
1 green pepper, chunked
2 medium fresh tomatoes, chunked
1 medium onion, sliced

Preheat oven to 325°. Line a large deep pan or casserole dish with heavy duty foil. Cover bottom of lined pan with melted oleo. Add lemon juice to bottom of pan. Place seasoned fish on top of this mixture. Sprinkle with oregano, bay leaves, potatoes, green chili peppers (mash in own juice), green pepper, tomatoes, and onion slices. Fold foil so that steam will not escape. Bake for 1½ hours; slit foil and fold back. Return to oven to reduce juice and brown. Try it . . . you'll like it!

Wild-n-Tame Fish-n-Game

Fillets of Sole Louise

3 medium-sized fillets of sole
3 tablespoons dry white wine or sherry
Juice of ½ lemon
½ bay leaf

⅛ teaspoon ginger
2 tablespoons butter
1 tablespoon onion, chopped fine
1 tablespoon parsley, chopped fine

Salt and pepper fillets of sole. In skillet place wine, lemon juice, bay leaf, ginger, butter, onion and parsley. Bring to boil; then turn down heat. Add fillets. Cover and cook for 5 minutes. Serve immediately.

Recipe may be used with fillets of most any type fish. This is a delicious gourmet dish easily prepared when you are running late.

Repast

Beer Batter

Good with vegetables (mushrooms, onions, bell peppers, all types squash, etc.). Also good with shrimp, fish, crab and crayfish tails.

1 cup flour
1 can beer
1 egg
1 tablespoon Worcestershire
   sauce

1 tablespoon mustard
2 cups crushed potato chips

Pour beer in flour until thin mixture. Add 1 beaten egg, Worcestershire and mustard. Dip vegetable or fish in batter; then roll through crushed potato chips. Drop into deep fryer at 300°. Cook 3–4 minutes until light brown.

"I'm Glad I Ate When I Did, 'Cause I'm Not Hungry Now"

Green Sauce

1 pint sour cream
1 jar Gerber's baby spinach
Juice of 1 lemon

1 large teaspoon horseradish
½ grated small onion
Salt and pepper

Mix all together thoroughly. Let stand for 3–4 hours. Especially good on crabmeat, shrimp or any fish.

Cuckoo Too

Poultry

Mission Espiritu Santo, founded in 1749 to Christianize the Indians, maintained first large cattle ranch in Texas. West of Victoria.

Chicken Stew

This savory filling, similar to Ninfa's, may be used in tacos, flautas, enchiladas, or toasted and buttered bolillos. My favorite way is to prepare a light, warm chicken salad, using fresh lettuce and garnishes of white Mexican cheese (the crumbly variety like farmer cheese) and fresh slices of papaya, avocado, or tomato. This makes a large quantity; half the recipe fills 12 enchiladas. It freezes quite well; however, you may wish to halve the recipe.

2 whole chickens	**2 cloves garlic**
1 bay leaf	**1 onion slice**
2 teaspoons salt	**Several cilantro sprigs**

In a large (4-quart) stockpot, cover the chicken with water and then add the bay leaf, salt, garlic, onion, and cilantro. Bring to a boil and then simmer until the chicken is tender, about 50 minutes. Remove the chicken and strain and reserve the stock. The stock may be used for a soup base or sauce; it freezes well.

When it is cool enough to handle, debone and shred the chicken.

1 medium-size onion, chopped	**¼ teaspoon salt**
2–3 tablespoons vegetable oil	**¼ teaspoon black pepper**
3 tomatoes, peeled and chopped, including juice	**1–2 teaspoons chile powder**
1 (4-ounce) can green chiles, chopped	**½ teaspoon garlic powder**
	¼–½ cup of chicken stock, if needed

In a large (12-inch) skillet or sauté pan, sauté the onion in oil until soft and translucent, about 5 minutes. Stir in the chopped tomatoes, chiles, and seasonings; then add the chicken. Return to a boil (if using chilled chicken); then cook over medium heat for 3 to 5 minutes. You may need to add a small amount of chicken stock to keep the mixture moist. Yields 8 cups.

Author's Note: Shred chicken while still warm and shred with the grain. After chicken is refrigerated, it becomes too gelatinous to shred well. Storing chicken in some of its stock will keep it tender and moist.

Storage, Freezing, and Advance Preparation: This filling may be refrigerated or frozen.

Creative Mexican Cooking

Chicken Madeleine
A Square House Luncheon Favorite

½ cup butter
½ cup flour
1 cup cream
1 cup chicken broth
1 cup milk
1 teaspoon salt
½ pound fresh mushrooms or 6
  ounces canned, sliced

2 cups diced cooked chicken
½ cup sherry wine
¾ cup toasted, slivered almonds
2 cups whole, seedless white
  grapes

Dice boned, cooked chicken. Melt butter; make a roux with flour; add cream, milk, chicken broth and cook until smooth and thick. Fold in mushrooms, chicken, toasted almonds and add sherry. Correct seasoning. Just before serving fold in white grapes.

To serve: make either cream puff (pâté à Chou) or crêpes. If the cream puffs are used, they can be made, baked and stored in the deep freeze. This is especially nice for the larger luncheons. *Be sure your cream puff is baked completely dry and that no moisture remains inside.* Reheat slowly to serve.

Square House Museum Cookbook

Chicken Squares

3 cups cooked chicken, diced
2 cups chicken broth
1 cup cooked rice
2 cups soft bread crumbs
⅓ cup diced celery
¼ cup pimientos
4 eggs, beaten
1 teaspoon salt

½ teaspoon poultry season
1 tablespoon onions, diced
Black pepper
1 (10¾-ounce) can cream of
  mushroom soup or cream of
  chicken soup
⅓ cup milk

Combine all ingredients, except soup and milk. Mix well. Bake in greased pan at 350° for 55 minutes. Serve with sauce made of soup and milk heated together.

Cowtown Cuisine

Gourmet Chicken Spaghetti

3 pounds chicken
8 ounces thin spaghetti
4 tablespoons butter
4 tablespoons flour
1 cup cream
1 cup chicken broth
1 cup mayonnaise
1 cup sour cream
1 cup Parmesan cheese

⅛ cup lemon juice
⅓ cup white wine
½ teaspoon garlic powder
½ teaspoon cayenne
1 teaspoon dry mustard
1 teaspoon salt
8 ounces fresh mushrooms
4 tablespoons butter

Boil and bone chicken. Break spaghetti into thirds and boil in chicken stock. Make basic white sauce. Melt butter; add flour and cook until bubbly. Add cream and chicken broth, stirring and cooking until thickened. Add mayonnaise, sour cream, Parmesan, lemon juice, wine and seasonings. Sauté mushrooms in butter. Place mushrooms, chicken and spaghetti in flat 3-quart casserole. Add sauce and mix well. Sprinkle paprika and additional Parmesan on top. Bake at 350° for 30–40 minutes. May be made ahead of time and frozen. Serves 8–10.

Lagniappe

Texas Quick Chicken and Dumplings

1 large chicken or 4 large breasts
  and 6 thighs

1 dozen flour tortillas
Salt and pepper to taste

Boil chicken in pot with plenty of water. Debone chicken and return to broth. Bring back to a boil and add flour tortillas while water is boiling. (Tortillas should be cut in wide strips about 2 inches long. You should get 8 dumplings per tortilla). Reduce heat and cover pot. Cook slowly for about 10 minutes.

"I'm Glad I Ate When I Did, 'Cause I'm Not Hungry Now"

Pollo Con Calavacita

1 fryer or selected pieces	1 large onion, chopped
3 pounds zucchini or calabassa	1 or 2 garlic cloves, chopped
4 ears corn	Generous pinch of comino
3 tomatoes or 1 (12-ounce) can	2 or 3 serrano or jalapeño peppers
1 green pepper, cut in strips	

Brown chicken lightly in a small amount of butter. Add onion, garlic, tomatoes, comino and hot peppers and a small amount of water. Simmer about ½ hour. Add squash, corn from the cobs, green pepper strips and simmer about another ½ hour. There should be very little moisture left, but it should not be dry. This is a delicious dish made with lean pork or a combination of pork and chicken. It is also better made the day before and reheated at serving time. Serves 6.

San Antonio Cookbook II

Pollo (POY yoh)—The Spanish word for chicken.
Calabacita (cah lah bah SEE tah)—A round, striped green squash, also called a zucchini squash.

Chicken and Dumplings

1 (3 to 4-pound) hen, cooked and deboned	½–1 cup ice water
	2 cups chicken broth
2 cups flour	2 cups milk
1 teaspoon salt	½ cup butter
½ cup shortening	Salt and pepper to taste

Blend flour, salt, and shortening until mixture resembles corn meal. Slowly add cold water until it makes a dough. Roll dough thinly on a floured board and cut into strips. In a Dutch oven add equal amounts of broth and milk. Add butter, salt, and pepper. Bring to a slow boil, lower heat, and simmer. Add one strip of dough at a time to this liquid. Do not stir. Push down with a spoon. Cook for 15 minutes, then add meat carefully. Serves 8.

Hospitality

Mexican Chicken Portuguese

6 cups cooked, chopped chicken
1 pound Velveeta cheese, cut in
  chunks
1 pound Longhorn cheese, grated
1 pint sour cream
1 (3-ounce) jar sliced pimentos
2 (10-ounce) cans tomatoes and
  green chiles

3 medium onions, chopped
1 clove garlic, minced
1 tablespoon oil
2 bell peppers, seeded and
  chopped (optional)

Cook the onion and garlic in oil until transparent. Add the tomatoes and green chiles and bring to a boil. Reduce the heat and
simmer until thick, about 20 minutes. Add the cheese and heat
slowly until melted. Then add the chicken and sour cream. Heat
until hot and smooth, but do not boil. Serve over a layer of rice
and a layer of crisp tostado strips.

  This is a great dish for buffet supper with roast beef or ham. For
luncheon serve simply with a green salad!

It's a Long Way to Guacamole

Snow on the Mountain

½ cup butter
1 cup fresh mushrooms, sliced
½ cup green pepper, chopped
½ cup flour
1 teaspoon salt

¼ teaspoon pepper
2 cups half and half
2 cups chicken broth
2 cups chicken, cooked and diced
  (1 [3-pound] fryer)

TOPPINGS:
Celery, diced finely
Tomatoes, diced
Cheese, coarsely grated
Green onion, chopped

Chinese noodles
Pineapple chunks
Almonds, unblanched, sliced
Coconut, grated

Sauté mushrooms and green pepper in butter. Blend in flour, salt
and pepper. Add and stir constantly half and half and chicken
broth until mixture boils. Add chicken and heat through. To
serve, cover plate with cooked rice and top with chicken mixture.
Add toppings desired, ending with coconut.

Scrumptious

Nancy's Chicken Mole

Here is a company dinner that's as easy as can be.

2 (3-pound) chickens, cut into
  serving pieces
Margarine
Salt
1½ cups chicken broth
1 bell pepper, chopped fine
¾ teaspoon anise seed
1 tablespoon sesame seed
3 cloves garlic, crushed
Dash powdered cloves
⅛ teaspoon powdered cinnamon

Dash black pepper
¼ teaspoon whole coriander,
  crushed
1 square unsweetened chocolate,
  melted
1½ tablespoons chili powder
3 large tomatoes, chopped fine
1 whole pimiento, chopped fine
⅓ cup almonds, crushed (or
  peanuts)
3 cups cooked rice

Arrange chicken pieces in a large, flat baking dish that has been well-greased with margarine. Salt the chicken lightly. Then mix together (in a processor, blender, or by hand) remaining ingredients, except almonds and cooked rice, to make a coarse purée. Pour evenly over chicken pieces and bake uncovered in a 350° oven for about 1 hour, or until chicken is tender throughout. Meanwhile, cook a pot of rice. Serve mole over rice with crushed almonds sprinkled on top. Feeds 8 in 1 hour.

An American Gumbo

 Mole (MOH lay)—A Mexican hot sauce of chili, spices, and sometimes chocolate.

Baked Chicken Nuggets

7–8 boneless chicken breasts,
  uncooked
2 cups fine breadcrumbs
1 cup grated Parmesan cheese

1½ teaspoons salt
1½ tablespoons dried thyme
1½ tablespoons dried basil
1 cup butter, melted

1. Cut chicken into 1½" pieces. 2. Combine next 5 ingredients. 3. Dip chicken in butter, then in breadcrumb mixture. 4. Place on baking sheet. 5. Bake at 400° for 20 minutes. Makes 14–16.

Easy Does It Cookbook

Almond Chicken

It is crunchy! The kind of dish the diet-people look for.

INGREDIENTS:

1½ cups raw chicken meat (about half a chicken) diced
2 ounces canned or fresh mushroom slices
4 ounces diced bamboo shoots or water chestnuts (quartered)
½ cup almonds
1 cup diced celery
½ cup chicken broth
2 garlic halves
3 tablespoons oil
1 teaspoon cornstarch mixed with 2 teaspoons water

A. SEASONING FOR CHICKEN:

2 tablespoons sherry
1 teaspoon salt
2 teaspoons soy sauce
½ teaspoon sugar
Pinch of MSG, optional
1 tablespoon cornstarch
1 egg white

B. SEASONING FOR VEGETABLES:

½ teaspoon salt
½ teaspoon sugar
Pinch of MSG

PREPARE AHEAD:

1. Marinate chicken with seasoning A; leave it for 10–15 minutes.

2. Place all vegetables in three sections on one plate, within easy reaching distance.

TO COOK: (5–6 minutes)

1. Heat one tablespoon oil over high heat, sauté celery first. After one minute, add bamboo shoots and mushrooms, toss fry quickly. Remove.

2. Heat two tablespoons oil over high heat, sauté garlic first, discard. Sauté chicken quickly until color of meat turns to white. Remove.

3. In the same fry pan, bring ½ cup broth to hot, thicken with the cornstarch mixture; return all cooked vegetables and chicken to the pan. Toss in almonds just before serving. Serve hot. Serves 4–6.

Hint: Egg white adds extra tenderness to the chicken.

Chinese Cooking the American Way

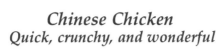

Chinese Chicken
Quick, crunchy, and wonderful

SAUCE:

¼ cup honey
½ cup soy sauce
¼ cup red wine vinegar
1 clove garlic, minced

2 tablespoons sesame seed, toasted
⅛ teaspoon red pepper

Combine all ingredients.

4 cups cooked, shredded chicken
½-1 head iceberg lettuce, shredded
1 (3¾-ounce) package bean threads or 1½ cups bean sprouts

2 tablespoons oil
2–3 bunches scallions

Marinate chicken in sauce 30 minutes. Using wok or large sauce-pan, sauté bean threads in oil over high heat 1 minute; drain. Mix chicken, marinade, scallions, and lettuce with bean threads. Toss briefly over low heat to blend thoroughly. Serve immediately so that vegetables remain crisp. Serves 4.

The Dallas Symphony Cookbook

Lemon Seasoned Chicken Breast
(Good for diets)
(Microwave)

1 tablespoon water
½ teaspoon Bouquet sauce
1 tablespoon lemon juice
½ teaspoon salt (optional)

2 whole bone-in chicken breasts, halved, skin removed
1–2 teaspoons parsley flakes

In small dish, combine all ingredients except chicken and parsley. Arrange chicken breasts, bone side up, on microwave roasting rack, with meatiest portions to outside of dish. Brush with ½ of seasoned mixture. Microwave on HIGH for 5 minutes. Turn pieces over and brush with remaining mixture. Microwave 10–15 minutes or until meat near bone is no longer pink. Rotate once during cooking. Top with parsley.

The Pride of Texas

Breast of Chicken in Cream and Apples

8 chicken breasts	1½ cups cider
3 tablespoons flour	½ cup brandy
8 tablespoons butter	2 cups whipping cream
4 tablespoons minced onion	Salt and pepper to taste
8 fresh apple rings, peeled and cut ½-inch thick	

Dust the chicken breasts with flour and sauté in the butter with the onion over a low heat. Poach the apple rings in the cider until soft. When chicken is nicely browned add the brandy and ignite. Drain the apple rings and add the cider used for poaching to the chicken. Cook at low heat until the chicken is tender, about 10 minutes. Add cream and continue cooking until the sauce is thickened. Season to taste. Place chicken on a serving platter, put a slice of apple on each piece, and pour sauce over all. Run under the broiler to brown. Serves 8.

Bravo, Chef!

Chicken Monterrey Cole
A delectable treat.

4 whole chicken breasts	¾ cup dry bread crumbs
8 ounces Monterrey Jack cheese	Butter
2 eggs, beaten	

Bone and skin and split the chicken breasts; flatten each half to ¼-inch thickness. Cut cheese in 8 sticks. Roll chicken breasts around cheese and secure with toothpicks. Dip chicken rolls in egg and then bread crumbs. Heat butter to 325° and brown chicken on all sides. Remove toothpicks and bake at 400° for 20 minutes. Makes 8 servings.

Crème of the Crop

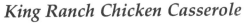

King Ranch Chicken Casserole

The King Ranch may be the most famous spread in America, and this just might be the best-loved recipe in Texas: it was sent in with only slight variations by good cooks all over the state. How the dish earned its name, its only connection to the illustrious ranch, nobody knows.

1 (10¾-ounce) can cream of
chicken soup
1 (10¾-ounce) can cream of
mushroom soup
2 cups chicken broth
1 (10-ounce) can Rotel Tomatoes
and Green Chiles

12 tortillas, cut in pieces
1 (3–4 pound) chicken, cooked
and cut into bite-sized pieces
1 large onion, chopped
2 cups grated American cheese

Combine soups, chicken broth and tomatoes and set aside. Oil a 3-quart casserole. Layer half of tortilla pieces, half of chicken, half of onion and half of cheese in the casserole. Pour half of chicken broth mixture over layers. Repeat layers of tortillas, chicken and onion, then pour remaining chicken broth over top with remaining cheese. Bake at 350° for 45–60 minutes. This can be frozen and reheated and will still taste great. Serves 8.

Tastes & Tales From Texas . . . With Love

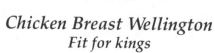
Chicken Breast Wellington
Fit for kings

1 sheet Pepperidge Farm puff
  pastry (comes frozen in a
  17¼-ounce box containing 2
  sheets per box) at room
  temperature
¼ cup butter
1 pound (4 count) boneless
  chicken breast

½ (8-ounce) package cream
  cheese, at room temperature
Knorr Swiss Aromat Seasoning
  for Meat to taste
Lawry's lemon pepper to taste
Melted butter

1. When puff pastry reaches room temperature, unfold it onto a floured surface, sprinkle top lightly with flour, and roll it out as flat as you can, but to where you can still handle the dough. Cut dough into 4 equal-sized squares.

2. Using medium heat, melt the butter, add chicken breasts, and cook 5 minutes per side.

3. Place each breast in the center of a pastry square, put 2 tablespoons of cream cheese on top of each breast.

4. Now sprinkle to taste with Seasoning for Meat and lemon pepper.

5. Pull the edges of the pastry square up and fold them over the breast as to seal the breast inside the puff pastry.

6. Brush the top of pastry with melted butter if you wish.

7. Bake uncovered in a preheated 350° oven for 30 minutes. Serves 4.

Leaving Home

Honey Bake Chicken

1 fryer, cut-up
4 tablespoons margarine
½ cup honey
¼ cup pineapple juice

1 tablespoon Dijon mustard
1 teaspoon salt
1 teaspoon curry powder

In large baking dish, melt margarine. Add honey, pineapple juice, mustard, salt and curry powder. Mix well. Coat chicken with mixture and arrange in baking dish. Bake uncovered about 1 hour at 375°. Turn once or twice. Serves 4.

San Antonio Conservation Society Cookbook

Chicken Spectacular

1 (1-pound) can French style
  green beans, drained
½ cup mayonnaise
1 cup water chestnuts, drained
  and sliced
2 tablespoons chopped pimiento
1 (6-ounce) can sliced mushrooms
2 tablespoons chopped onion

1 (6-ounce) package Uncle Ben's
  Long Grain and Wild Rice
1 can cream of celery soup
1 package slivered almonds
Salt and pepper to taste
1 stewed chicken, diced or 4 large
  breasts, cooked and diced

Stew chicken or breasts. Use chicken broth to cook 1 package rice. Toast almonds in butter and salt under broiler in oven. Mix remaining ingredients along with diced chicken and rice. Place in 2-quart casserole dish. Top with slivered almonds. Almonds can be mixed in with the casserole if desired. If dry looking before baking, pour chicken broth over it. This casserole freezes very well. If frozen, thaw, then bake uncovered for 30 minutes at 350°. Serves 6–8.

Entertaining in Texas

Broccoli Chicken

12 halves deboned chicken
  breasts (cook until tender)
3 packages frozen chopped
  broccoli, cooked
3 cans cream of chicken soup
1½ cups Hellman's mayonnaise

1 tablespoon lemon juice
1 teaspoon curry powder
1 cup grated sharp Cheddar
  cheese
1 stick oleo
1½ cups cracker crumbs

Place cooked, chopped broccoli in flat casserole dish. Place breasts on top. Make sauce of the chicken soup, mayonnaise, lemon juice and cheese. Heat through until cheese melts. Pour over the layers of broccoli and chicken. Sauté crumbs in oleo. Sprinkle over top and dust with paprika. Bake at 350° for 30 minutes or until sauce is bubbly. Serves 12.

The Cottage Kitchen Cookbook

Chicken Dijon

12 pieces of chicken	½ jar Dijon mustard
Salt, pepper, and garlic salt to taste	1 cup sour cream
	Italian flavored bread crumbs

Season chicken with salt, pepper, and garlic salt. Combine mustard and sour cream; spread each piece lightly with this mixture. Roll in bread crumbs: place chicken in baking dish and cover with foil. Bake at 400° for 30–40 minutes. Remove foil: bake an additional 20 minutes or until chicken is golden brown.

Enjoy!

Lemon Spring Chicken

8 chicken breasts	2 tablespoons salad oil
1 cup flour	1 teaspoon minced onion
2 teaspoons salt	2 minced garlic cloves
¼ teaspoon pepper	4 lemons, juiced
⅔ cup butter	½ cup finely chopped parsley

Dust chicken breasts with flour and seasonings. Heat butter and oil with onions and garlic. Add breasts and sauté lightly, about 20 minutes. Turn once. Continue cooking. Add lemon juice to pan. Boil 1 minute. Add parsley and pour over chicken. Serve at once and hot!

Through Our Kitchen Door

Chicken Taco Filling

This chicken dish is a delicious filling for the traditional taco, or try it in a soft taco. Prepare the shells for soft tacos by immersing corn tortillas in ½ inch hot oil only until they are soft. Drain on paper towels. Spoon filling down the center of each tortilla and fold in half or roll. Serve immediately with grated Monterrey Jack cheese, lettuce, and guacamole.

3 tablespoons oil	1½ cups canned tomatoes and
1 medium onion, chopped	green chilies with juice
1 large clove garlic, minced	½ teaspoon cumin (comino)
2 cups cooked chicken	Salt and pepper to taste

In a heavy skillet, heat oil and sauté onion, garlic, and chicken, using two forks to stir and shred chicken. Cook over medium heat until chicken starts to brown and gets crisp around the edges.

Add tomatoes and green chilies with juice, breaking the tomatoes into small pieces as you add them. Add cumin, salt, and pepper.

Continue cooking over medium heat until all liquid has cooked down—about 10 minutes. Scrape bottom of pan frequently to prevent sticking. Yields 8–10 servings.

Cooking Texas Style

Taco (TAH coh)—A kind of Tex-Mex sandwich, filled with combinations of ground meat, chile peppers, cheese, tomatoes, lettuce, and refried beans. Tacos are enclosed in a folded or rolled tortilla and served with salsa cruda.

Sour Cream Chicken Enchiladas

1 chicken, stewed and cut into
  bite-size pieces
1 large bunch green onions and
  tops, chopped
½ stick margarine, or ¼ cup
  butter
1 garlic clove, minced
1 (16-ounce) can tomato sauce
1 (4-ounce) can chopped green
  chiles, drained
1 teaspoon sugar

1 teaspoon cumin
½ teaspoon salt
½ teaspoon oregano
½ teaspoon basil
2 cups Monterrey Jack cheese,
  grated
2 cups Longhorn Cheddar cheese,
  grated
1 pint sour cream
12 tortillas

Set aside stewed, boned and cut up chicken. Sauté together onions, margarine and minced garlic. Add tomato sauce, chiles, sugar, cumin, salt, oregano, basil. Simmer approximately 15 minutes. In separate bowl mix together Monterrey Jack and Cheddar cheese. Mix the cubed chicken with enough sour cream to just moisten. Save remainder of sour cream.

    Dip each tortilla into hot tomato sauce to soften tortilla. Place a portion of the chicken mixture on the tortilla and add a portion of the grated cheeses. Roll up and place seam-side down in a greased baking dish. This will do 12 tortillas. Mix remaining tomato sauce with the remaining sour cream and smooth over top of casserole, allowing it to seep between tortillas. Sprinkle cheeses over top. Cover and bake at 350° for 30–45 minutes, or until hot. Preparation time: 1 hour with fresh chicken, ½ hour with canned chicken. Serves 6 and is very good warmed over.

Entertaining at Aldredge House

Mexican Cream

This is similar to a French *crème fraîche* and may be used as a substitute for sour cream. It will not curdle as easily as sour cream and is therefore excellent for topping enchiladas.

2 cups sour cream
1 cup heavy cream

2 teaspoons fresh lime juice

Stir ingredients together and let stand at room temperature for 2 hours. Refrigerate till ready to use. This will keep for 2 weeks. Yields 3 cups.

Creative Mexican Cooking

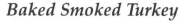

Baked Smoked Turkey

12–15 pound young turkey
Thin mesquite, or hickory chips,
   cooked to coals in covered
   outdoor grill

MARINADE:

½ cup celery
½ cup onions
½ cup bell peppers
¼ cup lemon juice
¼ cup Worcestershire sauce
⅓ teaspoon Louisiana Hot Sauce

¼ cup tomato sauce
½ teaspoon chili powder
½ teaspoon thyme
½ teaspoon oregano
1 teaspoon salt
½ teaspoon rosemary

Blend all in a blender. Simmer for 20 minutes. Cool. Marinate turkey for two or three hours in this marinade, rinsing first and rubbing cavity with small amount of salt. Remove from marinade and place in oven baking bag. Bake approximately three hours in 325° oven. Remove from bag. Add ½ cup Wesson oil to marinade and swab turkey with this mixture. Place bird on the barbecue grill, off center from the fire, with a drip pan beneath to catch drippings. (Do not let the drippings burn during the smoking, for the flavor would be ruined.) Allow only the smoke from the fire to cook the bird. Smoke the turkey for about one hour, swabbing with the marinade-oil sauce occasionally. Test for doneness by moving drumstick. If pliable and soft, the bird is done. Remove the smoked turkey from the grill and let rest for at least three hours, or place overnight in the refrigerator before slicing to serve.

The Cottage Kitchen Cookbook

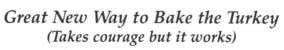

Great New Way to Bake the Turkey
(Takes courage but it works)

1 (14–18 pound) turkey

Salt and pepper inside and out. Place in roaster or turkey pan with six cups of water. Tightly cover with lid or heavy duty foil.

Bake the bird in a 500° preheated oven for one hour. Turn off oven and DO NOT OPEN THE DOOR FOR 12 HOURS. It does work and your turkey will be moist and tender. You will have lots of good juice for the dressing and gravy. Plus, your oven will be free for other baking if you do as I do and let him do his thing all night.

For a 20–22 pound turkey, cook 1 hour and 15 minutes.

Collectibles II

Apple Stuffed Cornish Hens
(Microwave)

⅓ cup water
3 tablespoons margarine
¼ cup chopped celery
1 teaspoon instant minced onion
1 cup dry herb stuffing mix (such as Pepperidge Farm)
¼ cup dry roasted peanuts

1 tart cooking apple, cored and diced
2 (10-ounce) Cornish game hens, defrosted
Oil
Kitchen Bouquet

Combine water, margarine, celery and onion in a 4-cup glass measure. Microwave on HIGH 1½ minutes, or until margarine melts and water is boiling. Stir in stuffing mix until liquid is absorbed. Stir in peanuts and apple.

Remove neck and giblets from hens. Wash in cold water and pat dry. Fill cavities with stuffing and truss to secure drumsticks. If any stuffing will not fit into hens, place in baking dish along with hens to cook. Place breast-side up in a 1½-quart rectangular dish. Brush with oil and Kitchen Bouquet. Garnish with paprika. Microwave on 70% (MEDIUM-HIGH) 18–20 minutes, turning each hen ½-turn around midway through cooking. Let stand 5 minutes before serving. Makes 2–4 servings.

Micro Quick!

Game

*The open range and a modern metropolis share the landscape in the
Panhandle of Texas. Amarillo.*

Smothered Quail

6 quail, dressed
6 tablespoons butter
3 tablespoons flour
2 cups chicken broth
½ cup sherry

Salt and pepper to taste
1 (3-ounce) can mushrooms, chopped
1 (6-ounce) box Uncle Ben's Long Grain Wild Rice

Brown quail in butter. Remove to baking dish. Add flour to butter. Stir well. Slowly add broth, sherry and seasonings. Blend thoroughly. Add mushrooms. Pour over quail. Cover and bake at 350° for 1 hour. Serve over rice prepared according to package directions. Serves 6.

Hullabaloo in the Kitchen

Fried Quail

12 quail
3 cups water
1 tablespoon salt
1 cup Pioneer pancake or biscuit mix

2 teaspoons onion powder
2 teaspoons seasoned salt
¼ teaspoon seasoned pepper
2 envelopes instant chicken broth

Cover quail with water to which 1 tablespoon salt has been added. Chill at least 1 hour. Combine remaining ingredients in a paper bag. Remove quail from water a few at a time and do not dry. Shake in mix. Fry in deep, hot oil only until quail float and are golden brown. Serves 4.

Flavors

Doves with Wild Rice

12 doves, cleaned, washed and dried
1 box Uncle Ben's wild rice

1½ cups red cooking wine
1 cup water
2 tablespoons butter or margarine

Sauté doves in roasting pan in 2 tablespoons butter or margarine until brown on all sides. Sprinkle seasoning from Uncle Ben's wild rice over birds. Add cooking wine and water. For best results birds should be breast down in the liquid. Make a nest in the middle and add the rice. Bake covered at 300° for 1½ hours. Serves 4–6.

Entertaining in Texas

Jalapeño Dove Breasts

10 dove breasts	1 can water chestnuts
30 jalapeño peppers, seeded	30 bacon slices

Carefully remove meat from each side of dove breast with a sharp knife and slice each half lengthwise into 2–3 pieces.

Cut jalapeño pepper lengthwise into strips about the same size as the dove breast. Be sure to remove the seeds. Cut canned water chestnuts into small bite-sized chunks, cut bacon slices into halves. Wrap 1 dove breast slice, 1 jalapeño slice, 1 water chestnut in half slice of bacon and skewer with toothpick. Cook in broiler or on barbecue coals until bacon is brown. Serves about 60.

Jacque Wynne and Steve Kanaly won both American Regional Cuisine and Gala awards with this recipe.

March of Dimes Gourmet Gala Cookbook

Stuffed Doves

12 doves, cleaned	¼ cup chopped parsley
1 onion, chopped finely	½ teaspoon thyme
6 tablespoons butter or margarine	4 slices bacon
1 cup fine bread crumbs (plain)	¼ cup each: melted butter and
1 cup chopped ham	white wine, mixed
½ cup pine nuts	

Sauté onion in butter until soft. Mix with crumbs, ham, nuts, parsley and thyme. Stuff birds. Arrange in lightly greased dish and cover each bird with ⅓ slice of bacon. Roast at 325° for 1¼ hours. Baste frequently with butter and wine (every 15 minutes). For more liquid, add wine. If breast up, take bacon off during last 15 minutes to brown. Serves 6.

Spindletop International Cooks

Duck à la Bourbon

1 duckling (4½ pounds)
1 teaspoon salt
1 orange, quartered
1 clove garlic

¼ cup plus 2 tablespoons
   bourbon, divided
¼ cup melted butter
½ cup orange marmalade

Preheat oven to 450°. Rinse duckling and pat dry. Fill duckling cavity with salt, orange quarters, garlic clove, and ¼ cup bourbon. Close cavity.

Place duckling on its back on rack in shallow roasting pan. Brush with butter. Roast uncovered 30 minutes. Reduce heat to 375°. Roast duckling 40 minutes, basting often with drippings. Turn duckling onto breast; roast 20 minutes, basting often. Turn duckling onto back; roast 30 minutes, basting often.

Combine marmalade and 2 tablespoons bourbon. Spread mixture on duckling breast and roast 10 additional minutes. Remove to warmed platter. Serve with bourbon sauce. Serves 4.

BOURBON SAUCE:

1½ tablespoons butter
1 duck liver
½ small clove garlic, finely
   chopped
3 tablespoons flour
⅛ teaspoon finely ground black
   pepper or to taste

½ teaspoon catsup
½ cup orange juice
½ cup chicken broth
¼ cup red wine
2 tablespoons orange marmalade
¼ cup bourbon
1 tablespoon grated orange zest

Melt butter in saucepan. Add duck liver and garlic. Cook over low heat until liver is browned on all sides. Remove liver and chop finely. Reserve drippings.

Add flour, pepper, and catsup to drippings. Blend well. Gradually add orange juice, broth, wine, marmalade, bourbon, and orange zest. Cook over low heat, stirring continuously until thickened. Add liver and cook additional 5 minutes. Yields about 1½ cups.

Houston Fine Arts Cookbook

Fried Wild Turkey

Breast of turkey (domestic turkey may be substituted)	2½ cups or more buttermilk
Salt, to taste	2 cups vegetable oil
Pepper, to taste	Flour

Bone the breast of turkey. Slice the breast in ¼-inch thick slices or thicker, if desired. Salt and pepper to taste. Soak turkey slices in buttermilk for 2–3 minutes. While turkey is soaking, heat vegetable oil in frying pan. Roll turkey slices in flour. Drop in heated oil (327°) and fry until golden brown. (Do not overcook.) Drain on a paper towel. Best served with cream gravy.

(Mrs. Madeline Russell) *Texas Celebrity Cookbook*

Sweet and Sour Rabbit

1 tame rabbit from market	1 cup sugar
½ cup flour	2 teaspoons cornstarch
⅓ cup salad oil	¾ cup white vinegar
1 teaspoon salt	1 teaspoon soy sauce
¼ teaspoon pepper	¼ teaspoon ginger
1 can sliced pineapple, drained and syrup reserved	1 chicken bouillon cube
	1 green pepper, sliced

Cut rabbit into serving pieces. Coat rabbit with flour. Heat oil in skillet and brown rabbit pieces on all sides. Arrange rabbit pieces in a shallow roasting pan; sprinkle with salt and pepper. Add enough water to pineapple syrup to equal 1¼ cups liquid. Combine sugar, cornstarch, pineapple liquid, vinegar, soy sauce, ginger, and bouillon cube in a saucepan. Bring to a boil, stirring constantly. Boil for 2 minutes. Pour over rabbit. Bake, uncovered, for 30 minutes at 350°. Add pineapple and green pepper, bake for 30 minutes longer. Serves 4.

Wild-n-Tame Fish-n-Game

Frog Legs Herkimer

8 frog legs, fairly large
2 tablespoons lemon juice
Flour, for dusting
Salt
Fresh cracked white pepper
5 tablespoons salted butter
2 teaspoons finely chopped garlic

2 tablespoons chopped mixed
   herbs (tarragon, parsley,
   chives)
1 tablespoon cognac
2 tablespoons dry white wine
Thin slices lemon

Wash frog legs well in lemon juice and water. Dry them on paper towels, and dust lightly with flour seasoned with some salt and white pepper.

Heat the 5 tablespoons butter in skillet until it foams, and add the garlic. Cook one minute. Put in frog legs and shake until golden brown on each side. Add salt, pepper and the mixed herbs. Cook another minute. In a separate little pan heat the cognac and the wine, ignite and pour it flaming over the frog legs. Serve immediately on a hot platter garnished with thin lemon slices. Serves 4.

Morgan Brittany and Laurence K. Herkimer created this recipe which was a Gala Winner.

March of Dimes Gourmet Gala Cookbook

Roundup Rattlesnake

1 Sweetwater rattler, dressed
   (enough to serve 6)
1 cup pancake mix
1 egg, slightly beaten

1 small bottle 7-Up
Salt and pepper to taste
Crisco oil

Combine pancake mix, egg, and 7-Up. Batter will be thin. Mix and set aside. (Sweetwater, Texas is the home of the world's most famous rattlesnake roundup).

Dip prepared snake meat in dry pancake mix and allow to stand dry for 20 minutes. Sprinkle the snake fillets with salt and pepper. Dip in batter and pan fry in deep hot Crisco oil until golden brown. This is delicious. The batter clings to the meat and puffs up as it cooks. "Kinda like yore old leg peffs up if you git bit by this here critter!!"

Wild-n-Tame Fish-n-Game

Venison à la "Old Texas Settlers"

5–7 pounds ribs or other boney
  pieces of deer
Juice of 2 lemons
½ cup wine or vinegar
3 thick slices of onion
¼ teaspoon pepper
1 teaspoon salt

1 tablespoon pickling spices, tied
  in a bag
Flour, salt and pepper
Bacon drippings or hog lard
2–3 tablespoons butter or
  margarine

Place pieces of venison in a deep dish with just enough water to cover. Add half of the lemon juice. Add wine, onion, pepper, salt and pickling spices. Cover and place in the refrigerator; let stand for 10–12 hours. Drain and wipe dry, reserving the onion slices and spice bag.

Roll meat in flour, salt and pepper. Brown in hot fat. Place meat in a heavy pot with a tight cover. Add butter, the reserved onion and spice bag, the remaining lemon juice and 1 cup of water. Cover and cook over low heat until fork-tender, adding water if needed. Use the drippings in the skillet to make your favorite water gravy. When meat is tender, add gravy and cook for 10–15 minutes longer. (Gravy should not be too thick.) Remove the spice bag and serve. Serves 6.

The Galveston Island Cookbook

Wok Mélange

2–3 pounds deer or elk steak, slivered
3 tablespoons oil
1 teaspoon Worcestershire sauce
3 tablespoons soy sauce
2 teaspoons sherry wine
2 garlic cloves, minced
Salt and pepper
½ cup shallots, chopped
1 cup celery, sliced diagonally
1 cup fresh mushrooms, sliced
1 bell pepper, seeded and sliced into strips
1 cup fresh broccoli, separated into fleurettes
1 cup cabbage, shredded
2 teaspoons cornstarch
Hot cooked rice

Place 2 tablespoons oil, Worcestershire sauce, 2 tablespoons soy sauce and garlic into Chinese wok on high heat. Add meat, stirring and cooking until all liquid is absorbed and meat is thoroughly browned. Add sherry. Transfer meat from wok to platter.

Pour the remaining oil and soy sauce into wok on high heat. Add vegetables and cook 7 minutes. Stir constantly to prevent sticking. Then, add cornstarch to mixture in wok. Return meat to wok and blend with vegetables. Salt and pepper to taste. Serve over hot cooked rice. Serves 5 or 6.

Elegant Elk-Delicious Deer

Chicken Fried Venison

I have known this way of cooking venison since I was very young and have taught many people to cook the meat this way.

2 pounds meat (may be nice
  slices ¼-inch thick, or the
  small bits you get when
  trimming out hocks) and then
  beat flat with board
13 ounces evaporated milk

Salt
Pepper
Flour
Garlic powder (optional)
Onion powder (optional)

Put the meat in a large bowl with the evaporated milk and enough water to completely cover the meat. Allow to stand for 1 hour. Take the meat out, drain only slightly and then season to taste and roll in the flour. Drop into hot grease (375°) and fry until brown. Do not overcook or the meat will become dry and tough. Serve with gravy made from the flour and some of the milk left over and good hot bread.

(Bertie Varner, Y.O. Ranch) *Texas Celebrity Cookbook*

Venison Scallopini

1½ pounds venison, sliced in
  small pieces
⅓ cup flour
⅓ cup olive oil
1 medium onion, chopped
2 tablespoons chopped green
  pepper
½ teaspoon salt

Dash each of rosemary, thyme,
  oregano
1 teaspoon seasoning salt
1 can tomato soup
½ cup water
½ cup port wine
1 (4-ounce) can mushrooms
½ cup grated Cheddar cheese

Roll meat in flour. Sauté onion and pepper in oil until soft. Remove, add meat and brown on all sides. Add seasonings, soup, water and wine. Return onions and peppers to mixture, add mushrooms and cover. Simmer until meat is tender, about 35–45 minutes. Sprinkle with cheese and heat until cheese is melted. Serve with rice. Serves 4–6.

A Texas Hill Country Cookbook

Chili Quick

5 pounds lean deer meat, ground   1 can chili quick
2 pounds melted suet

Braise the meat in the suet. When it's almost done, add the chili quick.

"The chuckwagon cook didn't have chili quick (you can buy it in any grocery store), so he substituted hot peppers, black pepper, salt, a little dab of flour, onions, and a can or two of tomatoes. You can add a little water if you want to thin it; it'll stand up on your plate if you don't."

Note: When we asked Clyde Hester how many this recipe would serve, he said, "Depends on how hungry they are. I guarantee if you serve it to a hungry man with a cold can of something he likes to drink, he's gonna take a nap right away after eating it." Also we tried to pin Clyde down as to the size pot he cooks it in, and he responded, "I don't know. A big one."

Company's Coming

Elk and Sausage Pie

1 pound ground elk
½ cup bread crumbs
1 teaspoon onion powder
1 (9-inch) unbaked pie shell
3 sweet Italian sausages

2 fresh tomatoes
1 cup grated Cheddar cheese
12 small green chile peppers
  (canned)

Combine ground elk, bread crumbs and onion powder. Mix well, and press into pie shell. Remove sausages from casings, mash, and spread evenly over meat mixture, leaving ½-inch edge. Bake at 350° for 30 minutes. Remove from oven.

Peel and slice tomatoes. Halve each slice and arrange around edge of pie. Sprinkle tomatoes with grated cheese. Arrange chile peppers spoke-fashion, inside circle of tomatoes. Return to oven at 350°, for 10 minutes more. Serve hot. Different and Delicious!

Elegant Elk-Delicious Deer

Venison Sausage and Rice Supreme

1 pound deer sausage
½ cup onion, diced
1 cup celery, chopped
1 (3-ounce) can mushrooms
½ cup toasted almonds

1 can water chestnuts
1½ packages chicken noodle
  soup (dehydrated kind)
2½ cups water, hot
3 cups cooked rice

Cook rice as directed on package. Rinse and drain water chestnuts and set aside. Slit skin on deer sausage and crumble into skillet. Brown, stirring frequently.

Remove meat and sauté onion and celery in drippings. Add mushrooms, almonds, water chestnuts, soup, hot water, cooked rice and cooked sausage. Mix all together and place in 1½-quart casserole. Cover and cook for 45 minutes to 1 hour at 350°.

Wild-n-Tame Fish-n-Game

Teriyaki Meatballs

1 pound elk or deer, ground
¼ cup onion, chopped
¼ cup flour
1 egg
1 teaspoon salt
¼ teaspoon black pepper
¼ cup soy sauce

1 tablespoon oil
3 teaspoons sherry wine
½ cup water
2 tablespoons brown sugar
⅛ teaspoon ginger, ground
1 teaspoon garlic salt
2 teaspoons cornstarch

Combine meat, onion, flour, egg, salt, pepper and 1 tablespoon soy sauce. Shape mixture into meatballs.

Heat oil and fry meatballs until lightly browned.

Combine soy sauce, sherry, water, brown sugar, ginger, garlic salt and cornstarch. Add meatballs and cook on low heat until sauce thickens. Yields 4 dozen.

Elegant Elk-Delicious Deer

Meats

Longhorn cattle drive on Exchange Avenue in Fort Worth. The Old West is captured in stores, restaurants, honky-tonks along the street.

Galveston Island Chili

1 pound suet, or beef tallow, diced
1 cup green onions and tops, chopped
2 large jalapeño peppers, chopped and stemmed
1 teaspoon black pepper
1 teaspoon salt
1 teaspoon dried parsley flakes
2 large white onions, chopped
6 pounds lean coarse grind chili meat
10 tablespoons paprika (2 [1¼-ounce] cans)

2 tablespoons cumin or cominoes
1 teaspoon dried red peppers
½ teaspoon sweet basil
1 teaspoon white pepper
2 quarts water
10 cloves garlic, finely chopped
2 tablespoons MSG
½ ounce Baker's chocolate
1 teaspoon Worcestershire sauce
1 (15-ounce) can tomato sauce
1 tablespoon salt

Use a large, well-seasoned iron pot of about 3-gallon capacity. Fry suet about 1 hour, save grease and throw away the pieces. This should leave about 2 cups grease.

Add to hot grease: green onions, jalapeño peppers, black pepper, salt, parsley flakes, white onions. Cook this mess at a fairly hot setting, stirring occasionally. While this is cooking make one "Brave Bull," double, by mixing 2 parts Cuervo Gold Tequila with one part Leroux White Cream De Cacao. Swirl this gently over a couple of ice cubes, and sip away.

Add ground meat. This may be beef or venison or a mixture of the two. The gristle and fat must be removed. Cook meat while stirring until it is all gray in color; cover. Please oil the inside of the iron lid before using. Don't bother to taste this stuff at this point. Try a "Brave Bull" instead.

Have another "Brave Bull," then add the following: paprika, cumin, red peppers, sweet basil, white pepper, water. Boil slowly, covered, for 2 hours (4 hours for venison). Add chopped garlic cloves, (don't crush them—that's barbaric), MSG, chocolate, Worcestershire sauce, tomato sauce and salt. Cook (simmer) for 1 more hour then taste and add salt to suit yourself. Be careful to not ever, ever let anything stick to the bottom of the pot. Use a wooden spoon.

Comment: This recipe combines the outstanding features of Dr. Tom F. Bryant's Original Galveston Island Two-Step Chili, Texas Jailhouse Chili, Mr. Wick Fowler's 2-Alarm Chili, and Mr. H. Al Smith's Pitiful Weak Comino Soup.

A Different Taste of Paris

Texas Chili

The smell of this chili cooking brought my family running.

3 pounds lean beef
¼ cup salad oil
6 cups water
2 bay leaves
6 tablespoons chili powder
1 tablespoon salt
10 cloves garlic, minced
1 teaspoon comino seeds
1 teaspoon oregano leaves,
  crushed

½ teaspoon red pepper
¼ teaspoon pepper
1 tablespoon sugar
3 tablespoons sweet Hungarian
  paprika
1 tablespoon dried onion flakes
3 tablespoons flour
6 tablespoons cornmeal

In a 6-quart saucepan, sear beef (cubed or coarsely ground) in salad oil until beef color is gray, not brown. Add water, bay leaves, chili powder, salt, garlic, comino seeds, oregano, red pepper, pepper, sugar, paprika and onion flakes. Simmer, covered, 2 hours. Cool. Refrigerate overnight so flavors will mellow. Remove top layer of solidified fat. Reheat. With a little cold water make a paste of flour and cornmeal. Add paste to chili. To obtain a smooth texture, cook and stir 5–7 minutes after thickening has been added. Remove bay leaves before serving. Serves 6.

Cook'em Horns

Gourmet Chili

1½ pounds ground beef, salted
1 large onion, chopped
4 strips bacon, fried crisp and
  diced
2 (4-ounce) cans mushroom stems
  and pieces
1 (1-pound) can tomatoes
1 (8-ounce) can tomato juice

1 (1-pound) can pinto beans
1 (1-pound) can red beans
1 (1-pound) can chili beans
1 package Williams Chili
  Seasoning
¼ cup parsley flakes
¼ cup chives

Brown beef with onion and bacon. Add mushrooms. Add remaining ingredients. Cook slowly for 1½ hours. Serves 8–10. Excellent and very easy.

Amarillo Junior League Cookbook

Sam's Chili

1½ pounds beef chuck roast, coarsely ground
1½ pounds pork shoulder, cut into ½-inch cubes
1 large onion, chopped
3 large garlic cloves, minced
3 (8-ounce) cans beer or 1½ cups water
1 cup Special Tomatoes (see recipe)

1 (8-ounce) can tomato sauce
½ cup chili powder
1 tablespoon salt
1 tablespoon cumin
1½ teaspoons paprika
2 tablespoons instant masa mix combined with 3 tablespoons warm water

Cook both meats, onion and garlic in dry heavy large saucepan over medium heat until meat is no longer pink. Stir in all remaining ingredients except masa. Cover and simmer until reduced to 12 cups, stirring occasionally, about 3 hours.

Degrease chili. Stir dissolved masa into chili. Cover and simmer 30 minutes. Best served the day after cooking. (Can be prepared 5 days ahead. Cover and refrigerate.)

SPECIAL TOMATOES:
(Rotel Tomatoes and Green Chilies)

1½ pounds tomatoes, peeled and coarsely chopped
1 serrano or jalapeño chili, minced

¾ teaspoon salt
¼ teaspoon freshly ground pepper

Combine all ingredients in heavy small saucepan over medium heat. Cook 10 minutes to blend flavors, stirring occasionally. (Invented for *Bon Appetit Magazine.*)

"I'm Glad I Ate When I Did, 'Cause I'm Not Hungry Now"

Son-of-a-Gun Stew

Son-of-a-gun stew is a kind of general name for a whole bunch of stews. Each cook had his own favorite recipe, or else used whatever came to hand. With seven basic staples—flour, beef, bacon, beans, coffee, syrup, and dried fruit—and at special times canned tomatoes or corn, or a few pickles, onions, or potatoes, "Cookie," or "Coosie" (from Cocinero) Brewton, could turn out good, nourishing, stick-to-the-ribs meals for hardworking outdoor men.

1 liver, coarsely chopped
Sweetbreads (calf), coarsely
  chopped
1 marrow gut (if it ain't got
  marrow gut, it ain't
  "Son-of-a-Gun Stew")

Vegetables (whatever you can
  get), cut up in chunks (onions,
  potatoes, canned corn, and
  tomatoes)

Cover the meat with water and boil slowly for 1½–2 hours. Add the vegetables, a good bit of salt, and boil it—the longer the better.

Dish it out boilin' hot with beans, biscuits, and plenty of HOT coffee.

Company's Coming

French Stew
"The best stew I've ever tasted"

2 pounds round steak, cubed
6 carrots, peeled and thinly sliced
1 onion, sliced into rings
1 cup chopped celery
1 (4-ounce) can mushrooms,
  drained
1 (16-ounce) can tomatoes,
  drained
⅛ teaspoon pepper

⅛ teaspoon rosemary
⅛ teaspoon thyme
⅛ teaspoon marjoram
Salt to taste
2 slices bread, cubed
1 (10-ounce) package frozen green
  beans
½ cup red wine, heated

Combine first 12 ingredients in a Dutch oven; mix well. Bake at 250° for 3½ hours. Add beans; bake 30 minutes. Stir in wine just before serving. Yields 12–14 servings.

Flavor Favorites

Veal Stew in a Pumpkin

This stew may be too good for children. Yes, their eyes do light up at the sight of a pumpkin tureen and, yes, they eat it as heartily as an adult, but the marriage of pumpkin and veal is a divine union lost on children.

1 pumpkin shell
1½ pounds boneless veal, cut
   into chunks
3 cups water
1 cup dry white wine
1 onion, sliced
1 carrot, scraped and cut into
   julienne slices
1 bay leaf

7 or 8 whole peppercorns
Salt to taste
2 cups pumpkin
4 tablespoons butter or margarine
¼ cup flour
Juice of half a lemon
Sprig of parsley, cut with scissors
Handful of pumpkin seeds

Choose a pumpkin that is about 10″ tall. Cut off the top third, scrape out all seeds and fiber using a tablespoon. Rinse the inside of both sections of the pumpkin with milk, then salt lightly and pepper generously. Replace the top, put the whole thing on a cookie sheet, and place it on the bottom rack of a 350° oven. Roast for 1 hour.

Meanwhile, in a large saucepot, combine stew meat with water, wine, onion, carrot, bay leaf, peppercorns, and salt to taste. Cover and simmer until the meat is thoroughly tender, skimming off foam as it appears. This may take anywhere from 1–2 to hours, depending on the tenderness of the veal.

While pumpkin and stew are cooking, separate seeds from fiber and roast the seeds on a cookie sheet in the oven.

Once roasted, the pumpkin will have some juice in the bottom. Pour this into the stew. Now, using a sharp, thin-bladed knife, cut cooked flesh from the top, in chunks, until you have about 2 cups, taking care not to cut through the skin of the pumpkin.

In a small saucepan over medium-high heat, raise butter to a boil. Add pumpkin chunks and cook and stir until liquid has evaporated and pumpkin chunks have taken up the oil and begun to glaze and brown. Sprinkle flour over the pumpkin chunks and cook and stir to make a golden roux. Stir in a few spoonfuls of the boiling broth from the stew pot to make a thick gravy. Add lemon juice.

CONTINUED

210

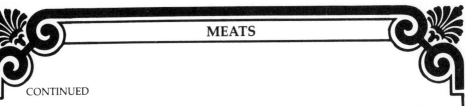
CONTINUED

When the veal is fork-tender, pour the pumpkin gravy into the stew, stirring to mix thoroughly. Soon you'll have a lovely thick stew. Taste for seasonings and adjust. Pour stew into pumpkin shell; sprinkle top with parsley and roasted pumpkin seeds. Put the top back on and serve at once.

If you don't wish to use the pumpkin as tureen, cut the back off a used jack-o'-lantern, rinse with milk, season with salt and pepper, cover with foil, and roast for about 30 minutes. Then proceed with directions for glazing pumpkin chunks. Feeds 4 in 2 hours and 30 minutes.

An American Gumbo

Veal Birds

½ cup chopped celery
¼ cup chopped onion
½ cup butter
¾ teaspoon salt
Freshly ground pepper
⅛ teaspoon sage
1 tablespoon chopped parsley
2 cups soft bread cubes
¼ cup milk

8 veal cutlets
Toothpicks
⅓ cup flour
¼ cup water
¼ cup dry white wine
2 tablespoons butter
4 ounces fresh mushrooms, sliced
1 cup sour cream
Cooked rice

Sauté celery and onion in ¼ cup of the butter until tender; mix with salt, pepper, sage, parsley, bread cubes, and milk. Divide dressing evenly among cutlets. Roll cutlets and fasten securely with toothpicks. Coat meat heavily with flour; brown on all sides in remaining ¼ cup butter. Add water and wine; simmer, covered, for 45 minutes or until tender. Remove to platter and keep warm. Add 2 tablespoons butter to pan; sauté mushrooms until tender. Blend in sour cream, stirring until heated and thickened. Serve birds on a bed of rice and pour sauce over all. Serves 8.

Enjoy!

Cholent

Cholent is a sort of stew which came into existence because Jewish housewives in Europe were faced with the necessity of preparing a hot meal for Sabbath afternoon in spite of the injunction against beginning to cook on the Sabbath itself. The stew was begun well before Sabbath and allowed to cook all Friday afternoon. Before Sabbath (sundown) it was put into a big commercial oven and allowed to simmer until lunch the next day.

"My father, Sam Perl, (says Frances Perl Goodman) lived in Galveston the first decade of this century and tells of the joy and responsibility of taking Grandma Perl's heavy cholent pot to the community's oven on Friday afternoon and then retrieving it on his way home from the synagogue Saturday noon. He says the aromas from all the different cholents were tantalizing and overwhelming, and he and other boys ran home with their cholents (being careful not to stumble and face disaster from mama!)."

The following recipe is my own from different sources:

3 pounds fatty boneless brisket
3 large onions, sliced
1 garlic clove, minced
¼ cup schmaltz (chicken fat) or
   shortening
Salt, pepper and paprika to taste
1 pound dried lima beans,
   soaked overnight

¾ cup uncooked barley
3 large potatoes, cut in thick
   slices
2 tablespoons flour
1½ cups boiling water

Brown meat with onions and garlic in the fat. Season well. Place in a heavy iron pot—with a tight-fitting lid—or a large earthenware bean pot. Cover with drained beans and barley. Add sliced potatoes and sprinkle with the flour, a little more melted fat, salt, pepper and paprika. Carefully pour boiling water down the sides of the pot. Cover tightly and place in 400° oven for 30 minutes. Then reduce oven to 250° and cook overnight. Makes 15–18 servings. No peeking and no basting!

The Melting Pot

Caldillo

3 pounds cubed beef
1½ cups diced onion
3 cups tomatoes, diced
1½ cups green chile strips
½ cup beef stock

2 tablespoons salt
2 tablespoons pepper
2 teaspoons garlic salt
2 teaspoons cumin
2 pounds potatoes

Sauté beef, onions in bacon fat; add tomatoes, chili strips and seasonings. Cover and cook over low heat until meat is tender. Add cubed potatoes during last 30 minutes. Caldillo may be frozen after preparation. Makes 1 gallon.

The Pride of Texas

Salpicón
(Mexican Shredded Beef)

8 pounds top sirloin or eye of
  round
2 cloves garlic
1 bay leaf
1 (12-ounce) can tomatoes
¼ cup fresh cilantro*
Salt and pepper to taste
1 bottle Wishbone Italian salad
  dressing

1 cup chopped green chiles (fresh
  or canned)
1 cup cooked garbanzo beans
½ pound Monterrey Jack cheese
  cut in ½-inch squares
2 avocados, cut in strips
1 bunch parsley

Place beef in heavy pot; cover with water and add garlic, bay leaf, tomatoes, cilantro, salt and pepper. Cook over medium heat about 5 hours. Remove broth, cool meat and cut into 2-inch squares. Shred and arrange in a 9 × 11-inch Pyrex dish. Cover beef with salad dressing and allow to marinate overnight in refrigerator. Before serving, arrange the following in layers over beef: beans, cheese, chiles, avocados. Decorate with parsley. Serves 16–20. This is a perfect dish for a buffet table.

*Cilantro is fresh coriander.

Seasoned With Sun

Garbanzo beans (gar BAHN zoh)—Seeds, larger than peas, which taste somewhat like dried beans or peas. Also called a chickpea, the garbanzo is used in soups and stews and as a sidedish instead of rice or frijoles.

Marinated Beef Tender

5–6 pounds beef tender, larded
  for roasting
All-season salt
Pepper

1 (25-ounce) bottle dry sherry
2 pounds mushrooms, optional
Margarine
Garlic powder

Sprinkle roast with all-season salt and pepper and marinate in sherry for 24 hours. Refrigerate. Remove from marinade, reserve. Place tender on rack in pan. Cook at 400° for 30 minutes and 350° for 20 minutes. It should be rare at this time. Cook marinade over high heat to allow alcohol to evaporate. Add pan juices from meat. Sauté fresh mushrooms in margarine and add to marinade juice. Season with salt, pepper and garlic powder to taste.

Slice tender thin and place in chafing dish and add sherry-mushroom mixture. Do not cover chafing dish or meat will continue to cook. Serve with Pepperidge Farm Parker House rolls or party rolls. This will serve 12 people if cut 1-inch thick or 20 people if cut thin.

"The key to this recipe is the quality of meat you buy. It is best to buy the best tender you can find at the most reliable store. Always go to a store that you know serves quality meat. It is better to pay a few cents more for that guarantee. Jamail's in Houston is such a store. Jamail's is a grocery store where you can find anything called for in a recipe. The women shop in minks and diamonds. Chauffeurs wait in Mercedes and Rolls Royces for the housekeepers to grocery shop. The housekeepers know the butchers on a first name basis. It is a status symbol to have a charge account at Jamail's. There is a waiting list to get an account since their number of accounts is limited to 500.

"One of the few times I have seen an employee of Jamail's shaken was when I asked for 15 five-pound tenders. The butcher blinked and courteously said, 'Ma'am, may I ask how many people you plan to serve?' I said, '250.' He said, 'You're just about right.' "

A Doctor's Prescription for Gourmet Cooking

Texas Brisket
Best brisket I've ever eaten.
I didn't use a knife, it was so tender.

1 brisket, 4 or 5 pounds	¼ teaspoon nutmeg
2 teaspoons meat tenderizer	¼ teaspoon garlic powder
1 bottle (4-ounces) liquid smoke	1 teaspoon onion salt
1 teaspoon celery salt	1 tablespoon brown sugar
1 teaspoon paprika	

Sprinkle brisket with meat tenderizer, cover with liquid smoke. Refrigerate overnight, covered with foil. Next day, sprinkle brisket with mixture of remaining ingredients. Cover tightly with foil, bake 2 hours at 300°. Loosen foil, bake 5 hours more at 200°. Remove meat from pan, set aside 1 hour before slicing. Strain any grease from pan juices (or chill in deep freezer for easy removal). Slice brisket very thin across grain, serve with hot degreased liquid or barbecue sauce of your choice. Serves 5 or 6.

Cook'em Horns

Deluxe Cherry Brisket

1 (5-pound) brisket	Caraway seeds
Soy sauce to taste	Celery seeds
Worcestershire sauce to taste	Rosemary
1 package Lipton onion soup mix	1 (20-ounce) can cherry pie filling

1. Season brisket with next 2 ingredients. Sprinkle soup mix on brisket, add rosemary, caraway seeds, and celery seeds. Marinate 2 days.

2. Wrap brisket and seasonings in 2 layers of aluminum foil and bake 4 hours at 325°. Let cool before unwrapping.

3. Pour gravy into one container and place meat in another; refrigerate.

4. Scrape off all seasonings and slice cold meat.

5. Put gravy in bottom of pan and put slices on top of gravy. Pour cherry pie filling over meat and bake in 350° oven for 30–45 minutes. Yields 6–8 servings. Preparation time: Make 2 days ahead of time.

Rare Collection

Barbecued Beef Brisket

Sam usually smokes 10–12 pound briskets overnight for large crowds. This is an adaptation for home barbecues.

6 cups mesquite chips	2 tablespoons Dry Rub (see
1 (4-pound) beef brisket,	recipe)
untrimmed	Barbecue Sauce (see recipe)

Soak mesquite in water to cover 1 hour. Drain.

Prepare barbecue grill, lighting fire at one end only. Rub brisket with Dry Rub. When coals are white, place meat over coals and sear 5 minutes on each side. Move meat to side of grill away from fire. Spread 4 cups mesquite over coals. Cover grill. Smoke brisket 1 hour, maintaining temperature at about 200° and sprinkling mesquite with water occasionally. Spread remaining 2 cups mesquite over coals and continue smoking meat 1 hour.

Preheat oven to 200°. Wrap beef tightly with heavy duty foil. Bake 8 hours. Slice meat across grain and serve with Barbecue Sauce.

SAM'S DRY RUB:

¼ cup salt	1½ teaspoons ground red pepper
1½ teaspoons freshly ground	
pepper	

Combine all ingredients in small bowl. (Can be stored several weeks in air-tight jar.)

BARBECUE SAUCE:

½ (4-ounce) bottle liquid smoke	1½ tablespoons chili powder
¾ (5-ounce) bottle Worcestershire	1½ tablespoons celery seed
sauce	1 cup brown sugar
¾ (5-ounce) bottle soy sauce	1 tablespoon Dijon mustard
1 or 2 teaspoons Tabasco	1 (32-ounce) bottle catsup
1 or 2 tablespoons garlic salt	

Mix all ingredients in saucepan; simmer for 15 minutes.

Note: I adapted this barbecued beef brisket for people who don't really have a proper outdoor grill. I always use a double bathtub cooker and smoke the brisket at low temperatures for 20–24 hours. It is the recipe that I developed for *Bon Appetit Magazine.* In the early days, brisket was dirt cheap. It was that part of the beef

CONTINUED

CONTINUED

that nobody really knew what to do with. The meat was either ground up into hamburger or thrown away. But now brisket has gained a great amount of popularity, and the prices aren't dirt cheap anymore. A lot of people make a mistake by buying brisket with the fat trimmed off. The brisket needs the fat to keep it juicy as it cooks. If you don't keep the fat, you'll just wind up with a big old dry piece of leather.

"I'm Glad I Ate When I Did, 'Cause I'm Not Hungry Now"

Party Tenderloin

1 (4-pound) beef tenderloin
½ teaspoon Lawry's seasoning
½ teaspoon garlic salt
½ teaspoon coarse black pepper

½ teaspoon salt
3 green onions, diced
2 slices bacon, cut in 4 pieces
  each (optional)

Rub meat with all seasonings and press into meat. Place in shallow roasting pan and broil on both sides until brown and crispy. Arrange bacon pieces on top of meat. Press diced green onions on top of tenderloin and bake at 400° for 35 minutes for rare. (Place slices of meat under broiler for a few minutes for those who prefer medium doneness.) Remove meat to serving platter and lightly cover to keep warm. Add small amount of water to pan drippings for *au jus* and season to taste. Serves 8.

Ready to Serve

Wibb's Beef Tender

1 whole beef tender
Lemon pepper
Gobs of butter

Sprinkle beef tender generously with lemon pepper. Brown on hot barbecue fire on all sides for about 20 minutes. Put in shallow pan in 200° oven with gobs of butter on it. It will hold for hours and still come out pink. Can be done before guests arrive.

Or try a portion of a tender for dinner for two.

A Texas Hill Country Cookbook

State Fair Chuck Roast
(Microwave)

2–4 pound beef chuck, boneless
  shoulder pot-roast
1 (10.5-ounce) can beef broth
½ teaspoon garlic powder
1 teaspoon instant minced onion

2 tablespoons Worcestershire
  sauce
¼ cup bottled liquid smoke
4 slices bacon

Place pot-roast in 4-quart microwave-safe container. Mix broth with seasonings. Pour over the roast. Allow meat to marinate at room temperature 30 minutes, turning roast over once during marinating time. Lay bacon strips over the roast, covering entire top of roast. Cover with glass lid. Microwave on MEDIUM-HIGH (70%) POWER 3 minutes per pound. For next cooking cycle, cook by Time Cooking or Temperature Cooking.

For Time Cooking: Microwave on LOW (30%) POWER 30 minutes per pound.

For Temperature Cooking: Use food temperature sensor set for food to reach an internal temperature of 160° on LOW (30%) POWER, holding at that temperature at least 30 minutes. Allow meat to remain covered 10–15 minutes before slicing. Slice thinly across the grain. Serves 6–8.

The Texas Microwave Cookbook

Gourmet Pot Roast

1 (3 to 4-pound) beef pot roast
1 tablespoon olive oil
3 (4-inch) pieces of celery
1 large carrot, cut in chunks
1 large onion, quartered
½ teaspoon rosemary
½ teaspoon thyme

1 slice bacon, cut in 5 or 6 pieces
⅓ cup Burgundy wine
½ cup water
2 bay leaves
1½ teaspoons salt
¼ teaspoon pepper
1 teaspoon flour

In Dutch oven, brown roast in oil. In skillet or saucepan cook celery, carrot, onion, rosemary, thyme and bacon pieces, stirring constantly and until onion is golden. Add to meat. Add wine, water, bay leaves, salt and pepper. Cover and simmer 2½ hours. Thicken liquid with flour blended with a little cold water or wine. Cook 30 minutes longer. Strain liquid, discarding vegetables and bay leaves. Serve gravy with sliced roast. Serves 6.

Ready to Serve

Pot Roast with Sour Cream Gravy

3 tablespoons shortening
3–4 pound pot roast
2 medium onions, sliced
1 (8-ounce) can water chestnuts,
  sliced

1 tablespoon salt
1½ teaspoons paprika
½ cup hot water
2 tablespoons flour
½ cup sour cream

Melt shortening in a Dutch oven and brown meat on all sides. Slip rack under meat. Add onions, water chestnuts, salt, paprika, and hot water. Cover and simmer 2½ hours or until meat is fork tender. Remove roast and rack. Skim fat from drippings. Fold flour into sour cream. Gradually add sour cream mixture to drippings, and cook until thick. Slice meat and serve with gravy.

Flavors

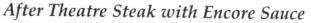

After Theatre Steak with Encore Sauce

5–6 pound center cut sirloin, 2
 inches thick
Kitchen Bouquet
Generous cracked pepper
½ pound butter
⅓ cup lemon juice

2 tablespoons Worcestershire
 sauce
2 tablespoons catsup
⅓ cup degreased meat drippings
Imported olive oil

Coat steak with Kitchen Bouquet and then cracked pepper to taste. Set aside for an hour or more.

To make Encore Sauce, mix together melted butter, lemon juice, Worcestershire sauce and catsup. Beat with a wire whisk to mix and set aside.

Sprinkle olive oil on steak and rub evenly. Preheat oven to 350° and cook steak uncovered for approximately 45 minutes. Turn heat off, open door slightly and leave another 15 minutes. Remove from oven and sprinkle with salt if desired. Go to the theatre.

Arrange meat on platter. Add meat drippings to Encore Sauce, whisk again and heat. Serve steak at room temperature with Encore sauce and biscuits, rolls or tiny hamburger buns.

A Different Taste of Paris

Steak Burgundy

Pan broil a sirloin steak. While steak is broiling, mix the following:

3 tablespoons butter, melted in a
 small pan
6 green onions, finely chopped,
 added to butter and sautéed 3
 or 4 minutes

1 tablespoon parsley
1 cup burgundy

Add 3 tablespoons butter to pan where steak has cooked. Melt and add this mixture to the wine mixture above. Simmer. Pour over steak and let marinate in warm oven for 30 minutes. Serves two.

Trading Secrets

Pepper Steak

¼ cup oil
1 clove garlic, crushed
1 teaspoon salt
1 teaspoon ginger
½ teaspoon pepper
1½ pounds sirloin, cut in thin strips
2 large green peppers, sliced
4 green onions, cut into 1-inch pieces
2 large onions, sliced
¼ cup cold water
¼ cup soy sauce
1 tablespoon cornstarch
½ teaspoon sugar
½ cup beef bouillon
1 (6-ounce) can water chestnuts, sliced
Cooked rice

In hot oil, sauté garlic, salt, ginger and pepper until garlic is golden. Add meat and brown 2 minutes. Remove meat. Add green pepper and onions. Cook 3 minutes. Mix water with cornstarch and add to mixture. Return meat to pan and add all remaining ingredients. Simmer until thick. Serve over hot rice. Serves 6.

Amarillo Junior League Cookbook

Anticucho Sauce

1 part red wine vinegar
3 parts water
2–3 serrano peppers
Salt
Whole black peppercorns
½–1 teaspoon garlic salt or 2–3 cloves garlic
Pinch oregano
Pinch comino
1–2 pounds beef (chuck, round or sirloin) cut into 1½-inch cubes
Bacon drippings

Place all ingredients except beef and bacon drippings in a blender. Blend well. Pour over meat. Cover and marinate several hours or overnight. Thread meat on sticks or skewers. Stir bacon drippings into remaining marinade. Grill anticuchos over hot charcoal fire and baste with marinade. Turn frequently until brown on all sides. The bacon drippings will make the meat smoke; therefore, the smoke will provide additional flavor. Serves 4–6.

San Antonio Conservation Society Cookbook

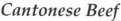

Cantonese Beef

2 (10-ounce) packages frozen
  broccoli spears, partially
  thawed, or 1 bunch fresh
  broccoli
1 pound flank steak or round
  steak, partially frozen, thinly
  sliced across grain
2 teaspoons cornstarch
1 teaspoon sugar

¼ teaspoon ground ginger
1 tablespoon soy sauce
1 clove garlic, crushed
5 tablespoons cooking oil
1 (8-ounce) can water chestnuts,
  drained and sliced
1 cup sliced fresh mushrooms
1½ teaspoons salt
Hot cooked white rice

Cut broccoli flowerets and stems into 1½-inch lengths, about ½-inch wide; set aside. If using fresh broccoli, break flowerets with stems from large stems. Peel skin from large and small stems. Cut steak slices into 2 × 1-inch pieces. In a small bowl combine 1 teaspoon cornstarch, ¼ teaspoon sugar, ginger, soy sauce, 1½ teaspoons water and garlic; blend well. Stir in beef and set aside.

Preheat wok or a large heavy skillet about 3 minutes. Pour in 2 tablespoons oil. Add beef; stir fry 1 minute, until meat loses its red color. Return beef to bowl. Heat remaining 3 tablespoons oil in wok or skillet. Stir in broccoli, chestnuts and mushrooms; stir fry 2 minutes. Add salt, remaining ¾ teaspoon sugar and 2 tablespoons water; mix well. Cook 1 minute, stirring occasionally. Add meat, cook and stir 1 minute. Blend together remaining 1 teaspoon cornstarch and 1 tablespoon water. Add to wok or skillet. Cook until thickened. Serve over rice. Serves 4.

Cookin' Wise

Carne Asada

4–6 sandwich steaks
Cooking oil
1 medium onion, finely diced

1 (10-ounce) can green chile, cut
  in strips (or fresh chiles,
  roasted and peeled)
Monterrey Jack cheese, grated

Sauté onion and chile strips in a small amount of oil. Drain and set aside. Fry steaks in oil adding more than necessary; place steaks on a cookie sheet. Top each with portions of chile, onion and grated cheese. Bake at 350° until cheese melts. Serves 4–6.

Seasoned With Sun

Lone Star Chicken-Fried Steak

No Texas cookbook can claim authenticity without including a chicken-fried steak recipe. There are many variations, but they are all breaded, tenderized steak, fried and served with cream gravy.

1½ pounds round steak,
  tenderized
1 cup flour
1 teaspoon salt

Pepper
2 eggs, slightly beaten
½ cup milk
Oil for frying

GRAVY:
6 tablespoons bacon or pan
  drippings
6 tablespoons flour

3 cups hot milk
Salt and pepper

Trim steak and cut into 5 pieces. Combine flour, salt and pepper. Dredge all steak pieces in flour mixture until lightly coated. Combine eggs and milk. Dip steak into egg mixture and dredge again in flour. Heat ½ inch of oil in a heavy skillet. Place steaks in skillet and fry until golden brown on both sides.

To make gravy, remove steaks to warm oven, retaining 6 tablespoons of drippings (or use bacon drippings). Add flour. Cook and stir until flour begins to brown. Add hot milk and stir until thickened. Season with salt and pepper to taste and pour over warm steaks. Serves 5.

Tastes & Tales From Texas . . . With Love

Fajitâs

One of the hot new trends in Tex Mex cuisine comes from an old favorite of the Texas Mexican. Skirt steaks, known in San Antonio as *fajitâs*, or "little girdles," have long been a standby for one very good reason. Up until very recently they were cheap. I mean dirt cheap.

The skirt is beef diaphragm muscle, and for many years it was considered by butchers as a sort of throwaway; but the flavor of the skirt far surpasses that of the beef tenderloin and has suddenly become fashionable.

Fajitâs are traditionally cooked outside over a charcoal fire, but Merle Ellis has discovered that you can use a heavy, dry cast iron skillet over high heat with good results—even though it is guaranteed to set off the smoke alarm.

The marinade in this recipe comes from my old friend, Bobbie Covey, of Austin, who knows more about the art of Tex Mex cuisine than anybody I've ever met.

1 skirt steak (1¼–1½ pounds)	**Juice of a lime**
Half can of beer	**1 dried red pepper, crushed**
½ cup cooking oil	**1 clove garlic, pressed**
1 thin-sliced onion	**Fresh-cracked pepper to taste**

Make a marinade of all the ingredients and soak the steak, covered, in the refrigerator about 1 hour. Meanwhile, make a charcoal fire outside (or use the cast iron skillet method).

When meat is ready to be cooked, slice it into about 6-inch pieces and grill quickly, turning once, no more than 3–4 minutes to the side. Cut on the diagonal into thin strips and fold into a warm flour tortilla with sour cream, guacamole, and salsa. Feeds 4 in 1 hour and 30 minutes (includes marinating time).

An American Gumbo

 Fajitas (fah HEE tahs)—Skirt steaks, actually the beef diaphragm muscle.

Tacos al Carbon

2 pounds flank or skirt steak	Steak seasoning
¼ cup oil	Flour tortillas
¼ cup soy sauce	Onion
¼ cup lime juice	Sour cream
2 tablespoons Pickapeppa sauce	Guacamole
Chili powder	Salsa

Slice steak into thin 1–1½-inch strips. Mix oil, soy sauce, lime juice and Pickapeppa. Pour over meat in a zip-loc bag. Sprinkle liberally with chili powder and steak seasoning. Marinate overnight. Put meat on skewers and cook on grill about 7 minutes on each side or until done.

Serve with grilled sliced onion, sour cream, guacamole, salsa, or Pico de Gallo, and let everyone roll his own into warm flour tortillas. Serves 4–6.

Lagniappe

Italian Cutlets

1 pound ground beef	3 slices Mozzarella cheese,
Salt and pepper to taste	halved
2 tablespoons chopped parsley	1 (1⅝-ounce) package Lawry's
Flour	spaghetti sauce mix, prepared
2 eggs, beaten	according to package directions
½ cup bread crumbs	½ cup grated Parmesan cheese
¼ cup vegetable oil	

Combine meat, salt, pepper, and parsley. Shape into 6 cutlets. Dredge cutlets in flour, dip in eggs, and roll in crumbs. Sauté cutlets in oil until brown and place in a baking dish. Put Mozzarella slices on each cutlet, cover with sauce, and sprinkle with Parmesan cheese. Bake at 400° for 20–25 minutes.

Flavors

Pick Pocket Tacos

1 pound ground meat
1 onion, chopped
¼ teaspoon salt
½ teaspoon garlic salt
2 teaspoons chili powder
¼ cup chili sauce (more if
  desired)

½ teaspoon cumin
Pocket bread
Cheese
Lettuce
Tomatoes
Avocados
Picante sauce

Brown in a skillet ground meat and onion. Add salt, garlic salt, chili powder, chili sauce and cumin. Cook and stir until all is blended well. Warm pocket bread and fill each with meat mixture, grated cheese, lettuce and tomatoes. Serve with slices of avocados, and picante sauce. Yields 6 servings.

Calf Fries to Caviar

Tacos

1 pound ground beef
1 onion, chopped finely
1 pod garlic, chopped finely
2 small jalapeño peppers,
  chopped
1 can Rotel tomatoes and chilies
  (or 1 large fresh tomato peeled
  and grated for pulp)
2 teaspoons cumin

1 teaspoon Lawry's seasoned
  pepper
1 package chalupa shells
1 package Lawry's taco seasoning
  mix (optional)
1 cup grated Cheddar cheese
1 cup shredded lettuce
½ cup chopped, fresh tomatoes

Mix beef, onion, garlic, pepper, tomatoes, seasoned pepper and cumin and cook until beef is done. Add Lawry's seasoned mix, if it is being used, when meat is almost done. Heat taco shells in oven and fill at the last minute with meat mixture. Add grated cheese and top with lettuce and tomatoes. Serves 4. A wonderful idea for a party is to put all ingredients out and let each person fix their own taco to their liking! Add sour cream to your list of condiments.

Cuckoo Too

Sour Cream Enchiladas

2 pounds ground beef
1 onion, diced
1 green pepper, diced
1 teaspoon salt
Pepper
2 tablespoons picante sauce
1 tablespoon chili powder
½ teaspoon cumin
1 tablespoon garlic powder

4 drops hot sauce
½ cup chopped ripe olives
½ cup margarine, melted
¼ cup all-purpose flour
1½ cups milk
2 cups sour cream
18 corn tortillas
2 cups grated Longhorn cheese

Brown beef in skillet; drain. Add onion and green pepper; cook until vegetables are soft. Add salt, pepper, picante sauce, seasonings, and olives; simmer 5 minutes and set aside.

Combine butter and flour in a saucepan; slowly add milk, stirring constantly. Cook and stir until thickened. Blend in sour cream; heat 1 minute. (Do not boil.)

Fill each tortilla with meat mixture; roll. Place in a greased 13 × 9 × 2-inch casserole. Cover with sour cream sauce; sprinkle with cheese. Bake at 375° for 25 minutes or until bubbly. Yields 18 servings.

Flavor Favorites

Easy Enchilada Casserole

2 pounds ground beef
1 stick margarine
1 onion, chopped
1 (10¾-ounce) can cream of
   mushroom soup
1 (10¾-ounce) can cream of
   chicken soup

1 (8-ounce) can taco sauce
1 (15-ounce) can enchilada sauce
2 cups Cheddar cheese, grated
1 package corn tortillas

Brown ground beef. Sauté onion in the margarine. Add sauces and soups to the onion and meat mixture. Layer the meat mixture and tortillas in a large casserole (9 × 13-inch) and top with grated cheese. Bake at 350° for approximately 30 minutes.

Tortillas can be torn into fourths and added to the meat mixture instead of layering. Bake as above.

For microwave, cover with plastic wrap and cook 15 minutes on roast.

La Piñata

Green Enchiladas

½–¾ pound ground beef
½ medium onion, finely chopped
1 clove garlic, finely chopped
1 teaspoon chili powder (increase
    to taste)
Salt and pepper to taste
1 large onion, chopped
1½ cups grated Velveeta or
    Monterey Jack cheese

Salad oil
1 dozen corn tortillas
¼ cup margarine
3 tablespoons flour
½ teaspoon salt
2 cups milk
1 (4-ounce) can chopped green
    chilies

Brown meat, the half onion, and the garlic together until meat is thoroughly cooked. Add chili powder, salt and pepper and set aside. Soften tortillas by frying in ½ inch of hot salad oil for only a few seconds. Do not allow them to become crisp. They may be stacked as they are cooked.

To prepare enchiladas, place a spoonful of meat mixture on a tortilla. Add a tablespoon each of onion and cheese. Roll up and place seam side down in a 9×13-inch baking dish. Prepare remaining tortillas in the same manner. Any remaining meat or cheese may be sprinkled on top of enchiladas. More cheese may be used if desired. Melt margarine on medium heat and add flour and salt. Stir until bubbly and add milk. Stir until smooth and only slightly thickened. Add green chilies and remove from heat. Pour over enchiladas and bake the casserole at 350° for 10–15 minutes, or until thoroughly heated. Enchiladas may be prepared the day before serving or may be frozen. If preparing ahead, add sauce just before cooking in oven. Serves 4–6.

San Angelo Junior League Cookbook

Aunt Martha's Tamale Pie

1½ pounds ground beef	1 (6-ounce) can tomato paste
1 onion, chopped	1 cup water
1 green pepper, cut into strips	½ cup sliced ripe olives
1 clove garlic, minced	2 tablespoons chili powder
1 (12-ounce) can whole kernel	1 teaspoon salt
corn, undrained	1 cup grated Cheddar cheese

Sauté beef, onion, green pepper and garlic. Drain excess grease. Stir in corn, tomato paste, water, olives, chili powder and salt. Simmer 20–25 minutes. Stir in cheese until melted. Pour into 2-quart casserole.

TOPPING:
¾ cup yellow cornmeal
½ teaspoon salt
2 cups water

Combine ingredients; cook at medium heat 15 minutes, stirring constantly until mixture thickens. Spoon over meat, bake 35–40 minutes at 375°. Serves 6.

Variation: Omit cheese from base. Add ½ cup cornmeal mixed with ½ cup water during last 10 minutes of simmering the sauce. Substitute Spoon Bread Topping and use 3-quart casserole.

SPOON BREAD TOPPING:
1½ cups milk	½ cup cornmeal
1 teaspoon salt	1 cup grated Cheddar cheese
2 tablespoons butter or margarine	2 eggs, lightly beaten

Heat milk, salt and butter; slowly stir in cornmeal. Cook, stirring until thickened. Remove from heat, stir in cheese and eggs. Pour over meat mixture. Chill 1½ hours. Bake 35–40 minutes at 350°.

Cook 'em Horns

Tamales (tah MAH lays)—Made by spreading a thick layer of masa on dried corn husks, then filling with shredded meat and cooking until soft.

Elvira's Tamales

1 (13-pound) Boston pork butt
5 (6-ounce) packages corn shucks
10 pounds masa
1 pound ancho chili pods
2 whole garlic bulbs (16–20 garlic cloves)

1 tablespoon comino
Salt
2–3 tablespoons chili powder
1½–2 pounds lard
Water

Day before: Cover pork with water; simmer until tender (about 1¾ hours). Cool. Chop fine, using knife and cutting board. Reserve broth; refrigerate meat and broth. Pour boiling water over corn shucks and soak overnight.

Early in day: Mix masa with water and broth, according to package directions; set aside.

Stem and seed chili pods. Rinse under running water. Simmer in covered pot of water about 45 minutes. Cool. Scrape pulp from skins. Chop pulp in blender, adding enough water to make a tomato-sauce consistency. Discard chili skins, but save water gravy.

Peel garlic cloves; mix with comino and grind in a molcajete, adding enough broth to make a smooth mixture. Combine this mixture with salt to taste and about ¾ of chili pulp with the chopped meat. Knead with hands, mixing thoroughly for about 30 minutes.

Put masa in a large bowl. Add 1–2 tablespoons chili powder, salt to taste, and remaining chili pulp. Begin melting a pound of lard at a time, mixing it into the masa mixture. Continue adding melted lard ½ pound at a time, working it in with your hands, until masa is greasy and fluffy. Test by pressing back of your hand into mixture. The masa is ready when it no longer sticks to your hand.

Clean corn shucks as you need them because they dry out quickly. Put layer of the corn shuck scraps about 2 inches deep in the bottom of a 12-quart steamer. Place small, inverted metal bowl in center of the corn shuck layer.

Choose large corn shucks; open them flat with a spatula or table knife and spread a heaping tablespoon of masa in a thin layer over ⅔ of the wide end of the shuck. Next, spread ¼ cup of meat filling down middle of masa. Roll the tamale in the corn shuck, like a cigarette. Fold narrow end of shuck up toward the middle of tamale.

CONTINUED

230

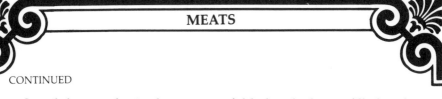

CONTINUED

Stand the tamales in the steamer, folded ends down, filled ends resting on inverted bowl so water can't get inside the shucks. The steamer will hold about half of tamales at a time.

In a 1-quart container, mix 2 parts broth with 1 part water. Pour into steamer, being very careful not to get it in open end of shucks. Cover tamales with scraps of shucks, then with damp towel. Cover pot and steam about 1 hour, adding more liquid as necessary. Tamales are ready when masa peels cleanly away from the shuck. Repeat steaming process with remainder of tamales. Makes 20–25 dozen.

"This is an all-day production. It speeds things up on the day you're going to make them if several ladies work like a production line. It is a lot of fun! They may be made ahead of time and frozen in a freezer . . . *not* in the freezer compartment of a refrigerator. To serve, you simply heat them in a steamer."

Company's Coming

 Masa (MAH zah)—A coarse corn flour used to make tortillas. *Molcajete* (mohl cah HAY tay)—A mortar used to grind ingredients.

Texas Tamale Pie

1 pound hamburger
1 medium onion, chopped
1 (16-ounce) can tomatoes
1 (8-ounce) can tomato sauce
1 (14½-ounce) can red kidney
  beans
1 package frozen succotash
1 small package of corn muffin
  mix
Salt, pepper and chili powder to
  taste

Brown hamburger and onion in a small amount of oil. Add tomatoes and tomato sauce. Simmer. Add kidney beans and succotash. Cook 10 minutes. Season to taste. Mash a few of the kidney beans against side of skillet for thickening. Pour into casserole. Mix corn muffin mix according to directions on package, adding extra milk so it is thinner than usual. Spoon on top of hamburger mixture. Bake at 375° until cornbread is done, about 25 or 30 minutes. Serves 6.

San Antonio Cookbook II

Husband's Delight
(Mine, for sure!)

1 (8-ounce) package cream
  cheese, softened
2 cups sour cream
3 green onions and tops, chopped
1½ pounds ground beef
2 tablespoons butter or margarine
2 (8-ounce) cans tomato sauce

1 teaspoon sugar
1 teaspoon salt
Dash of pepper
Dash of Worcestershire sauce
2 (5-ounce) package noodles
½ cup shredded cheese

In a bowl mix cream cheese, sour cream and onions; set aside. Brown the meat in butter; add tomato sauce, sugar, salt, pepper and Worcestershire. Cook noodles according to package directions. In a 2-quart casserole alternate layers of noodles, beef mixture, and sour cream mixture. Top with shredded cheese and bake at 350° until brown and cheese is melted. Yields 8 servings.

Keepers

Beef-Noodle Stroganoff
(Microwave)

1 pound ground beef
1 small onion, chopped
½ cup chopped celery
4 cups uncooked noodles (about 5
  ounces)
1 (10½-ounce) can condensed
  beef broth
¼ cup dry red wine or water

1 tablespoon dried parsley flakes
¼ teaspoon each, salt and pepper
1 (4-ounce) can mushroom pieces
  and liquid
1 teaspoon (heaping) prepared
  mustard
1 cup dairy sour cream

Crumble ground beef into a hard-plastic colander and sprinkle onion and celery on top. Set colander in a 2–3-quart casserole. Microwave on HIGH 6–7 minutes, stirring once. Discard fat. Place noodles in bottom of same casserole. Add meat, broth, water, parsley, salt, pepper and mushrooms. Cover and Microwave on HIGH 12–14 minutes or until noodles are almost tender. Stir two times during cooking. Blend mustard into sour cream and stir into beef-noodle mixture. Cover and Microwave on 70% (MEDIUM-HIGH) 2–2½ minutes. Let stand 5–7 minutes before serving. Serves 6.

Microwave Know-How

Crazy Crust Pizza

BATTER:

1 cup flour
1 teaspoon salt
1 teaspoon Italian seasoning or
  leaf oregano

⅛ teaspoon pepper
2 eggs
⅔ cup milk

TOPPING:

1½ pounds ground beef or 1 cup
  thinly sliced pepperoni
¼ cup chopped onion
1 (4-ounce) can mushrooms
  (optional)

1 cup pizza sauce or Hunt's Herb
  Sauce
1 cup shredded Mozzarella
  cheese

In medium skillet, brown ground beef, seasoning to taste with salt and pepper. (No need to brown pepperoni, if used.) Drain well. Set aside. Lightly grease and dust with flour 12 or 14-inch pizza pan or 15 × 10-inch jelly roll pan. Prepare batter. Combine flour, salt, Italian seasoning, pepper, eggs, and milk. Mix until smooth. Pour batter into pan, tilting pan so batter covers bottom. Arrange topping of meat, onion, and mushrooms over batter. Bake on low rack in oven at 425° for 25–30 minutes until pizza is deep golden brown. Remove from oven. Drizzle with pizza sauce and sprinkle with cheese. Return to oven for 10–15 minutes. Serves 3 or 4.

The Blue Denim Gourmet

Texas Hash

½ large onion
½ green pepper
3 tablespoons Crisco
1 pound ground beef
2 cups tomatoes

½ cup uncooked rice
1 teaspoon chili powder
1 teaspoon salt
¼ teaspoon black pepper

Cook onions and green pepper slowly in Crisco. Add ground beef and sauté until browned. Add remaining ingredients and bake covered at 375° for 45 minutes.

The Blue Denim Gourmet

Cheesy Meat Loaf
(Microwave)

1½ pounds ground beef
1 egg, slightly beaten
1 tablespoon Worcestershire
   sauce
¼ teaspoon pepper
¼ teaspoon salt

½ cup milk
¼ cup chopped onion
⅓ cup dry bread crumbs
1 cup grated Cheddar cheese
1 (4-ounce) can mushroom pieces,
   drained

TOPPING:
5 tablespoons brown sugar
1 teaspoon dry mustard

½ cup catsup

Combine beef, egg, Worcestershire sauce, pepper, salt, milk, onion and bread crumbs. Mix well. Roll out on wax paper into rectangular shape about ½-inch thick. Sprinkle cheese and mushrooms on top of beef mixture. Roll lengthwise like a jelly roll by picking up edge of wax paper and allowing meat to roll over on itself. Place on platter and microwave on a carousel or turn occasionally for 25–30 minutes on ROAST. Blend brown sugar, mustard and catsup. Spread over top of loaf as soon as it comes out of microwave. Serves 6–10.

Variation: Substitute Monterey Jack for Cheddar cheese.
Hullabaloo in the Kitchen

Mini-Mex Meat Loaves
(Microwave)

4 (6-inch) corn tortillas
1 pound lean ground beef
½ cup dry bread crumbs
⅓ cup picante sauce

1 egg, well beaten
1 teaspoon chili powder
Shredded Cheddar cheese,
   chopped lettuce and tomatoes

In outer edge of each tortilla, make 4 (2-inch) cuts toward center. (Make a cut at 3, 6, 9 and 12 o'clock positions.) Place a tortilla in each of 4 (10-ounce) custard cups.

Combine meat, bread crumbs, picante sauce, egg and chili powder; blend well. Divide meat mixture into four equal portions. Press each meat portion into a tortilla-lined custard cup. Make an indentation in center of each mini loaf. Place cups on a microwave-safe tray; cover with waxed paper. Microwave on 70% (MEDIUM-HIGH) 8–9 minutes, rotating cups midway through cooking. Top each meat loaf with cheese and let stand 2–3 minutes. Garnish with lettuce and tomatoes to serve. Makes 4 servings.

Micro Quick!

Jalapeño Cheeseburgers
(Microwave)

4 shaped beef patties, lean
   ground
4 thin slices jalapeño-flavored
   cheese

4 toasted hamburger buns

Place empty browning skillet in microwave. Microwave on FULL (100%) POWER 5 minutes. Place beef patties into hot skillet. Microwave on FULL (100%) POWER 1 to 2 minutes, or until each patty is seared. Turn each patty over in skillet. Microwave on FULL (100%) POWER another 1 to 2 minutes. Place one slice of cheese on each patty. Microwave on MEDIUM (50%) POWER 30 seconds or just until cheese is melted. Serve on toasted buns. Serves 4.

The Texas Microwave Cookbook

Cheeseburger Pie

Pastry for 1 (9-inch) one-crust pie,
  unbaked
1 pound ground beef
½ teaspoon ground oregano
½ cup crushed soda crackers

1 (8-ounce) can tomato sauce
¼ cup chopped onion
¼ cup chopped green pepper
¾ teaspoon salt
¼ teaspoon pepper

Brown meat. Drain. Stir in remaining ingredients and pour into pastry shell.

CHEESE TOPPING:
1 egg, beaten
¼ cup milk
½ teaspoon salt
½ teaspoon dry mustard

½ teaspoon Worcestershire sauce
2 cups grated Cheddar cheese

Combine egg and milk. Stir in seasonings and cheese. Spread topping evenly over filling. Cover edge of pie crust with 2–3-inch strip of aluminum foil to prevent excessive browning. Remove foil the last 15 minutes of baking. Bake in 425° oven for 30 minutes. Serves 6–8.

Amarillo Junior League Cookbook

"Juicy Pig" Sandwiches

2 pounds ground beef
2 teaspoons chili powder
2 teaspoons salt
¾ teaspoon ground cinnamon
1 (16-ounce) can stewed tomatoes
2 medium-sized green peppers,
  chopped

3 medium onions, chopped
¾ cup vinegar
½ cup sugar
1 cup prepared mustard
Hamburger buns

Combine meat, chili powder, salt, and cinnamon in a skillet; cook until meat is well-browned.

Combine tomatoes, green pepper, onion, vinegar, and sugar in a saucepan; cook until onions are tender.

Combine meat and vegetables mixtures; simmer 40–50 minutes, stirring occasionally. Stir in mustard, mixing well. Spoon onto hamburger buns. Freezes well. Yields 12–15 servings.

Flavor Favorites

Italian-Style Cabbage Rolls

¾ pound ground beef
¾ pound pork sausage
1 teaspoon salt
1 teaspoon monosodium
  glutamate

¼ teaspoon black pepper
1 small onion, chopped finely
1 cup cooked rice
2 eggs
1 medium head cabbage

Combine meats, salt, monosodium glutamate, pepper, onion, rice and eggs, mixing well. Form into 10–12 fat rolls (about as long as your thumb). Meanwhile, pour boiling water over 10 or 12 large cabbage leaves. Let stand 5 minutes. Roll one meat roll into a cabbage leaf, securing with a toothpick. Place in baking dish. Continue making remaining meat rolls. Place all in baking dish and cover with Garlic-Tomato Sauce. Bake covered 1½ hours at 350°. Serves 4–6.

GARLIC-TOMATO SAUCE:

3 tablespoons cooking oil
1 small onion, chopped
½ teaspoon (or to taste) garlic
  powder
1 teaspoon monosodium
  glutamate

¼ teaspoon black pepper
2 tablespoons parsley
1 (16-ounce) can tomatoes, cut up
1 cup water

Sauté onion in cooking oil until golden brown. Add seasonings, tomatoes and water. Cover and simmer for 15 minutes. Pour over cabbage rolls.

Tasteful Traditions

 MSG—Monosodium glutamate, a powder taken from glutamic acid in plants. Used as a flavor enhancer. Some recipes use the brand, Accent.

Marinated Lamb

Marinate lamb chops, ground lamb patties wrapped in bacon, rolled roast, or leg of lamb (on spit) in the following for 2 hours:

¼ cup red wine
¼ cup (plus) olive oil
¼ cup lemon juice

½ cup rosemary
1 clove garlic, crushed

The best starting place if one is learning to acquire a taste for lamb is with your charcoal barbeque. Marinate meat and cook as you would beef.

To cook leg of lamb in the oven follow same instructions and method for beef, *except* season with rosemary, crushed garlic, salt and pepper.

For lamb patties, make patties, wrap in bacon and brown in real butter in a skillet. After patty is browned, turn the heat down and sprinkle with Bouquet Garni and add ½ cup of Crosse and Blackwell mint sauce (not jelly). Cover and cook for about 30 minutes on low heat.

In stroganoff substitute lamb chunks for beef for a very delicate flavor. Serve with green rice and Waldorf salad.

Spindletop International Cooks

Rack of Lamb Persillade

1 small rack of lamb
2 teaspoons Dijon mustard
1 cup bread crumbs
½ teaspoon salt
½ teaspoon pepper

3 garlic cloves, crushed
1 twig fresh thyme
1 tablespoon olive oil
1 cup chopped parsley

To make persillade, combine all ingredients except lamb and mustard in a processor. Process, allowing mixture to stay very green. Do not overprocess. Roast the rack of lamb at 450° for 20 minutes (medium rare). Five minutes before removing from oven, brush with Dijon mustard and persillade. Serve the rack with natural lamb juices. Rack of four chops.

Any of the flavorful Bordeaux wines will be good with the Lamb.

The Adolphus Cookbook

 Persillade (per seh LAHD)—A French word which tells that a dish contains parsley or is garnished with parsley.

Liver Fantastique

6 pieces bacon
1½ pounds calves liver, sliced
⅓–½ cup seasoned flour
1⅓ cups brown sugar
1½ cups vinegar
1 teaspoon onion salt

1 teaspoon marjoram
1 teaspoon rosemary leaves,
  crushed
Pepper
1 bell pepper, sliced
1 onion, sliced

Fry bacon until crisp––drain and keep warm. Add enough bacon drippings or salad oil to drippings in pan to make ⅓ cup. Dredge sliced liver in seasoned flour and brown in drippings. Drain on paper towels and set aside. Make a roux of ⅓ cup seasoned flour and bacon drippings. Add all the remaining ingredients, except bell pepper and onion. Stir till thick as gravy consistency and add up to 1⅓ cups hot water if desired. Add liver to gravy mixture and cook over low heat for 30–40 minutes. Add pepper and onion during the last 15 minutes. Serve with bacon crumbled on top. Yields 4–6 servings.

La Piñata

Sausage Con Queso

A dandy lunch dish when served over heated large round tostados.

2 pounds hot pork sausage
2 pounds Velveeta cheese, cubed
1 cup evaporated milk
1 (.7-ounce) package Good
  Seasons garlic salad dressing
  mix

1 (.7-ounce) package Good
  Seasons bleu cheese salad
  dressing mix

Brown sausage well and drain thoroughly. Melt cheese with the milk in the top of a double boiler; stir in salad dressing mixes and meat. To reheat, add additional evaporated milk. Serve with warm tostados. Fills a standard chafing dish.

Crème of the Crop

Sausage Mushroom Strudel

1 pound Italian sausage
1 pound mushrooms, finely
  chopped
1 tablespoon chopped shallots
1 (8-ounce) package cream
  cheese, softened

8 frozen strudel sheets
1 cup butter, melted
¾ cup dry breadcrumbs
3 tablespoons butter, melted

Preheat oven to 400°. Fry sausage in large saucepan; crumble and remove from pan. Pat dry. Drain all but 2 tablespoons of drippings. Add mushrooms and shallots to pan and sauté until all liquid is evaporated. Return sausage to pan; stir in cream cheese and cool. Using 4 strudel sheets for each roll, unfold 1 sheet, brush with butter and sprinkle with breadcrumbs. Repeat with second and third sheets; top with fourth sheet. Spoon half of mixture along long side of sheets. Tuck short ends toward center to keep filling intact; roll like a jelly roll. Place roll on buttered baking sheets and brush with butter. Bake 20 minutes. Serves 10.

This freezes well, but must be thawed thoroughly before baking.

The Dallas Symphony Cookbook

Pork with Corn Dressing

4–6 pork loin chops (1-inch thick)
1¾ cups canned white cream
  style corn (Del Monte)
1½ cups bread crumbs

2 eggs, slightly beaten
¼ cup onion, chopped
Paprika to taste
Salt and pepper

Trim fat from chops and render in skillet. Season chops with salt and pepper and brown in fat. Remove chops to casserole dish. Discard fat scraps and excess fat from pan. Deglaze pan with small amount of water and pour around chops. Combine remaining ingredients, except paprika. Spoon over and around chops. Cover and bake at 375° for 45 minutes. Remove cover, sprinkle with paprika and brown under broiler. Serves 4–6. Serve with steamed Brussels sprouts or broccoli and a crunchy salad.

Variation: Add ½ cup chopped and sautéed bell pepper and ½ teaspoon thyme to corn mixture.

A Different Taste of Paris

Pork Tenderloin à la Cream
Typically European style

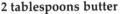

2 tablespoons butter	½ teaspoon cracked black pepper
1 pound pork tenderloin(s), cut in half lengthwise	¼ teaspoon garlic powder
8 new potatoes, washed and cut in half	8 ounces fresh mushrooms, washed, drained, and cut in half
2 cups carrots, peeled and sliced	2 medium onions, chopped
2 teaspoons parsley flakes	¾ cup whipping cream, do *not* whip
1 teaspoon Knorr Swiss Aromat Seasoning for Meat	2 tablespoons dry red wine
½ teaspoon thyme	1 bay leaf, broken into 4 pieces

1. In a skillet, melt the butter and using medium heat brown the outside of the tender(s) until grey in color. Remove from heat and put aside.

2. Bring 8 cups of water to a boil, add the potatoes and carrots, return to a boil and cook for 10 minutes; drain immediately.

3. In the bottom of a baking dish, put the parsley, seasoning for meat, thyme, pepper and garlic powder and mix it together with your fingers.

4. Roll the tender(s) in this mixture so that the spices stick to the tender, and place in bottom of baking dish.

5. Add all the remaining ingredients to the baking dish, plus the partially cooked potatoes and carrots.

6. Bake in a preheated 350° oven for 45 minutes or until tenders are cooked to the desired degree of doneness. Serves 4–6.

Leaving Home

Stir-Fried Shredded Pork With Spicy Garlic Sauce

INGREDIENTS:

12 ounces pork tenderloin or butt
6 water chestnuts
3 tablespoons dry black fungus, optional

½ cup bamboo shoots, shredded
2 teaspoons chopped garlic
2 cups vegetable oil

SEASONINGS TO MARINATE PORK:

1½ tablespoons soy sauce
1½ tablespoons sherry
1½ tablespoons cornstarch

1 tablespoon cooking oil
2 teaspoons chopped ginger

SEASONING SAUCE:

1 tablespoon Hoisin sauce
1½ tablespoons soy sauce
1 tablespoon sesame oil
1 tablespoon cooking wine or sherry
2 teaspoons brown sugar

2½ teaspoons cornstarch
1 tablespoon water
Dash of pepper
1 tablespoon wine vinegar
1 tablespoon chopped green onion

TO PREPARE:

1. Cut pork in string style, marinate with soy sauce, sherry, oil, cornstarch and chopped ginger.

2. Soak black fungus in hot water about 10–15 minutes. Rinse and clean. Slice them when expanded. Also slice the water chestnuts very fine.

3. Mix all seasoning sauce in a cup or bowl.

TO COOK:

1. Heat oil in wok or frying pan, then add pork shreds. Just stir for ½ minute, then remove and put aside. Drain off oil from pan. Reserve for stir-frying vegetables or other meats.

2. Heat 3 tablespoons remaining oil to stir fry garlic, then add water chestnuts, bamboo shoots, fungus, and pork strings; stir thoroughly. Add the ready prepared seasoning sauce, stir evenly and serve hot or warm. Serves 4–6.

Hint: This dish can be made ahead and reheated in a frying pan. If the sauce is too dry during reheating, just add 2–3 tablespoons stock or sherry.

Chinese Cooking the American Way

Honey-Glazed Ham Slice

This will bring them buzzing' round the table . . .

1 slice smoked (fully-cooked) ham, cut 1-inch thick	¼ cup honey
	1 teaspoon prepared mustard
¼ cup orange juice	

Combine orange juice, honey and mustard and cook slowly for 10–12 minutes, stirring occasionally. Place ham in broiling pan about three inches from heat. Brush with orange glaze. Broil 8 minutes on first side, then turn, brush with glaze, broil 6–8 minutes longer.

From My Apron Pocket

Barbecued Cabrito

6–8 pounds cabrito

MARINADE:

½ cup fresh lemon juice	¼–⅓ cup snipped fresh chives
2 teaspoons Dijon mustard	Salt and pepper to taste
1½ cups olive oil	

Mix thoroughly all ingredients. This marinade may also be used as a salad dressing.

BARBECUE SAUCE:

¼ cup red wine vinegar	½ cup butter or margarine
½ cup water	1 tablespoon prepared mustard
1 teaspoon salt	2 tablespoons Worcestershire sauce
½ teaspoon garlic powder	
1 tablespoon caramelized sugar	¼ cup tomato paste
¼ teaspoon black pepper	1 teaspoon liquid smoke
⅛ teaspoon cayenne pepper	

Combine all ingredients and simmer for 20 minutes. Do not boil. Brush meat with marinade, wrap in double thickness of heavy foil; refrigerate for at least 2 hours or overnight. Open foil, pour barbecue sauce over cabrito, reclose tightly. Bake for 3–3½ hours at 350°. Serve with Hopping John, coleslaw and cornbread. Serves 8–10.

San Antonio Conservation Society Cookbook

 Cabrito (cah BREE toh)—A young goat.

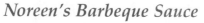

Noreen's Barbeque Sauce

2 (1 pint–10 ounce) bottles Heinz
ketchup
1 (10-ounce) bottle Worcestershire
sauce
¾ cup (packed) McCormick's dry
mustard
¼ cup vinegar (pour in 1 ketchup
bottle to rinse)
3 cups water (use to rinse both
ketchup bottles)
⅓ cup dark brown sugar, packed
⅓ cup sorghum molasses
2 cups water (use to rinse out
molasses)
2 medium onions (quarter and
drop in sauce)
6 medium garlic cloves (quarter
and drop in sauce)
¼ cup Mazola
1 teaspoon salt

Pour all ingredients into large (approximately 6-quart) kettle with cover. Use water and vinegar to rinse out ketchup bottles and molasses measuring cup. Cook slowly at about 225–250° with cover on for 2 hours, then take off cover. Stir occasionally, adjusting seasonings to taste.

After sauce has thickened as desired, strain into jars, removing onions and garlic. Sauce will keep several weeks or longer if refrigerated, if not used sooner.

Hint: Perfect on pork backbone or ribs: Place 4 pounds lean backbone or ribs in glass casserole, salt both sides. Slice 1 or 2 big onions and place on top. Lay several stalks of celery on top of the onions. Cover with 2 cups Noreen's Barbecue Sauce. Bake 3 hours in 250° oven. Turn and cook 3 more hours. Heat the sauce and serve with meat. Eat all you can and freeze the rest for later.

Through Our Kitchen Door

Barbecue Sauce

3 tablespoons water
1 pint vinegar
1 pound margarine, melted
1 (6-ounce) jar prepared mustard
1 (6-ounce) bottle Worcestershire
sauce
Garlic salt to taste

Mix thoroughly. Sauce will store indefinitely in refrigerator. *Good on any type of barbecued meats, especially chicken.*

Hospitality

Easy 'Hot' Sauce

5 pounds hot green chili peppers   1 cup vinegar, white
1 large onion, peeled   Salt and pepper
12 garlic cloves, peeled
12 (16-ounce) cans whole
    tomatoes

Quarter the onion and place all ingredients in blender. Season with salt and pepper to taste. Makes 2 gallons.
    (Richard Gonzales, King Ranch) *Texas Celebrity Cookbook*

Hot Chili Sauce

10 pounds ripe tomatoes   1 pound sugar
5 large onions   1 teaspoon ground cinnamon
2 cups Mexican peppers   1 teaspoon cloves
1 scant cup salt   1 teaspoon allspice
2 green sweet peppers   2 tablespoons each celery and
2 red peppers, seeded and   mustard seed, tied in a bag
    chopped finely   1 quart vinegar

Peel and cut up ripe tomatoes, onions and Mexican peppers. Cook until tender. Add sugar, salt, green and red peppers, cinnamon, cloves and allspice and stir until thoroughly mixed. Let simmer gently with bag of celery and mustard seed. Add vinegar and boil briskly for 15 minutes. Put in jars and seal while hot. Mixture will thicken on cooling. This sauce is very hot!
                                 A Taste of Victoria

Jalapeño Jelly

1 pound bell pepper	1¼ cups white vinegar
¼ pound fresh jalapeños	⅓ cup lemon juice
5½ cups sugar	1 (6-ounce) bottle of Certo

Grind green pepper and jalapeño pepper in a food grinder. (If a grinder is unavailable, it is possible to chop it up in a blender.) Add sugar and vinegar. Bring to a boil for 5 minutes, stirring constantly. Add ⅓ cup lemon juice; bring to a boil. Add bottle of Certo and bring to a rolling boil for one minute. (A rolling boil is when no amount of stirring can make the boiling subside.) Pour into hot, sterile jelly jars. Wait 2 weeks before using. Makes seven half-pint glasses.

Note: If you would like the jelly to have a green color, add about 3 drops of yellow food coloring and 2 drops of blue. You can just add green coloring instead, but the yellow and blue give a more attractive tint.

This is definitely a meat jelly, not a breakfast jelly. It is used as a complement for turkey and dressing, fajitas, and most any kind of meat. A dab of jelly added to cheese spread on a cracker makes a quick and tasty hors d'oeuvre.

My mother never made jalapeño jelly, but I gave her a jar each Christmas and other times I visited her. This makes an excellent little gift for friends and neighbors at Christmastime.

Mrs. Blackwell's Heart of Texas Cookbook

Cranberry Jalapeño Jelly
(Microwave)

Red instead of the usual green.

6 jalapeño peppers	6 ounces liquid fruit pectin
2½ cups cranberry juice cocktail	1 cup vinegar
7 cups granulated sugar	Red food coloring, optional

Wearing lightweight rubber gloves, quarter and remove seeds from peppers. Place peppers and cranberry juice in blender and process until peppers are very finely chopped. Combine with sugar in a 4-quart simmer pot. Cover with plastic wrap (so that you can see mixture as it cooks). Microwave on HIGH 18–20 minutes, or until mixture comes to a full rolling boil. Add pectin and Microwave on HIGH 2–3 minutes, or until mixture returns to a boil. Add vinegar and food coloring, if desired. Pour mixture into sterilized jelly glasses and seal. Yields 8 (8-ounce) jars.

Serving Suggestion: Spread ½ cup of jelly over an 8-ounce block of cream cheese. Serve with assorted crackers.

Micro Quick!

Champagne Ice

1 cup sugar	Juice of 1½ oranges
4 cups water	Grated rind of 1 orange
1 bottle dry Champagne	2 tablespoons brandy

Cook the sugar and water to a rolling boil and boil for 6 minutes. Add the Champagne and heat to volatize the alcohol. Remove from the heat and stir in the orange juice, rind and brandy. Pour into the container of an ice cream freezer; pack with salt and ice and freeze. This may be made in the refrigerator freezer in ice trays or in a cake pan. When almost frozen, beat with hand electric beater. Do this two or three times to break up ice crystals for a better texture. Serves 8–10.

We suggest serving as a palate refresher between courses.

Entertaining at Aldredge House

Agarita Jelly

5½ cups agarita juice
7½ cups sugar
1 (1¾-ounce) box Sure-Jell

Mix juice and Sure-Jell in a 6–8-quart saucepan. Bring to a boil, stirring constantly. Add sugar quickly and bring to a full rolling boil (a boil that cannot be stirred down), stirring constantly. Remove from heat; skim off foam and quickly pour into sterilized jars or glasses. Cover at once with hot melted paraffin. Cool. Put on lids. Yields about 8 cups.

The agarita is a small, low shrub that grows wild in the Hill Country. The red berries ripen in May. The bush is thorny and it is impossible to gather the berries by hand. The best solution is to spread an old sheet on the ground under the bush. Then with a fairly long stick (I use an old tennis racket), gently beat the bush till the berries fall. You'll have twigs, leaves and insects too. Remove as many as possible, then wash many, many times. You will need approximately 1½ gallons of berries for the juice. Cook berries with 1½ cups water on medium heat for about 20 minutes. Strain in a jelly bag or through a clean white cloth. If you do not have enough juice, add water to make the correct amount. Don't use more than 1 cup water though.

Another word of advice. Spray yourself well with insect repellent before beating that bush. Chiggers are no fun! Too, be sure none of those long, wiggly creatures are hiding under that bush!

A Texas Hill Country Cookbook

Cakes, Cookies, Candies

Houston's Astrodome is the site of major entertaining and sporting events.

Texas Buttermilk Pound Cake

1 cup shortening	½ teaspoon salt
3 cups sugar	1 cup buttermilk
6 egg yolks	2 teaspoons lemon flavoring
3 cups flour	6 egg whites
¼ teaspoon soda	

Preheat oven to 325°. Cream shortening and sugar together. Add egg yolks, one at a time, mixing after each addition. Sift together the flour, soda and salt, and add alternately with buttermilk. Add lemon flavoring and fold in stiffly beaten egg whites. Pour this mixture in an ungreased tube or bundt pan and bake at 325° for 1 hour and 20 minutes.

SWEET MILK VARIATION:
Substitute 1 cup sweet milk for buttermilk, and substitute 2 teaspoons vanilla for lemon flavoring. Bake in greased and floured bundt pan at 350° for 1 hour and 15 minutes. Pour buttermilk glaze over cake.

BUTTERMILK GLAZE:

½ cup sugar	½ stick butter or margarine
¼ cup buttermilk	

Combine in a saucepan and cook 6 minutes. Pour over cake.

Cookin' Wise

Cream Pound Cake

2 sticks of softened butter	½ pint whipping cream
3 cups sugar	1 teaspoon vanilla
6 eggs, room temperature	1 teaspoon lemon extract
3 cups cake flour	¼ teaspoon almond extract

Cream butter and sifted sugar thoroughly. Beat in eggs one at a time on high speed. Beat well. Add flour which has been sifted 3 times, alternately with whipping cream, adding flour first and last. Add vanilla.

Cook in greased floured pan in 325° oven from 1½–2 hours until tested done. Do not open oven during first hour. Cool slightly before removing from pan.

Square House Museum Cookbook

Mama's Easy Pound Cake

There was a time when a Texas lady's skill as a homemaker was judged by the delicacy of the flavor of her pound cake. This delicately-flavored family recipe is Mrs. Billie Pate's legacy from her mother.

3 sticks margarine	1 pound flour
1 (1-pound) box powdered sugar	1 teaspoon vanilla
6 eggs	

Use powdered sugar box as measure for 1 pound flour. Beat margarine and sugar until creamy. Add eggs, one at a time. Fill sugar box with unsifted flour and add to mixture. Blend well. Add vanilla. Bake in 325° oven for 1 hour in a greased and floured Bundt pan or loaf pan.

Our Favorite Recipes

Better Than Sex Cake

1 box yellow butter cake mix (without pudding)	½ cup oil
1 (6-ounce) package chocolate chips	¼ cup water
¾ cup pecans, chopped	1 teaspoon vanilla
4 eggs	1 small box instant vanilla pudding
	1 (8-ounce) carton sour cream

Coat chocolate chips and pecans with a little of the dry cake mix. Mix remainder of cake mix, eggs, oil, water, vanilla, vanilla pudding and sour cream thoroughly. Fold in chocolate chips and pecans. Pour into a greased and floured tube pan and bake for about 50 minutes at 350°. Cool before frosting.

CHOCOLATE FROSTING:

1 (16-ounce) box powdered sugar	¾ stick margarine, softened
3 squares baking chocolate, melted	Milk

Prepare chocolate frosting by combining all ingredients except milk. Add enough milk to make the frosting of a spreading consistency. Frost and serve—then *judge for yourself!!*

Ready to Serve

Frozen Kahlúa Cake
A must!

¾ cup butter, softened
2 cups sugar
¾ cup cocoa
4 egg yolks
1 teaspoon baking soda
2 tablespoons cold water

½ cup cold coffee
½ cup Kahlúa
1⅓ cups flour
2 tablespoons vanilla extract
4 egg whites, beaten

Preheat oven to 325°. Cream butter and sugar. Add cocoa and egg yolks. Dissolve soda in water and combine with coffee and Kahlúa; add to batter, alternating with flour. Add vanilla and fold in stiffly beaten egg whites. Grease and flour bundt pan. Pour in batter; remove air bubbles. Bake 1 hour.

GLAZE:
1 cup powdered sugar
½ cup Kahlúa

Combine glaze ingredients and pour over warm cake; cover with foil and freeze.

TOPPING:
1 cup whipping cream, whipped

About 1 hour before serving, remove from freezer and ice with whipped cream. Serves 12.

The Dallas Symphony Cookbook

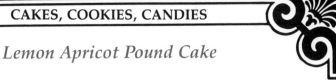
Lemon Apricot Pound Cake

CAKE:

1 (3-ounce) package instant lemon pudding mix	4 eggs
1 cup apricot nectar	¾ cup oil
1 box lemon supreme cake mix	1 tablespoon lemon extract

Place pudding into bowl with apricot nectar and let sit while mixing the rest of ingredients. Combine the cake mix, eggs, (beating well after each addition of egg) oil, lemon extract and then add the pudding mixture. Beat well with mixer and pour batter into greased and floured tube or bundt pan. Cook at 350° for 40–50 minutes. Remove from oven and take out of pan immediately. Prick top with a toothpick and spoon glaze over the cake.

GLAZE:

¼ cup fresh lemon juice	1½ cups powdered sugar
¼ cup apricot nectar	

Mix lemon juice, apricot nectar, and powdered sugar until smooth. Yields 24 servings. Freezes.

Delicious with glaze alone, but for a special treat add this icing over glaze: a box of Fluffy Lemon Frosting and 1 cup whipping cream. Mix until stiff and ice.

La Piñata

Mandarin Orange Cake

1 package butter cake mix	1 (11-ounce) can mandarin orange sections, cut up and undrained
4 eggs	
1 cup cooking oil	

Mix all ingredients. (Do not use mixer.) Spoon into three (8-inch) greased and floured cake pans. Bake at 350° for 15 minutes.

ICING:

1 (9-ounce) carton whipped topping	1 (20-ounce) can crushed pineapple, drained
1 (3-ounce) instant vanilla pudding mix	

Mix ingredients well. Ice cake. Keep cake in refrigerator

Tasteful Traditions

Celebration Cake

1 cup butter or margarine
2 cups sugar
4 eggs, separated
1 teaspoon vanilla
¼ teaspoon almond extract
½ cup water
1 teaspoon baking soda

6 tablespoons Droste's cocoa or 9
   tablespoons Hershey's cocoa
2 cups + 3 tablespoons all-purpose
   flour
½ teaspoon salt
1 cup buttermilk

Cream butter and sugar. Add egg yolks, one at a time. Add vanilla, almond extract and water. Sift cocoa, flour, soda and salt together. Add dry ingredients alternately with the buttermilk. Beat egg whites and fold into batter. Pour into 3 paper-lined 9-inch pans. Bake at 350° for 30 minutes.

ICING:

3 cups sugar
3 tablespoons Droste's cocoa or
   4½ tablespoons Hershey's
   cocoa
3 tablespoons white Karo
1 cup milk
3 tablespoons maraschino cherry
   juice

1 beaten egg
3 tablespoons butter
1½ teaspoons vanilla
¼ teaspoon almond extract
½ cup chopped maraschino
   cherries
1 cup chopped nuts

Stir sugar, cocoa, Karo, milk, cherry juice and egg until sugar is dissolved and ingredients are blended. Cook slowly to 238° on a candy thermometer or soft ball stage. Add remaining ingredients.

The secret to this is the Droste's cocoa!! Droste's is available at the Neiman-Marcus Gourmet Shop or the Emporium.

The Galveston Island Cookbook

Mexican Chocolate Cake
(Microwave)

Converted from our *Houston Chronicle* Food Editor, Ann Criswell's book.

½ cup margarine (1 stick)	2 cups flour
2 (1-ounce) squares unsweetened	2 cups sugar
baking chocolate	2 eggs, beaten
½ cup oil	1 teaspoon baking soda
¾ cup water	1 teaspoon cinnamon
½ cup milk	1 teaspoon vanilla
1½ teaspoons vinegar	

Place margarine and chocolate in a glass mixing bowl. Microwave on HIGH 2 minutes, or until melted. Add oil and water; blend. To sour the milk, combine with vinegar. Add sour milk, flour, sugar, eggs, baking soda, cinnamon and vanilla to chocolate mixture. Stir well with a wooden spoon.

Using solid shortening, grease two (2-quart) 8 × 12-inch rectangular glass pans. Shield corners. Pour half of batter into each pan. Cooking one pan at a time, Microwave on 70% (MEDIUM-HIGH) 7½–8½ minutes, rotating several times during baking. Leave cakes in pans. Cool slightly. Frost cakes while still warm using Mexican Chocolate Frosting, below. Makes 2 cakes, 8 servings each.

MEXICAN CHOCOLATE FROSTING: Great on any cake!

½ cup margarine (1 stick)	1 pound powdered sugar
2 (1-ounce) squares unsweetened	1 teaspoon vanilla
baking chocolate	½ cup chopped pecans
6 tablespoons milk	

Place margarine and chocolate in a glass mixing bowl. Microwave on HIGH 2 minutes, or until melted. Add milk, sugar and vanilla. Beat until smooth. Stir in pecans. Frosts two layers.

Micro Quick!

Wini's Carrot Cake

2 cups sugar
4 eggs
1½ cups Wesson oil
3 cups flour
2 teaspoons soda
3 cups grated carrots
1 cup broken pecans

1 teaspoon lemon flavoring
1 teaspoon coconut flavoring
Curacao or Triple Sec Liqueur or
  2 cups sugar
1½ cups fresh orange juice
2 tablespoons grated orange
  rind

Blend sugar, eggs and oil. Add flour and soda. Mix thoroughly. Fold in carrots, pecans, lemon and coconut flavorings. Pour into greased and floured bundt pan. Bake for 1½ hours at 300°. As soon as cake is removed from oven, pour Curacao or Triple Sec, any amount desired, over warm cake. Or, mix together 2 cups sugar, orange juice and orange rind, and brush over all sides of warm cake. Let cool completely in pan. Yields 16 servings.

Keepers

Black Bottom Cup Cakes

1 (8-ounce) package cream cheese
½ cup sugar
1 egg, beaten
⅛ teaspoon salt
1 (6-ounce) package chocolate
  chips
1½ cups flour
1 cup sugar

¼ cup cocoa
1 teaspoon soda
½ teaspoon salt
1 cup water
⅓ cup salad oil
1 tablespoon vinegar
1 teaspoon vanilla

Combine cream cheese, sugar, egg, and salt. Stir in chocolate chips and set aside. This is topping for batter. Sift flour, sugar, cocoa, soda, and salt. Add water, salad oil, vinegar, and vanilla. Fill muffin pans ⅓ full of cocoa batter. Top with 1 tablespoon of cream cheese mixture. Bake at 350° for 20–25 minutes. Yields 18 cup cakes.

Hospitality

Sauerkraut Kuchen
(Sauerkraut Cake)

⅔ cup butter	1 teaspoon soda
1½ cups sugar	2¼ cups sifted flour
1 teaspoon vanilla	1 cup water
3 eggs	⅔ cup drained, thoroughly rinsed
½ cup cocoa	and chopped sauerkraut
1 teaspoon baking powder	
½ teaspoon salt	

Preheat oven to 325°. Grease and flour 3 (8-inch) cake pans. Cream butter and sugar until smooth. Add vanilla and eggs, one at a time. Sift dry ingredients together and add alternately with water. Mix well. Fold in drained sauerkraut. Turn into cake pans. Bake in preheated oven for approximately 30 minutes or until cake springs back at the touch. Remove from pans immediately, cool on a rack, then frost with Cocoa Buttercream Frosting. Serves 10.

COCOA BUTTERCREAM FROSTING:

¾ cup cocoa	½ cup butter
Pinch salt	1 teaspoon vanilla
2 cups powdered sugar	¾ cup whipping cream

Combine cocoa, salt, and sugar. Cream butter and vanilla. Add cream. Combine sugar mixture and cream mixture a little at a time, then beat 2 minutes at high speed with an electric mixer. Spread on cooled cake.

The Only Texas Cookbook

Turtle Cake
Cake version of Turtle Candy.

1 German chocolate cake mix	1 can Eagle Brand milk
1 stick margarine, softened	1 pound bag caramels
1½ cups water	Pecans
½ cup oil	

Combine and mix well cake mix, margarine, water, oil, and ½ can Eagle Brand milk. Pour ½ of the batter into a greased and floured 13 × 9 × 2-inch baking dish. Bake in a preheated 350° oven for 20–25 minutes.

Melt and mix together caramels and ½ can Eagle Brand Milk. Spread over the baked layer. Sprinkle generously with chopped pecans. Cover with remaining cake batter. Bake 25–35 minutes longer. Frost with Turtle Cake Frosting.

TURTLE CAKE FROSTING:

1 stick margarine	1 box powdered sugar
3 tablespoons cocoa	1 teaspoon vanilla
6 tablespoons evaporated milk	

Melt in a small saucepan margarine, cocoa, and evaporated milk. Remove from heat and add powdered sugar and vanilla. Spread over cool cake.

Calf Fries to Caviar

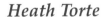

Heath Torte

6 egg whites
2 cups sugar
1 teaspoon vinegar

1 teaspoon vanilla
⅛ teaspoon salt

1. Beat egg whites with vinegar, salt, and vanilla until very stiff.
2. Add sugar and beat until very stiff.
3. Pour into 2 (9-inch) cake pans, buttered on sides and greased brown paper on bottom.
4. Bake in 300° oven for 1 hour. Cool.

FILLING:
1 pint heavy cream, whipped
10–15 Heath bars, finely ground
1 tablespoon vanilla

2 tablespoons powdered sugar
Nuts, chopped

FILLING:
1. Whip cream and add sugar and vanilla. Fold in ground Heath bars.
2. Place half of filling between layers and other half on top.
3. Cover top with chopped nuts. Cover with plastic wrap. Refrigerate overnight. Yields 15 servings. Preparation time: 1 hour.

Rare Collection

Texas Pecan Torte

3 cups pecans
6 eggs, separated
1½ cups sugar
3 tablespoons flour
1 teaspoon salt

3 tablespoons rum
½ cup whipping cream
2 tablespoons powdered sugar
1 cup chocolate chips
½ cup sour cream

Chop pecans very fine in a blender, 1 cup at a time. Beat egg yolks until light and beat in sugar, flour, salt, 2 tablespoons rum and nuts. Set aside. Beat egg whites until stiff and fold into the nut mixture. Pour into 3 (8-inch) or 2 (10-inch) layer cake pans, buttered and lined with waxed paper. Bake for 25 minutes in 350° oven. Allow to cool. (May be kept overnight). A few hours before serving time, whip cream with powdered sugar and 1 tablespoon of rum. Spread filling between layers. Melt chocolate chips, fold in sour cream and spread over the cake top for icing.

San Antonio Cookbook II

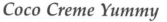

Coco Creme Yummy

My school chum Margaret Ferro's comment of the Coco Creme Yummy . . . "This has got to be the most sinfully, scrumptious cake ever; you can't resist licking the pan."

PASTRY:

1⅓ cups granulated sugar
2¼ cups sifted cake flour
4¼ teaspoons baking powder
1 teaspoon salt
¾ cup butter, softened

½ cup whole milk
2 teaspoons vanilla extract
1 cup Coco Lopez Cream of
   Coconut Milk
6 egg whites, unbeaten

Preheat oven to 350°. Grease and flour a 13×9×2-inch baking pan.

Sift flour, sugar, baking powder and salt together. Add the butter, whole milk and vanilla. Beat for 2 minutes at medium speed. Add the 1 cup cream of coconut milk and unbeaten egg whites. Beat thoroughly at medium to high speed. Pour into prepared pan. Bake for 30 minutes. Lower heat to 325° and bake for an additional 5–10 minutes or until cake tester comes out clean. Remove cake from oven. Cool for 15–20 minutes.

SYRUP:

1 (15-ounce) can Coco Lopez
   Cream of Coconut Milk

1 (14-ounce) can condensed milk

Blend cream of coconut milk with condensed milk. Perforate full depth of cake at about ½ inch intervals with ice pick. Slowly pour cream of coconut milk and condensed milk mixture over the cake evenly. Allow to cool completely at room temperature.

TOPPING:

1 (9-ounce) "La Creme" whipped
   topping

1 (7-ounce) package angel flake
   coconut

Once cool, spread the La Creme whipped topping evenly over cake. Sprinkle coconut on top.

Sweets. . . . From Marina With Love. . . .

Nita's Hidden Treasures

The following recipe was known just as Lemon Bars until it was discovered that our daughter Nita was secretly wrapping them in waxed paper and hiding them in her bureau to eat unshared when she was alone! Anyone who has lived in a large family knows how quickly Nita's Hidden Treasure secret was exposed! However the name has become permanent—and here is Nita's favorite cookie. Do be sure to make enough to share!

⅔ cup butter
1 cup dark brown sugar, firmly
  packed
1 cup regular oats
1½ cups sifted all purpose flour

1 teaspoon baking powder
½ teaspoon salt
1 (14-ounce) can condensed milk
½ cup lemon juice
1 teaspoon lemon rind

Preheat oven to 350°. Generously butter a 9″ × 12″ baking pan.

Thoroughly cream the butter and sugar together until light. Stir in the oats blending well. Sift together the flour, baking powder and salt and mix in until texture is evenly crumbly. Reserve half the crumb mixture and spread the remaining half evenly over the bottom of the prepared baking pan pressing lightly into place. Mix together the milk, lemon juice and rind until very smooth and creamy. Spread carefully and evenly over the crumb layer and cover the cream layer with the remaining reserved crumbs. Bake for 25–30 minutes until lightly golden in color. Remove from oven and cool on wire rack. When completely cool cut into 48 squares.

Sweets. . . . From Marina With Love. . . .

Christmas Stollen
(Christmas Fruit Loaf)

1 cup sugar	1 teaspoon almond extract
½ cup melted butter	3 cups mixed candied fruit, or
2 teaspoons salt	fruit cake mix
2 cups scalded milk	8 cups sifted flour
½ cup warm water	1 cup raisins
2 cakes yeast	1 cup chopped pecans
2 beaten eggs	

Put sugar, salt, melted butter and hot milk in large bowl. Cool this mixture. Meanwhile dissolve yeast in warm water. Mix these together. Add beaten eggs and almond extract. Add about ⅔ of the flour, approximately 5 cups and beat until smooth. Stir in the rest of the ingredients, fruit, raisins and nuts and remaining flour. Turn onto floured board and knead, adding whatever flour is necessary to handle. Place in greased bowl and let rise. When double in size, turn onto floured board and shape into 4 loaves. Let rise until double again. Bake at 400° for 10 minutes and then turn oven down to 350° for 30 minutes. When cool, dust with powdered sugar.

Guten Appetit!

Party Cheesecakes

18 vanilla wafers	1 tablespoon lemon juice
2 (8-ounce) packages cream	1 teaspoon vanilla extract
cheese, softened	½ can fruit pie filling (cherry,
¾ cup sugar	blueberry, etc.)
2 eggs	Whipped cream (optional)

Place paper liners in 18 muffin cups; put 1 vanilla wafer in bottom of each. Combine cream cheese, sugar, eggs, lemon juice and vanilla; beat until smooth and creamy. Fill each muffin cup ⅔ full. Bake at 350° for 15–20 minutes. Cool thoroughly. Put a teaspoon of pie filling on top of each cheesecake. If desired, top with whipped cream. Yields 8 servings.

La Piñata

Cheesecake

The cheesecake offered at The Adolphus has many variations, but the four main flavors are lemon, vanilla, almond and chocolate. The same recipe is used for each kind. Be sure to use genuine extracts of lemon, vanilla and almond and real semisweet chocolate. The cheesecake will be tall in a 10-inch pan (springform, if you have it). Piallier makes 16 at once. This recipe is for one.

2 pounds plus four ounces cream cheese	1 cup dry bread crumbs
1⅔ cups granulated sugar, mixed with ½ cup cornstarch	Flavoring: (Use only one.)
3 extra large eggs	2 tablespoons almond essence, or
2 cups milk, mixed with 1½ cups sour cream	2 tablespoons lemon extract, or
	3 tablespoons vanilla, or
	1 cup melted semisweet chocolate

Preheat oven to 425°. Press 1 cup dry bread crumbs on the bottom of a well-buttered 10-inch pan. Starting with all ingredients at room temperature, beat softened cream cheese with electric mixer. Mix cream cheese with sugar and cornstarch for three minutes. Add whole eggs, one at a time, mixing after each at medium speed. Mix again for three minutes. Whisk milk and sour cream together and fold into the mixture with a wooden spoon, scraping sides as well until smooth and creamy. Add flavoring. For chocolate flavored cheesecake, fold 1 cup of melted semisweet chocolate into 2 cups of cake batter, then combine with remaining batter. Spoon mixture into the prepared pan.

Place cheesecake pan in the center of a large pan of hot water and bake for 50 minutes at 425°, then reduce heat to 375° and bake for 5 minutes. After the first 25 minutes, if the top seems to be getting light brown, set a loose sheet of foil over it.

Allow cake to cool completely, at least three hours, before cutting. For best results, refrigerate for one hour before removing from pan. If not using the springform pan, heat the pan briefly on direct heat just long enough to melt the butter cooked into the crumb base. Invert the cake onto a plate or tray, then back to right side up. At the Adolphus, they return the cake right side up onto a sweet pastry crust, but the only purpose is to make a neat serving.

Some diners enjoy a Port as a counterpoint to this rich cheesecake.

The Adolphus Cookbook

CiCi's Chocolate Amaretto Cheesecake
(Microwave)

Sinfully rich—heavenly easy!

4 tablespoons margarine
1¼ cups vanilla wafer cookie
  crumbs
2 tablespoons Amaretto liqueur
8 ounces semi-sweet baking
  chocolate
3 tablespoons milk

2 (8-ounce) packages cream
  cheese
1⅓ cups sugar
3 eggs
1 cup sour cream
½ teaspoon cinnamon
½ teaspoon almond extract

Place margarine in a 9-inch round high-sided layer-cake pan which is microwave safe. Microwave on HIGH 30–45 seconds, or until melted. Stir in cookie crumbs and pat mixture on bottom only. Microwave on HIGH 2 minutes. Sprinkle Amaretto liqueur over crust. Set aside.

Unwrap squares of chocolate and place in large glass mixer bowl along with milk. Microwave on 50% (MEDIUM) 4 minutes; stir. Add cream cheese and Microwave on 50% 4 minutes, or until cheese is softened. Place bowl on mixer stand and beat mixture on MEDIUM HIGH. Add sugar; beat well. Add eggs, sour cream, cinnamon and extract; blend. Pour into prepared crust.

Microwave on 70% (MEDIUM-HIGH) 12–14 minutes, rotating once midway through cooking. Center should jiggle slightly when set. Cheesecake will firm considerably after refrigerating. Chill two hours or more before serving. Makes 12–16 servings.

Serving Suggestion: Serve topped with whipped cream flavored with 1–2 tablespoons Amaretto liqueur. Garnish with sliced toasted almonds.

Micro Quick!

Praline Cheesecake

1 cup graham cracker crumbs
3 tablespoons sugar
3 tablespoons margarine, melted
3 (8-ounce) packages cream
  cheese, softened
1¼ cups firmly-packed dark
  brown sugar

2 tablespoons all purpose flour
3 eggs
1½ teaspoons vanilla
½ cup chopped nuts

Combine graham cracker crumbs, sugar, and margarine, mixing well. Press in the bottom of a 9-inch springform pan. Bake at 350° for 10 minutes. Cool.

Combine cream cheese, brown sugar, and flour; beat until smooth and fluffy. Add eggs, one at a time, beating well after each addition. Blend in vanilla and nuts. Pour over crust; bake at 350° for 50–55 minutes. Cool. Serve with whipped cream. Yields one (9-inch) cake.

Flavor Favorites

Refrigerator Ginger Muffins

1 cup shortening
½ cup sugar
4 eggs
1 cup dark molasses
4 cups cake flour, sifted
3 teaspoons ginger

1 teaspoon cinnamon
1 teaspoon allspice
2 teaspoons soda
1 cup buttermilk
1 teaspoon vanilla

Cream together the shortening and sugar and add the eggs and molasses. Sift together the flour, ginger, cinnamon, allspice, and soda and add to the molasses mixture alternately with the buttermilk. Mix well and add vanilla. Place in a covered bowl. Will keep in a refrigerator for two weeks. When ready to bake, fill greased muffin tins ⅔ full. Bake at 350° for 25–30 minutes. Yields about 36.

La Piñata

Pumpkin Roll

3 eggs	½ teaspoon salt
1 cup sugar	1 teaspoon ginger
⅔ cup pumpkin	1 teaspoon nutmeg
1 teaspoon lemon juice	1¼ cups powdered sugar
¾ cup flour	1 (8-ounce) package cream cheese
2 teaspoons cinnamon	¼ cup butter, softened
1 teaspoon baking powder	½ teaspoon vanilla

At high speed on mixer, beat eggs for 5 minutes. Gradually add sugar and beat well. Stir in pumpkin and lemon juice. Combine flour, cinnamon, baking powder, salt, ginger and nutmeg. Add to pumpkin mixture and blend well. Spoon batter into a well greased and floured 15 × 10 × 1-inch jelly roll pan. Spread to corners. Bake in a 375° oven for 15 minutes. Turn cake out onto a towel sprinkled with ¼ cup powdered sugar. Beginning at narrow end, roll up cake and towel together. Cool 1 hour. Combine 1 cup powdered sugar, cream cheese, butter and vanilla. Beat until smooth and creamy. Unroll cake and spread with filling. Roll cake up again and chill seam side down. Will freeze. Cut with an electric knife. Serves 20.

Amarillo Junior League Cookbook

Crunchy Bars

1 stick butter	1 cup flaked coconut
1 cup graham cracker crumbs	1 cup Grapenuts
1 (6-ounce) package semi-sweet chocolate chips	1 (14-ounce) can Eagle Brand condensed milk

1. In 325° oven melt butter in 9 × 13-inch pan. 2. Remove from oven and sprinkle evenly over butter in this order: graham cracker crumbs, chocolate bits, coconut, Grapenuts. 3. Drizzle can of milk over all. 4. Bake at 325° for 30 minutes. 5. Cut into bars.

Double recipe for freezing day. Freezes well. You may want to cut into squares and separate into packages of 6–8 before freezing for easy defrosting.

Easy Does It Cookbook

Southern Pecan Bars

1 cup flour
½ cup margarine
½ cup brown sugar
½ cup chopped pecans
2 eggs
1 cup brown sugar or ¼ cup
    brown sugar and ¾ cup dark
    brown Karo syrup

1 teaspoon vanilla
2 tablespoons flour
Pinch of salt
1 teaspoon baking powder
1½ cups coconut (optional)
½-1 cup pecans

Mix first 4 ingredients together to make a smooth paste and pat into a greased baking pan. Bake 10 minutes in a 350° oven. Cool while preparing topping.

    Beat eggs; add sugar and vanilla. Beat again. Mix flour, salt, and baking powder. Sift over coconut and pecans, then add to egg mixture. Pour onto baked crust. Bake 20–25 minutes at 350°.

Our Favorite Recipes

Sour Cream Apple Squares

2 cups flour
2 cups brown sugar, packed
½ cup butter or margarine
1 cup nuts, chopped
1 or 2 teaspoons cinnamon
1 teaspoon soda

½ teaspoon salt
1 cup sour cream
1 teaspoon vanilla
1 egg
2 cups (2 medium) peeled apples,
    chopped fine

Preheat oven to 350°. Combine flour, brown sugar and margarine. Blend until crumbly. Stir in nuts. Press 2¾ cups mixture into 13 × 9-inch pan. To remaining mixture add cinnamon, soda, salt, sour cream, vanilla and egg. Blend well. Stir in apples. Spoon evenly over base. Bake 25–35 minutes until toothpick comes out clean. Cut into squares. Serve with whipped cream.

Repast

Full-of-Fudge Bars

1 package yellow cake mix
1 cup peanut butter

½ cup butter, melted
2 eggs

Combine cake mix, peanut butter, butter and eggs. Press ⅔ of mixture in ungreased 9 × 13-inch pan. Save the rest for topping.

FILLING:
1 cup chocolate chips
1 can Eagle Brand milk (1⅓ cups)
2 tablespoons butter

1 package coconut pecan icing
mix

Combine all filling ingredients and melt together in saucepan. Spread over first layer in pan, then crumble or press out thinly the reserved cake mixture on top of filling layer. Bake at 350° for 20–25 minutes. Cool and cut into bars. Very rich!

Cookin' Wise

Deluxe Brownies

1 package Duncan Hines brownie
   mix
Milk
½–1 cup chopped pecans

Chocolate chips
Butter or margarine
Light brown sugar

Mix brownies according to package directions for chewy brownies, substituting milk for water. Add pecans, reserving a few to sprinkle on top. Place brownie mixture in a pan. Sprinkle chocolate chips over batter. Melt equal parts butter and sugar, 2–4 tablespoons each depending on size of mix, and drizzle over batter. Bake according to package directions.

Flavors

Peppermint Brownies

2 squares unsweetened chocolate
½ cup margarine
2 eggs
1 cup sugar

¼ teaspoon peppermint extract
½ cup sifted flour
Dash of salt
½ cup nuts

Melt chocolate and margarine over hot water. Beat eggs until frothy. Beat in sugar, and add chocolate-margarine mixture and extract. Add flour, salt and nuts. Mix well. Pour into 10-inch greased and floured pan. Bake 20–25 minutes in 350° preheated oven. Cool well.

FROSTING:
2 tablespoons margarine
2 cups sifted powdered sugar
3 tablespoons milk

½ teaspoon peppermint extract
Red food coloring

Combine all ingredients in mixer. Frost cooled brownies, and refrigerate.

GLAZE:
1 tablespoon margarine
1 square unsweetened chocolate

Mix margarine and chocolate over hot water. Pour over frosted brownies. Do not use knife to spread. Roll and tilt pan until glaze covers frosting. Refrigerate, and serve cool. Makes 18 (2-inch) brownies.

Noted Cookery

Black Forest Cookies

½ cup butter or margarine,
  softened
1 cup sugar
1 egg
1 teaspoon vanilla
1½ cups flour

½ cup cocoa
¼ teaspoon salt
¼ teaspoon baking powder
¼ teaspoon soda
1 (10-ounce) jar maraschino
  cherries

In a large bowl, cream butter, sugar, egg and vanilla until light and fluffy. Add remaining ingredients, except cherries, and blend at low speed until a stiff dough forms, about 1 minute. Shape dough into 1-inch balls, using a heaping teaspoon of dough for each. Place 2 inches apart on ungreased cookie sheet. Push one whole cherry halfway into each ball. When all cookies are molded and cherries are pushed in, prepare frosting and use immediately.

FROSTING:

1 (6-ounce) package semi-sweet
  chocolate chips (not milk
  chocolate)
½ cup sweetened and condensed
  milk

¼ teaspoon salt
1–1½ teaspoons maraschino
  cherry juice

In small, heavy saucepan, melt chocolate and condensed milk over low heat, stirring constantly. Remove from heat. Add remaining ingredients and stir until smooth. Frost each cherry by spreading ½ teaspoon of frosting over each cookie. Bake frosted cookies for 8–10 minutes at 350° until puffy. Store tightly covered. Yields 4 dozen.

Ready to Serve

Frosty Apple Bites

COOKIES:

2 cups sifted all purpose flour
½ teaspoon soda
½ teaspoon salt
¼ teaspoon nutmeg
½ cup margarine or butter
1 cup firmly packed brown sugar

1 egg, unbeaten
1 teaspoon vanilla
⅔ cup evaporated milk
1 cup walnuts, chopped
1 cup apples, pared and chopped
½ cup semi-sweet chocolate chips

Sift together all the dry ingredients. Then cream margarine and brown sugar and then add the unbeaten egg and vanilla. Beat well. Add the dry ingredients alternately with evaporated milk, beginning and ending with dry ingredients. Stir in walnuts and apples and chocolate chips. Drop by teaspoonfuls onto lightly greased cookie sheets. Bake at 375° for 12–15 minutes. Frost while warm with cinnamon glaze.

CINNAMON GLAZE:

2 cups powdered sugar, sifted
3 tablespoons butter, melted

1 teaspoon cinnamon
2–3 tablespoons evaporated milk

Combine sugar, butter and cinnamon. Add evaporated milk until of spreading consistency. Yields 4 dozen cookies.

Cowtown Cuisine

Pecan Crunchies

The contributor of this recipe says she has never taken these cookies anywhere without people asking for the recipe. The happy surprise is that they are so easy to make.

½ (16-ounce) box graham crackers
½ pound butter

1 cup dark brown sugar
1 cup pecans, chopped

Lightly oil a jelly roll pan and line with graham crackers. Melt butter in a medium saucepan. Add brown sugar and stir until mixture bubbles vigorously. Add pecans and quickly spread over the graham crackers. Bake at 350° for 10 minutes. Cut along indentations of the crackers; leave in pan and freeze for 1 hour. Do not eliminate freezing because this is what makes these so crunchy. Yields 5½ dozen.

Tastes & Tales From Texas . . . With Love

Bizcochos
(Mexican Holiday Cookies)

2 cups lard*
1 cup sweet wine or any fruit
 juice
1 cup sugar
1 tablespoon cinnamon

1 tablespoon anise seeds
2 egg yolks
3 cups flour
1 cup sugar
4 teaspoons cinnamon

Whip lard until creamy. Mix wine, 1 cup sugar, 1 tablespoon cinnamon and anise; add this to the lard and mix with wooden spoon. Add egg yolks; mix well. Add sufficient flour to make a soft dough; roll out ½-inch thick. Cut in desired shapes and place on greased cookie sheet. Bake 15 minutes at 350°; check often to prevent burning. Mix remaining cinnamon and sugar. Dredge cookies in this mixture while still warm. Yields 8–10 dozen.

*In authentic Mexican cooking, lard (not shortening) is used.

Seasoned With Sun

Skillet Cookies

1 stick butter
3 eggs
1 cup sugar
1 teaspoon vanilla
⅛ teaspoon salt

1 cup chopped nuts
½ pound dates, finely cut
3 cups Rice Crispies
1 can Angel Flake coconut

Melt butter over low heat. Beat eggs with sugar and vanilla, salt, nuts and dates. Add to butter in skillet. Increase heat. Cook until thick, or until mixture pulls away from pan, stirring constantly. Cool 20 minutes. Add Rice Crispies. Divide into three portions. Shape into small rolls, about 12 inches long. Spread coconut on wax paper, coat the rolls in coconut. Wrap in foil and refrigerate overnight. Lasts several weeks in refrigerator. Slice into cookies as needed. Makes 40–50 cookies.

The Cottage Kitchen Cookbook

Cream Cheese Cookies

½ cup butter or margarine,
  softened
1 (3-ounce) package cream
  cheese, softened

1 cup sugar
1 cup flour
½ cup chopped pecans
1 teaspoon vanilla

Blend butter with cream cheese. Mix in flour and sugar. Add nuts and vanilla. Drop from teaspoon onto ungreased cookie sheets. Bake in 350° oven for 10–12 minutes or until edges of cookies are brown. Makes about 5 dozen chewy cookies.

Hullabaloo in the Kitchen

Molasses Cookies

¾ cup Crisco
1 cup sugar
1 egg
¼ cup molasses
2 cups flour, sifted
3 teaspoons soda

1 teaspoon cinnamon
1 teaspoon ground ginger
1 teaspoon ground cloves
1 teaspoon salt
Natural sugar

Cream Crisco and sugar. Add egg and molasses. Stir in flour, 1 cup at a time, along with other dry ingredients. Chill ½ hour. Shape dough into marble-sized balls, roll in natural sugar, and place 1 inch apart on baking sheet. Bake at 350° for 8–10 minutes. Yields 3–4 dozen. May be halved or doubled.

Flavors

The Pfeiffer-Whites' House Best Cookies

In addition to creating a little world of hospitality in this old home, Marilyn is an excellent cook. Awaiting every guest in his or her room is "a jar of these cookies along with a basket of fruit. Guests seem to really enjoy the 'homemade and old-fashioned taste,' and they are always a topic of conversation!"

1 cup flour
1 cup sugar
½ cup Crisco shortening
1 egg
1 tablespoon molasses
1 teaspoon cinnamon

1 teaspoon salt
1 teaspoon vanilla
¾ teaspoon baking soda
1 cup oatmeal
1 cup chocolate chips

Combine all ingredients. Bake at 350° for approximately 8–10 minutes. Do not overcook. Marilyn allows for exactly 9 minutes in her oven. Make certain that you check at 8 minutes. They will look almost undercooked. Remove from oven when they are just turning tan on top, yet still soft. Yields 4 dozen.

(Pfeiffer House, Bastrop) *Texas Historic Inns Cookbook*

Butter Mint Delights

Now we've come to *my* favorite cookie . . . they are *soo-oo-ooo good!* They used to spread in a very uncontrolled manner, but I have really worked at getting them to behave. This is the reason for the chilling and freezing. I like to use a pretty cookie stamp on the tops before they go to the freezer, as without it, they look rather plain. And if your candy tooth has as much weakness as mine does, you will have a difficult time to keep that full cup of mints when it's time to add them!

1 cup ground butter mints	**2 cups all purpose flour**
1 cup softened butter	**1 tablespoon granulated sugar**

Preheat oven to 300°. Line a 9-inch square baking pan with waxed paper.

Grind the butter mints to a medium fine texture in an electric blender. Knead the butter into the flour until thoroughly blended. Add the ground mints and continue kneading until dough is of a soft but solid consistency. Pat dough evenly into the prepared baking pan and refrigerate for 1 hour. Remove from refrigerator and sprinkle surface of pastry with the granulated sugar. Cut the pastry into small 1-inch squares. Lift the waxed paper with the cookies intact from the baking pan and place cookies about 1 inch apart on an ungreased baking sheet. Place in freezer for 30 minutes. Bake frozen cookies for 16–18 minutes. *Butter Mint Delights* should not brown at all. Remove from oven and cool on wire rack.

I used to crush these delicious mints between two sheets of waxed paper with a rolling pin but it wasn't enough protection for the mints—*from me!* This is not only my favorite cookie—the butter mints are my favorite candy, too. I wonder if that could have anything to do with my being willing to make them at *any* time!

Sweets. . . . From Marina With Love. . . .

Peanut Butter Chocolate Balls

1 stick margarine, softened
1 box powdered sugar, sifted
3 cups rice krispies
1 (6-ounce) package chocolate
   chips

½ square paraffin
2 cups crunchy peanut butter

Cream margarine and powdered sugar. Add peanut butter and rice krispies, mixing well. Form into small balls. Melt chocolate chips and paraffin. Roll balls in chocolate and place on waxed paper to cool.

Entertaining in Texas

Mexican Pecan Candy

2 cups sugar
1 cup milk
2 tablespoons butter
2 tablespoons white corn syrup

½ teaspoon salt
¼ teaspoon soda
1 cup chopped pecans
1 teaspoon vanilla

Mix all ingredients except pecans and vanilla in large saucepan and bring to a boil. When mixture comes to a boil, add pecans and cook until it reaches 234° or until soft ball when dropped in cold water. Add vanilla and beat until creamy. Drop by spoonfuls on wax paper.

The Cottage Kitchen Cookbook

Carnival Popcorn
(Microwave)

2 quarts popped popcorn
2 cups brown sugar, packed
½ cup white corn syrup

1 cup margarine or butter
6 ounces roasted, salted peanuts

Set aside popped corn in large bowl or bag. In 4-quart microwave-safe container, combine brown sugar, corn syrup, and margarine. Microwave on FULL (100%) POWER for 10 minutes. Remove container from oven. Add peanuts and popped corn. Mix well to coat surfaces of corn. Spread onto greased flat tray. Cool. Store in covered container. Yields 2 quarts.

The Texas Microwave Cookbook

Aunt Bill's Brown Candy

I got into a terrible argument about the origin of this recipe. I thought it was my grandmother's. One of my friends thought it was her grandmother's. I guess we both thought there was some long-lost relative of ours named Aunt Bill. Turns out this recipe was in an Oklahoma newspaper 50 years ago and everybody wanted to be related to Aunt Bill because her candy was so good.

6 cups white sugar
2 cups cream (or half and half)
¼ pound butter
¼ teaspoon soda
1 teaspoon vanilla
2 cups pecans

Place 2 cups of the sugar in a cast-iron skillet over low heat. Stir constantly until the sugar begins to melt and caramelize. When it has liquefied completely, remove from heat. At the same time (this is one of those recipes where you'll wish you had 4 hands) cook 4 cups of sugar and 2 cups cream in a large stainless steel stewpan. As soon as the sugar has caramelized, pour it in a small stream into the boiling cream and sugar. Cook to soft-ball stage (236°). I always use a candy thermometer, because this syrup heats up faster than other types of boiled candies, and you don't want it to get too hot. The instant it reaches 236°, remove from heat (it helps to set the pan on a cool dish cloth). Add soda, stirring all the time, then the butter and vanilla. Cool until you can put your hand on the bottom of the pot. Beat with a wooden spoon until mixture is thick and dull. Add pecans and pour quickly into a buttered dish or onto waxed paper. Cut into squares when cool.

The Only Texas Cookbook

Velveeta Cheese Fudge

1 pound margarine or butter
1 pound Velveeta cheese
1 cup cocoa
4 pounds powdered sugar
2 cups nuts, chopped
2 teaspoons vanilla

Melt margarine and cheese together. Mix in remaining ingredients. Spread in greased pan. Cool. Cut in squares. Keep in refrigerator. Makes enough for a big party!

Tasteful Traditions

Candy-Pecan Clusters

This has got to be the best chocolate candy recipe in the whole wide world—makes a bunch!

1 (7-ounce) jar marshmallow
 creme
1½ pounds Hershey's milk
 chocolate kisses (no substitute)

5 cups of sugar
1 (13-ounce) can evaporated milk
½ cup margarine
6 cups pecans

Place marshmallow creme and kisses in a large bowl; set aside. Combine milk, sugar and butter in a sauce pan. Boil mixture to a high point, let boil 8 minutes (or until a soft ball stage). Pour over marshmallow and kisses, blend well. Add pecans and mix. Drop by the teaspoon on waxed paper. An easy never-fail recipe. Makes 12 dozen clusters.

Collectibles II

Micro Brittle
(Microwave)

1 cup raw peanuts, pecans,
 almonds, walnuts or cashews
1 cup sugar
½ cup white corn syrup

⅛ teaspoon salt
1 tablespoon butter
1 teaspoon baking soda
1 teaspoon vanilla

Stir together nuts, sugar, syrup and salt in 4-cup glass measure. Place in microwave and cook 7–8 minutes on HIGH. Add butter and blend well. Return to oven. Cook 2–3 minutes more on HIGH or until nuts are golden brown. Add baking soda and vanilla. Gently stir until light and foamy. Pour onto greased cookie sheet. Let cool. When cool, break into pieces and store in airtight container.

Tasteful Traditions

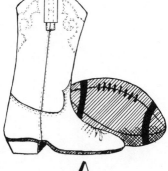

Pecan Log

3 tablespoons butter or
margarine, melted
4 tablespoons milk
1½ cups pecans, chopped

1 (15¼-ounce) package creamy
white frosting mix
28 vanilla caramels (8 ounces)
2 tablespoons milk

Combine butter and 2 tablespoons milk. Stir in frosting mix until well blended. Form into two 8 × 1½-inch logs. Wrap each in aluminum foil and chill for 2 hours.

Melt caramels with remaining 2 tablespoons milk on *low* setting. Spread melted caramel on top and sides of the chilled rolls, reserving ¼ of the mixture. Sprinkle 1 cup pecans on 2 sheets of aluminum foil and invert 1 log onto each sheet. Spread remaining caramel mixture on each log. Coat logs evenly with ½ cup pecans and reshape as needed. Wrap each log, seal and chill before serving.

When ready to serve, remove from refrigerator and let stand about 30 minutes, then slice into ¼-inch pieces. Yields 64 slices.

The Dallas Pecan Cookbook

Carmelitas

32 light candy caramel squares
¼ cup half and half cream or
evaporated milk
1 (16-ounce) roll chocolate chip
refrigerator cookies

1 (6-ounce) package milk or
semi-sweet chocolate pieces
½ cup chopped pecans

Melt caramels and cream in top of double boiler. Slice cookie dough ¼-inch thick and place in greased 8 or 9-inch square pan. Bake at 375° for 20–25 minutes. They will be puffy when removed from oven. Cool slightly. Sprinkle chocolate pieces over warm cookies. Carefully spread caramel mixture over top of chocolate, then sprinkle with chopped pecans. Refrigerate 1–2 hours. Yields 36 squares.

Ready to Serve

Grand Granola

Granola, which is easy to make and delicious, can be made in large batches and stored in air tight containers. It is a delightful substitute for processed breakfast cereals. For those of you who already are "weaned" from sweets, we suggest that you omit the oil and the honey or maple syrup in the following recipes and proceed as directed.

For young children and older people who have difficulty chewing, grind the granola in a nut mill, blender or food processor before serving.

4 cups rolled oats	½ cup sunflower seeds
1 cup bran	¼ cup chopped cashews
½ cup shredded coconut	⅓ cup raw clover honey
¾ cup chopped pecans	½ cup water
¼ cup sesame seeds	¼ cup unrefined oil

In large mixing bowl, combine dry ingredients and mix well. Stir together oil, water and honey. Pour over dry mixture and stir to coat. Pour into roasting pan. Bake at 350° for 30 minutes. Stir twice during baking. Remove and let cool.

Store in covered containers. May add dates, raisins or fresh fruit before serving. Yields 8 servings.

Nature's Kitchen

Nutty Fruit Treats

3 cups pitted dried fruit	½ cup unsweetened shredded
½ cup chopped nuts	coconut
½ cup sesame seeds	1 grated orange rind

Blend all ingredients in food processor. Shape into 1-inch balls and store in covered container.

Good to satisfy after-meal craving for sweets or for snacks.

Nature's Kitchen

Pies and Desserts

Thousands of showrooms attract merchants from all over the world to the World Trade Mart in Dallas.

Bing Cherry Pie
Always gets great reviews

1 (14-ounce) can sweetened
  condensed milk
1 (16-ounce) can dark sweet
  cherries, drained
¾ cup pecan pieces, toasted
½ cup lemon juice

½ teaspoon red food coloring
1 cup whipping cream, whipped
  until it stands in peaks
1 (9-inch) graham cracker crust,
  baked and cooled

1. In a mixing bowl, combine and mix together the milk, cherries, pecans, lemon juice, and red food coloring.

2. Whip the cream and gently fold the whipped cream into the other mixture.

3. Place in graham cracker crust, chill and serve. Makes 1 (9-inch) pie.

Leaving Home

Praline Apple Pie

2½ cups sliced peeled pie apples
⅓ cup sugar
¼ teaspoon nutmeg
¼ teaspoon cinnamon
1 beaten egg

Unbaked 9-inch pie shell
2 tablespoons honey
½ cup brown sugar, packed
2 tablespoons butter
½ cup pecans

Combine apples, sugar, and spices. Place apples mixture in unbaked pie shell. Bake at 400° for 15 minutes. Mix honey, brown sugar, and butter in a saucepan. Bring to a boil. Add egg and nuts. Remove the pie from the oven and pour honey mixture over the top. Return the pie to the oven for 10 minutes at 400°, then reduce the heat to 325°. Bake 25–30 minutes until set and apples soft. Serve warm.

The Blue Denim Gourmet

Gourmet Peach Pie

½ pint whipping cream
1 cup powdered sugar, divided
6 ounces cream cheese

1 (9-inch) baked pie shell
Sliced peaches

Whip cream with ½ cup of powdered sugar. Beat cream cheese with rest of powdered sugar. Fold together the whipped cream mixture and the cream cheese mixture. Spread in the cooled pie shell. Cool in refrigerator for at least 2 hours. Cover cream mixture with sliced fresh peaches.

GLAZE:
1 cup sugar
2 tablespoons corn starch
1 cup mashed peaches

1 cup water
Yellow food color

Make a glaze by mixing together the sugar, corn starch, mashed peaches, water and about 2 drops of food coloring. Boil until clear, stirring constantly. When cool, pour over pie. Canned cherry pie filling may be substituted for the fresh peaches when they are out of season.

Trading Secrets

Dutch Peach Pie
A Stonewall, Texas "Peach Jamboree" recipe

1 (9-inch) unbaked pastry shell
10–12 ripe peaches
1 egg, slightly beaten
1 cup sour cream
¾ cup sugar

¼ teaspoon salt
2 tablespoons flour
½ teaspoon cinnamon
½ teaspoon nutmeg

Preheat oven to 350°. Peel peaches, slice, and arrange in pastry shell. Mix egg with sour cream, sugar, salt, flour, cinnamon and nutmeg. Pour over peaches and bake for 20 minutes. Mix topping (recipe below) and sprinkle over pie and continue to bake 12–15 minutes.

TOPPING:
¼ cup brown sugar
3 tablespoons flour

2 tablespoons butter
½ cup chopped nuts

A Texas Hill Country Cookbook

Pumpkin Pecan Pie

4 slightly beaten eggs
2 cups canned or mashed cooked
  pumpkin
1 cup sugar
½ cup dark corn syrup

1 teaspoon vanilla
½ teaspoon cinnamon
¼ teaspoon salt
1 unbaked (9-inch) pie shell
1 cup chopped pecans

Combine ingredients except pecans. Pour into pie shell—top with pecans. Bake at 350° for 40 minutes, or until set.

With best wishes, Nancy Reagan.

March of Dimes Gourmet Gala Cookbook

Pecan Pie

1 (9-inch) pie crust
3 eggs
1 cup sugar
½ teaspoon salt
2 tablespoons melted butter

½ cup dark corn syrup
½ cup whipping cream
1 teaspoon vanilla
¼ cup brandy
1 cup chopped pecans

In a bowl beat the eggs, sugar, salt, melted butter, corn syrup and whipping cream. When well blended, stir in vanilla, brandy and pecans. Pour into 9-inch pie crust and bake in preheated 375° oven for 40–50 minutes until set. Top with whipped cream if desired.

Bravo, Chef!

French Coconut Pie
(Microwave)
(Original recipe from the Nutt House in Granbury)

1 deep pie shell in 9-inch
  microwave-safe pie dish

COCONUT CUSTARD FILLING:

2 eggs	2 teaspoons white vinegar
1 cup sugar	1 teaspoon vanilla extract
⅓ cup margarine, melted	⅔ cup flaked coconut

Place paper towel on top of pastry shell. Microwave pastry shell on MEDIUM (50%) POWER 4–5 minutes. Remove paper towel.

In medium mixing bowl, beat eggs until light. Add sugar, melted margarine, vinegar, vanilla extract, and ⅔ cup coconut. Mix well. Pour into pre-baked pastry shell. Microwave on MEDIUM (50%) POWER 7–9 minutes.

TOASTED COCONUT TOPPING:
⅓ cup flaked coconut

Place ⅓ cup coconut on paper plate. Microwave on FULL (100%) POWER 2 minutes, stirring often. Sprinkle toasted coconut over cooked coconut filling. Serves 6.

The Texas Microwave Cookbook

Skillet Caramel Pie

2 cups sugar	2 cups milk
5 tablespoons flour	3 tablespoons butter
¼ teaspoon salt	1 teaspoon vanilla
5 eggs, separated	1 (9-inch) baked pie shell

Put 1 cup sugar in heavy skillet over low heat to melt. Mix other cup of sugar, flour and salt. Combine egg yolks and milk; add to flour mixture and beat lightly. Pour this into skillet with melted sugar, stirring constantly. Cook until mixture is smooth and thick. Add butter and vanilla. Pour into baked pie shell and cover with meringue. Brown at 350° for 5–10 minutes.

Tempting Traditions

Pineapple Pie

1 (9-inch) pie shell, unbaked
4 eggs
1½ cups sugar
2 tablespoons flour

1 stick butter
1 small can crushed pineapple,
    well drained

Prepare pie shell and brush with a small amount of slightly beaten egg white. Set aside. Cream butter and sugar; add eggs, one at a time, beating well after each addition. Stir in flour. Add pineapple and mix until all ingredients are well blended. Pour mixture into pie shell and bake at 350° 30–40 minutes. Shake pan gently every few minutes during the last several minutes of baking time. The center should just be beginning to seem firm, but should still move. Remove from oven and set on a solid surface for pie to continue to set. Serves 6–8.

My aunt, Bonnie Robertson, is one of the most thoughtful ladies in the world. I couldn't count how many of these pies she has made and most of them were to fill the need of another. She always has one for my husband when we visit her.

Of Magnolia and Mesquite

Mince Pie and Hot Rum Sauce

1 package Nonesuch Mincemeat
1 cup hot water
½ cup maple flavored syrup

1 cup applesauce
1 cup crushed pecans

Dissolve mincemeat in hot water and syrup. Cook until thick. Add applesauce and pecans. Pour into unbaked pie crust and top with another crust. Sprinkle with sugar and bake.

HOT RUM SAUCE:
1 cup sugar
1 cup water

½ cup butter
¼ cup rum

Cook sugar and water to 230° or thread stage. Add butter and rum. Serve hot on warm mince pie.

Square House Museum Cookbook

Satin Rum Pie

2½ dozen ladyfingers
3 cups whipping cream
⅔ cup whole milk

36 large marshmallows
5½ tablespoons light rum
Finely ground pecans

Cut off tips of one end of split ladyfingers. Stand around edge of spring form pan, cut side in, sides touching. Cover bottom with remaining split ladyfingers and fill in with cut off pieces.

Melt marshmallows and milk in top of double boiler; cool, stirring occasionally. Whip cream to stand in peaks; fold in rum. Add to cool mixture and pour into prepared spring form pan. Sprinkle top with finely ground pecans. Refrigerate at least 24 hours. Decorate center top. Remove spring form and serve with pride. Serves 20.

The Pride of Texas

Whiskey Pie
Gala Winner

MERINGUE SHELL:

4–6 egg whites, room temperature   1 teaspoon white vinegar
½ teaspoon baking powder   1 teaspoon water
⅛ teaspoon salt   1 cup sugar
1 teaspoon vanilla

Combine all ingredients except sugar in large bowl. Beat until soft peaks form. Add sugar gradually, 1 tablespoon at a time. Beat until sugar is dissolved, about 7 minutes. Heap on lightly greased large pie plate. Bake in lower third of a 275° oven for 1 hour. Cool on rack. Meringue will be soft inside and will shrink.

FILLING:

8 egg yolks   7 tablespoons bourbon whiskey
8 tablespoons sugar

Beat yolks with electric mixer until very light. Add sugar slowly, 1 tablespoon at a time. Still beating, add whiskey 1 tablespoon at a time. Continue beating while you cook mixture over low heat (double boiler best). Cook until slightly thickened (170°). It is done when one can see definite folds in the mixture and the sides show roughness. Overcooking curdles it. Remove from heat and continue to beat 2 minutes. Cool. Chill.

1 cup heavy cream   1 teaspoon unflavored gelatin
¼ cup sugar   softened in ¼ cup water, then
½ teaspoon vanilla   heated to dissolve

Beat cream until it starts to thicken. Add sugar gradually, then vanilla, then softened gelatin. Fold into egg mixture. Fill meringue shell. Chill several hours before serving. Or break meringue into chunks being careful not to crush. Fold meringue into egg mixture and put into sherbet glasses to serve.

Mrs. Robert Applewhite was a Gala Winner with this recipe.
March of Dimes Gourmet Gala Cookbook

Buttermilk Pie

A smooth, creamy, delicious pie, and a recipe worth trying—despite any preconceived notions you may have about buttermilk. Originally this pie was a makeshift dessert for times when the pantry or cellar was bare and there were no fruits in season. It has now become much more—a classic Texas dessert.

4 tablespoons flour
1¾ cups sugar
½ teaspoon salt
½ cup butter, melted
3 eggs, beaten
1 cup buttermilk

½ teaspoon vanilla
½ teaspoon lemon extract
1 (9-inch) unbaked pie shell
Cinnamon and nutmeg to taste
  (optional)

Combine flour, sugar, and salt in a mixing bowl. Add melted butter and beaten eggs and stir with a whisk or fork until well blended. Stir in buttermilk, vanilla, and lemon extract and mix well. Pour into unbaked pie shell and dust with cinnamon or nutmeg, if desired.

Bake in center of 350° oven for 55–60 minutes or until filling is set and lightly browned. Yields 1 (9-inch) pie.

Cooking Texas Style

Easy Fudge Pie

2 squares Hershey's baking
   chocolate
⅔ stick of butter
4 eggs
2 cups sugar

1 teaspoon vanilla
Pinch of salt
⅔ cup chopped pecans
1 unbaked (9-inch) pie shell

Melt chocolate and butter over low heat. Beat eggs with a mixer until light; add sugar, vanilla and salt. Continue beating until well blended. Add chocolate and pecans. Bake at 350° for 40 minutes.

The Galveston Island Cookbook

Bourbon Chocolate Pie

1 cup sugar
2 eggs
4 tablespoons cornstarch
½ cup butter, melted
3 tablespoons bourbon
1 cup semi-sweet chocolate chips

1 cup pecans, chopped
1 (9-inch) unbaked pie shell
½ pint heavy cream
2 tablespoons powdered sugar
½ teaspoon bourbon

1. Combine sugar, eggs, cornstarch, butter, and 3 tablespoons bourbon. Stir in chocolate chips and pecans.

2. Pour into pie shell and bake in 350° oven 30–35 minutes or until puffy and brown. Cool completely.

3. Whip cream with powdered sugar and bourbon to form stiff peaks. Serve over individual pieces of pie. Do not freeze. Yields 6–8 servings.

Rare Collection

Kay's Lime Pie

1 envelope unflavored gelatin
½ cup sugar
¼ teaspoon salt
4 egg yolks
½ cup fresh lime juice
¼ cup water
1 teaspoon grated lime peel

Few drops green food coloring
4 egg whites
½ cup sugar
1 cup heavy cream, whipped
1 (9-inch) pie shell, pastry or
  crumb

1. Thoroughly mix gelatin, sugar, and salt in saucepan.

2. Beat together egg yolks, lime juice and water and stir into gelatin mixture. Cook over medium heat, stirring constantly until mixture comes to a boil.

3. Remove from heat and stir in grated peel. Add food coloring sparingly to give a pale green color.

4. Chill, stirring occasionally until mixture mounds slightly when dropped from a spoon.

5. Beat egg whites until soft peaks form; gradually add ½ cup sugar, beating to stiff peaks. Fold gelatin mixture into egg whites. Fold in whipped cream and pile into crust.

6. Chill until firm. Spread with additional whipped cream and edge with grated lime peel. Garnish with wedges of lime.

Morning, Noon and Night Cookbook

Peach Cobbler

A true West Texas version. Ranch cooks, usually cooking with canned fruit, could not get along without this recipe and the variations listed below.

2 cups fresh sliced peaches
2 cups sugar
6 tablespoons margarine
¼ teaspoon salt

1 teaspoon baking powder
¾ cup flour
¾ cup milk

Mix peaches and 1 cup sugar together and let stand while making batter. Melt margarine in a 2-quart casserole. In a bowl, mix 1 cup sugar, salt, baking powder and flour. Beat in milk until lumps are gone. Pour batter on melted margarine. Do not stir. Spoon peaches over top of batter. Again, do not stir. Bake at 350° for 45 minutes or until golden brown. Almost any canned, frozen or fresh fruit may be used. If canned or pre-sweetened fruit is used, omit the cup of sugar that fruit stands in. Also, be sure to drain the juice. Serves 6.

San Angelo Junior League Cookbook

Cherry Pudding

1 cup sugar
1 tablespoon real butter
1 egg, beaten
1 cup all purpose flour
½ cup chopped pecans

½ teaspoon baking soda
1 cup canned pitted sour cherries, drained
Heavy cream, whipped

Heat oven to 350°; cream sugar and butter. Add egg and mix until well blended. Blend 1 tablespoon flour into nuts; set aside. Mix remaining flour and baking soda. Add cherries alternately with flour mixture to batter. Stir in nuts. Pour pudding into a well greased 9 or 10-inch tube cake pan. Bake for 45 minutes. Serve with whipped cream. Serves 8–10.

The Dallas Pecan Cookbook

Sweet Potato Cobbler

2 sweet potatoes, medium size
Water to cover
⅔ cup sugar

½ teaspoon nutmeg
Lump of butter
Pinch of salt

Peel and slice 2 medium-size sweet potatoes. Cover with water. Add salt and let boil until tender. Add a lump of butter, nutmeg, and sugar. Prepare crust while potatoes are cooking.

CRUST FOR COBBLERS:

1½ cups flour
½ teaspoon salt
⅓ cup shortening

Water, enough to make stiff
dough (about ¼ cup)

To make crust, combine flour, salt, and shortening. Add enough water to make a stiff dough. Roll out on floured board until crust is ⅛-inch thick. In a deep pan, put potatoes sparingly but with plenty of juice. Sprinkle with sugar. Then add a layer of crust. Continue this procedure until all potatoes and crust are used. Sprinkle top with sugar and bake in moderate oven until slightly brown on top.

Mrs. Blackwell's Heart of Texas Cookbook

"Pavlova" or Fairy Cake

4 egg whites
1 pinch of salt
8 ounces granulated sugar
1 teaspoon cornstarch
2 teaspoon white vinegar

1 pint whipped cream
2 bananas, peeled and sliced
1 pint strawberries, stemmed and
sliced (other fruit if desired)

Stiffly beat egg whites with salt. Add sugar gradually, beat well until smooth and glossy. Add cornstarch and vinegar. Pour onto ovenproof pie plate which has been sprinkled with a little cornstarch. Bake in oven 250° for 1½ hours. When cool, fill with cream and fruits.

A Taste of Victoria

Pavlova—A light, whipped dessert, made with fruit, which has been called "as light on the stomach as the Russian ballerina was on her feet."

Marigolds

These are very petite, lemony tarts. Great for parties, showers and receptions. They can be frozen and thawed two hours prior to serving. Gloria Estrada, my wonderful friend, says of these, "I award you a Blue Ribbon!" Bake these and I guarantee you will win Blue Ribbons, too.

PASTRY:

¾ cup butter, softened
1½ cups all purpose flour, sifted
6 tablespoons confectioners'
   sugar

½ teaspoon vanilla extract

Preheat oven to 350°. Cream the butter with the flour and confectioners' sugar (I do this with my hands, as it does the job best). Mix until well blended. Add the vanilla and again blend thoroughly. Divide dough evenly between 3 dozen miniature muffin tins. With fingers smooth and press the dough into place on the bottom and sides of muffin tins to form shells and just to edge of muffin tin, not letting any dough extend beyond top of the tin. Place in freezer for 15 minutes. Remove from freezer and put 1 tablespoon of cleaned pinto beans in each tin. This will eliminate dough from shrinking. Place in oven and bake for 12–15 minutes. Remove from oven and with a demitasse coffee spoon remove the beans carefully. Lower oven temperature to 325°. Fill each shell gradually until all filling is used. Return to oven and bake for another 12–15 minutes or until just firm. Remove from oven and place in a draft-free area. Cool. Remove shells from tin carefully, loosening edges with thin knife. Place shells on cooling racks. When completely cool frost tops with pastry brush.

FILLING:

3 eggs, slightly beaten
1½ cups granulated sugar
2 tablespoons flour

½ teaspoon baking powder
¼ cup lemon juice
1½ teaspoons lemon rind

To the slightly beaten eggs add the granulated sugar, flour and baking powder. Blend well with spatula. Add the lemon juice and lemon rind and continue to blend only with a spatula until well combined.

CONTINUED

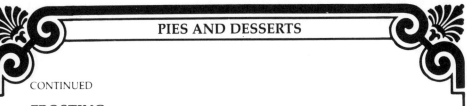
CONTINUED

FROSTING:

⅔ cup confectioners' sugar   2 tablespoons lemon juice

Blend the confectioners' sugar with the lemon juice until smooth.

Sweets. . . . From Marina With Love. . . .

Nancy's Fruit and Cheese Tart

Here is a dessert for company, a fruit and cheese course all rolled into one. This dessert can change with the season depending on whatever lavish fruit you find in the produce section. Try it once, and you'll be hooked. As Nancy says, it looks like you've slaved all day and maybe just completed an apprenticeship with a master baker.

¼ pound margarine or butter
¼ cup sugar
¼ teaspoon salt
1 cup (about 3–4 ounces) Swiss cheese, shredded
1¼ cups flour

2 tablespoons milk
1 cup shredded coconut
2 cups fruit
⅓ cup jelly or marmalade
½ teaspoon brandy, bourbon, or crème de menthe (optional)

Preheat oven to 375°. If you have a processor, you can simply add the ingredients (except coconut, jelly, and fruit) to the bowl in order, giving a spin after each addition, and within minutes you'll have what looks like a good ball of short dough. To mix in the traditional manner, cream butter with sugar and salt, then cut in shredded cheese followed by alternate additions of flour and milk until you have a short dough that makes a ball.

Spread the dough by hand into a 12-inch pizza pan or tart pan, smoothing with your hands and creating a slight lip around the edge.

Place in preheated oven and bake for 5 minutes. Remove from oven, sprinkle with coconut evenly, then return to oven and continue baking for 15 minutes, or until the crust is lightly browned. Without removing from pan, cool on a rack.

While the crust is baking, slice seasonal fruit or a combination of fruits. Place sliced fruit on crust while it is still warm. Dissolve jelly in a saucepan over low heat, add brandy, then drizzle over top of tart. Good warm or cold. Feeds 10 in 40 minutes.

An American Gumbo

Sopapillas

1 package active dry yeast
½ cup warm water (110°)
1 teaspoon sugar
3 cups flour
1 tablespoon melted butter,
  cooled

1 teaspoon salt
1 egg
Oil for frying

Dissolve yeast in warm water with sugar.

Mix flour, butter, salt, and egg. Pour into yeast mixture. Add enough water to make firm, springy breadlike dough.

Knead 15 minutes. Cover with towel or plastic wrap. Place in warm, draft-free area; let rise 30 minutes or longer until doubled in bulk.

Punch down dough. Roll half of dough to ¼-inch thickness on lightly floured board. Cut into 2-inch squares.

Heat oil to 375°. Stretch squares gently and drop into hot oil. Hold down in oil until dough begins to puff; then turn squares over. Fry only three or four at a time and turn often until golden. Drain on absorbent paper. Repeat with remaining dough. Serve hot with butter and lots of honey. Yields 3 dozen.

Houston Fine Arts Cookbook

 Sopapilla (soh pah PEE yah)—A dessert made of deep-fried dough, usually served with honey.

Flaky Empanadas
"Ojaldradas"

I grew up knowing these marvelous pastries as "Ojaldradas" (O hal drra' das). It's one of those words that can't really be translated exactly . . . it's not just "flaky" it's *more* than "flaky" and they truly *are* more than flaky! You'll really enjoy these . . . they're most special.

PASTRY:

3½ cups all purpose flour, sifted	½ teaspoon salt
1 cup melted pure lard, cooled	½ cup beer, room temperature

Preheat oven to 400°. Mix flour and salt with the melted lard. Add the beer and blend well. Dough should be nicely pliable but avoid working it more than necessary. Divide dough into small spoon-size portions. On a well floured board roll each portion of dough into a circle about 3 inches in diameter. Dust each circle well with flour on each side. Fold into quarters and roll out again. Place 1 teaspoon filling in center of circle. Fold top half over so it is ¼-inch from the edge of the bottom half. Turn bottom edge up over top edge and seal. Brush a little melted lard on top of empanada and sprinkle lightly with granulated sugar. Place pastry on baking sheets and bake for 15 minutes until light golden brown. Remove from oven and cool on wire racks.

FILLING:

2 (9-ounce) cans crushed pineapple, drained	⅔ cup granulated sugar
	2 tablespoons cornstarch

In a medium saucepan combine sugar and cornstarch. Add pineapple, mix well and simmer over medium heat until thick and clear. Remove from heat and cool slightly before using. Marmalade, any flavor, may be substituted for pineapple filling. I like to use "ate de Guayaba" which can be purchased at a Mexican grocery store.

Sweets. . . . From Marina With Love. . . .

Dacquoise au Chocolat

MERINGUE:
6 egg whites
⅔ cup sugar
1 cup chopped pecans

Preheat over to 300°. Grease and flour non-stick baking sheets and outline 3 non-overlapping 9-inch circles, using a cake pan as a guide. Whip egg whites to a froth, gradually beating in sugar. When stiff, fold in nuts. Spread meringue mixture evenly over circles; bake 45–55 minutes or until lightly toasted. The meringues must be loosened from the pans before they cool. If centers of layers are not crisp when cool, return to oven a few minutes.

CHOCOLATE BUTTER CREAM:

6 egg whites
1¾ cups sugar
2 cups unsalted butter, room
    temperature

3 ounces semi-sweet chocolate
Chocolate (garnish)

Place egg whites in top of double boiler and beat until frothy. Put over slightly simmering water and gradually beat in sugar. Increase heat and continue beating until thickened. Mixture should be warm to the touch and sugar completely dissolved. Remove from heat; set in a pan of cold water. Beat until mixture is room temperature. Gradually add butter, beating constantly. Melt chocolate and cool slightly. Blend into butter cream.

To assemble, select the nicest meringue for top layer. Spread each layer with butter cream, stacking one on top of the other. Spread a layer of butter cream on top of dacquoise. Garnish with finely chopped chocolate or chocolate curls. Serves 10.

The Dallas Symphony Cookbook

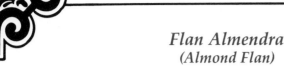

Flan Almendra
(Almond Flan)

This flan will keep in the pan up to a week in the refrigerator. It is silky smooth. The almonds rise to the top so that when you turn it, you have an almond crust. It is easy to make and elegant to boot.

½ cup sugar
1⅔ cups sweetened condensed
   milk
1 cup milk
3 eggs

3 egg yolks
1 teaspoon vanilla extract
1 cup slivered almonds, coarsely
   ground

Sprinkle the sugar evenly in a 9-inch cake pan and place over medium heat. Using oven mitts, caramelize the sugar by shaking the pan occasionally until the sugar is melted and has turned a light golden brown. (A little stirring may be necessary when caramelizing the sugar over a gas burner.) Allow to cool; the mixture may crack slightly.

Blend the remaining ingredients at high speed for 15 seconds. Pour over the caramelized sugar. Cover the pan with aluminum foil and place it in a larger, shallow pan containing about 1 inch of hot water. Bake at 350° for 55 minutes or until a knife inserted near the center comes out clean.

Remove the pan from water and uncover; let it cool on a wire rack at least 30 minutes. Loosen the edges with a spatula. Place a serving plate upside down on top of the cake pan and quickly invert the flan onto it. Serves 6–8.

The Only Texas Cookbook

Gran Sally's Bread Pudding

Ruthmary refers to this old-time dessert as "a rich version of a Depression Era staple from my childhood."

1 dozen brown-and-serve rolls, cooked and dried	1 teaspoon vanilla
	½ teaspoon nutmeg
Approximately 1 cup whole milk	½ teaspoon cinnamon
½ cup sugar	4 eggs, beaten

Crumble rolls in small pieces. Cover with milk. Add remaining ingredients and mix well. Grease baking dish with generous amount of butter or margarine and heat in oven until very hot. Then pour bread mixture into hot dish immediately and return to 350° oven to bake until a knife comes out clean, approximately 25 minutes. Pride House uses individual gelatin molds for baking dishes.

To serve: Spoon praline sauce in bottom of individual dishes. Place serving of pudding over the praline sauce and top with rich cream.

PRALINE SAUCE:

1 (16-ounce) box dark brown sugar	¼ cup Karo syrup, light or dark
	2 tablespoons butter
¾ cup cream	¼ teaspoon vanilla

Mix sugar, cream, and syrup and boil 5 minutes. Add butter and vanilla. Cool and refrigerate. Serves 6.

(Pride House, Jefferson) *Texas Historic Inns Cookbook*

Mexican Kahlua Soufflé

1 tablespoon cornstarch	1 tablespoon unflavored gelatin
1 cup evaporated milk	½ cup Kahlua
3 eggs, separated	¼ teaspoon vanilla
5 tablespoons sugar	Pinch of salt

Mix cornstarch with a little water and add to milk. Cook over low heat, stirring constantly until thickened. Beat egg yolks lightly with 4 tablespoons of the sugar. Soften gelatin in ¼ cup of water. Add yolks and gelatin to milk and cook for 5 minutes, stirring constantly. Allow to cool slightly and add Kahlua and vanilla. Add salt and 1 tablespoon of sugar to egg whites and beat until standing in peaks. Fold into the yolk mixture, pour into soufflé dish and chill until set. Serves 6.

San Antonio Cookbook II

White Magic Mousse

¼ cup sugar	¼ cup white crème de cacao
1 envelope unflavored gelatin	4 egg whites
1¼ cups milk	2 tablespoons sugar
4 ounces white chocolate, chopped	½ cup whipping cream, whipped
	White chocolate curls
4 egg yolks, beaten	Fresh strawberries

In saucepan combine ¼ cup sugar and gelatin. Stir in milk; add white chocolate. Cook and stir over low heat until chocolate melts. Gradually stir half of mixture into egg yolks; return to saucepan. Cook and stir 1–2 minutes or until mixture thickens slightly; do not boil. Remove from heat; stir in white crème de cacao. Chill gelatin mixture until partially set, stirring occasionally.

Beat egg whites until soft peaks form; gradually add 2 tablespoons sugar, beating until stiff peaks form. Fold into white chocolate along with whipping cream. Attach a buttered foil collar to a buttered and sugared 1-quart soufflé dish. Turn mixture into soufflé dish; chill until firm. To serve, remove collar and garnish with white chocolate curls and strawberries. Serves 6–8.

The Dallas Symphony Cookbook

Jeannine's Fruit Pizza

1 box yellow cake mix
¼ cup water
¼ cup margarine
¼ cup brown sugar
½ cup pecans, finely chopped
1 (8-ounce) package cream cheese
   at room temperature

1 pint whipped cream
Sliced strawberries, blueberries,
   bananas
Chunked pineapple, sliced in
   half
1 small jar apricot preserves
1½ tablespoons water

Combine cake mix, water, margarine, brown sugar and pecans. Press into 2 pizza pans which have been greased and floured. Bake at 375° until brown. Whip cream cheese and fold into whipped cream. This takes awhile. Spread over cake crust. Drain fruit several hours before using. Soak bananas in pineapple juice and drain. Arrange fruit on crust in pie wedge design or in rows. Combine apricot preserves with water. Glaze fruit. This is a beautiful dessert; looks like a stained glass window.

"Doctors, like school teachers, are recipients of cherished gifts and sayings from children. One of my favorite patients, Susie, age 5, gave me a coffee mug with the picture of a cow grazing in the field. The inscription said 'Someone Outstanding in the Field.' As she handed it to me she said, 'Here, Dr. Hill, to someone standing out in the field.'"

A Doctor's Prescription for Gourmet Cooking

Jay's Glory

1½ cups crumbled almond
   macaroons
½ cup sugar

½ cup Cognac or Tia Maria
1 pint heavy cream, stiffly
   whipped

Mix first 3 ingredients and fold in whipped cream. Place in dessert or custard cups and put in freezer for at least 3 hours. Mixture stiffens but will not freeze. Add a drop or two of food coloring for whatever season or reason. Serves 8.

Hospitality

Strawberry Yum Yum

CRUST:

1 cup flour
½ cup butter

¼ cup brown sugar
½ cup nuts, chopped

Mix crust ingredients until crumbly. Pat into 7 × 11-inch pan. Bake in a 350° oven for 15–20 minutes. Cool or chill.

FILLING:

1 cup sugar
2 egg whites
1 (16-ounce) package partially
　thawed strawberries

2 teaspoons lemon juice
1 (4-ounce) package Cool Whip

Mix filling ingredients, except Cool Whip, until blended in mixer. Turn on high for 15–20 minutes. Fold in Cool Whip. Pour over crust mixture. Put rest of crumb mixture on top. Freeze.

Cowtown Cuisine

Strawberries Giovanni

¼ cup butter or margarine
½ cup sugar
Zest of 1 lemon or orange
　(optional)

½ cup Kirsch
1 pint strawberries, sliced

In skillet melt butter; add sugar. Stir until sugar is dissolved and mixture bubbly. Add orange zest. Stir in Kirsch. Cook, stirring until bubbly again; add strawberries. Heat through. Serve while hot over vanilla ice cream. Yields 4 servings.

This is a favorite of all strawberry fanciers.

Keepers

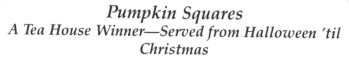
Pumpkin Squares
A Tea House Winner—Served from Halloween 'til Christmas

1 (1-pound) can pumpkin (2 cups)
1½ cups sugar
1 teaspoon salt
1 teaspoon ginger
1 teaspoon ground cinnamon

½ teaspoon nutmeg
1 cup chopped pecans
½ gallon vanilla ice cream (soft)
1 box ginger snaps

Combine pumpkin, sugar, salt, ginger, cinnamon and nutmeg. Then add pecans. Fold pumpkin mixture into ice cream or vice-versa.

Line a 9 × 13-inch pan or Pyrex dish with one-half of the ginger snaps. Top with one-half of the pumpkin-ice cream mixture. Cover with the remaining ginger snaps and spread the balance of the pumpkin mixture over the second layer of ginger snaps.

Freeze, when firm, cut into squares. Top with whipped cream or Cool Whip. Serves 18.

Collectibles II

Brandied Peaches

12 perfect ripe freestone peaches
6 cups water

4 cups sugar
Brandy

Boil water and sugar together 10 minutes. Peel peaches by dipping quickly in hot water and slipping skins off. You may leave whole or halve them. Simmer peaches in syrup until tender, about 5 minutes for whole, less for the half. Test with a toothpick and do not overcook. Remove from syrup with spoon and pack into sterilized jars. Add 2 tablespoons brandy to each pint and fill to cover peaches with syrup. Seal jars. Let ripen 1 month before using. Yields 3–4 pints.

Whole ones are nice served cold with cold baked ham and the halves with a little of the syrup are ooo-la-la in a saucer glass filled with champagne.

A Texas Hill Country Cookbook

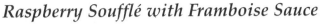
Raspberry Soufflé with Framboise Sauce

1 envelope unflavored gelatin
2 tablespoons water
1 cup raspberries defrosted, puréed in a blender and strained

¾ cup sugar
7–8 egg whites (to make 1 cup)
8-ounce container heavy cream

One quart soufflé dish—make collar of foil to 1½–3 inches above dish. Oil well. Soften gelatin in water. Add strained berries and sugar. Heat stirring until gelatin and sugar dissolves. Chill ½ hour (cold but not set). Beat egg whites very stiff but not dry. Fold into berry mixture. Beat cream until stiff and fold in mixture (egg whites must be folded in first). Chill overnight. Can freeze ahead and take out early in the afternoon and refrigerate. Remove foil at the last minute and serve.

FRAMBOISE SAUCE:
1 (10-ounce) package frozen raspberries partly defrosted or use fresh raspberries

¼ cup sugar
3 tablespoons Framboise

Blend raspberries, sugar and strain. Add Framboise. Serves 10–12. Preparation time: 50 minutes.

Entertaining at Aldredge House

 Framboise (frahm BWAHS)—A French liqueur made from raspberries.

Oreo Smush

1 stick butter
1 (19-ounce) package Oreos, crushed
½ gallon vanilla ice cream, softened

2 jars fudge sauce
1 large carton LaCreme or Cool Whip

Melt butter in 9 × 13-inch pan. Reserve about ½ cup crushed Oreos for top and mix remaining with butter to form a crust in pan (press in pan). Spread softened ice cream over crust; then add layer of fudge sauce. Top with carton of whipped topping. Sprinkle with remaining crumbs. Freeze until ready to serve. Taster says this is an ice cream lover's delight!

Tempting Traditions

"Auntie L's" Homemade Ice Cream
Definitely worth the trouble.

6 eggs
2 cups sugar
2 cups heavy cream

2 teaspoons vanilla
Milk or half and half cream

Separate into two bowls 6 eggs. Add to egg whites and beat until very fluffy 1 cup sugar. Set aside.

Add to egg yolks and beat until fluffy 1 cup sugar. Set aside.

Beat until stiff 2 cups heavy cream. Blend all mixtures together and add 2 teaspoons vanilla.

Pour into prechilled freezer can. Finish filling with milk or half and half cream. Freeze according to manufacturer's manual. Try this once! You will never make ice cream any other way. Yields 1 gallon.

Calf Fries to Caviar

Apple Ice Cream Sauce

½ cup firmly packed brown sugar
1 tablespoon cornstarch
½ teaspoon cinnamon
¼ teaspoon nutmeg
½ teaspoon grated lemon rind
   (optional)

1 teaspoon lemon juice
1 (20-ounce) can pie-sliced
   apples, undrained

Combine the first 7 ingredients in a saucepan; blend well. Stir in apples; cook, stirring constantly, until thickened. Serve hot over vanilla ice cream. Yields about 6 servings.

Flavor Favorites

Ancho (AHN choh)—A kind of chile pepper often used in Tex-Mex recipes, frequently as flavoring in chili con carne.

Bain marie (ban mah REE)—A French phrase which describes a steam table which has openings for several pots or pans so that their contents can be warmed by hot water or steam circulating around them.

Ballottine (bah leh TEEN)—A French dish of meat, fish, or fowl which has been boned and stuffed with a combination of meats, vegetables, and herbs, then rolled and tied in a bundle shape and cooked in rich stock. Although ballottine can be served cold, it is generally a hot dish.

Barquett or *barquette* (bar KET)—A small pastry shell shaped like a boat.

Bell pepper—A mild sweet pepper often used in Tex-Mex cooking.

Bisque (BISK)—A kind of creamy soup made with a purée of seafood, meat, and/or vegetables.

Bolillo (boh LEE yo)—A small, long roll of bread.

Cabrito (cah BREE toh)—A young goat.

Calabacita (cah lah bah SEE tah)—A round, striped green squash, also called a zucchini squash.

Caldillo (cahl DEE yoh)—A kind of gravy or sauce.

Ceviche (say VEESH)—A dish or appetizer made essentially of fish marinated in lime or lemon juice.

Chalupa (chah LOO pah)—Tortilla dough shaped into an oval or boat, filled with shredded meat and other ingredients.

Chervil (CHUR vuhl)—A plant belonging to the parsley family. The salad chervil is used as a salad green, a garnish, or seasoning, while the turnip-rooted chervil is found in stews or as a boiled or fried vegetable.

Chile (CHEE lay)—A pepper. The flavor of chiles ranges from mild to very hot. The American spelling is chili.

Chile pequin (CHEE lay pay KEEN)—A very small pepper that is extremely hot, often used in powdered form.

Chile rellenos (CHEE lay ray YAY nohs)—Stuffed peppers.

Chili con carne (CHEE lee cohn CAR nay)—Chili with meat. Most often called simply chili.

Chili con queso (CHEE lee cohn KAY soh)—Chili with cheese.

Chili meat—Coarsely ground round steak or well-trimmed chuck meat, usually ground on the ¾-inch plate on butcher's grinder.

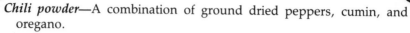

Chili powder—A combination of ground dried peppers, cumin, and oregano.

Chorizo (cho REE zoh)—A kind of spicy Mexican sausage.

Cilantro (seh LAN troh)—A member of the parsley family. Its small seedlike fruits are used as a seasoning in curry, pickle, and pastries. The extract of the fruit is used as a flavoring.

Cumin (CUHM in) or *comino* (coh MEE noh)—An herb plant whose seeds are used as a flavoring. Cumin is a member of the parsley family.

Duxelles (dukes ELL)—A combination of mushrooms, chopped shallots, and herbs, simmered in butter. It has the consistency of a hash, and is often used to flavor sauces, soups, and stuffings.

Enchilada (ain chee LAH dah)—A corn tortilla, filled with cheese and shredded meat. The tortillas for enchiladas are fried lightly in oil so that they remain soft.

En croute (ahn CROOT)—A dish that is cooked in a crust.

Fajitas (fah HEE tahs)—Skirt steaks, actually the beef diaphragm muscle.

Framboise (frahm BWAHS)—A French liqueur made from raspberries.

Frijoles (free HOH lays)—Beans.

Frijoles refritas (ray FREE tahs)—Refried beans, a favorite Tex-Mex dish. Beans are first cooked with tomatoes, onions, chili peppers and other seasonings, then mashed and fried.

Fritters—Pieces of fruit, vegetable, meat, or poultry dipped in batter, then cooked in hot fat or oil.

Garbanzo beans (gar BAHN zoh)—Seeds, larger than peas, which taste somewhat like dried beans or peas. Also called a chickpea, the garbanzo is used in soups and stews and as a sidedish instead of rice or frijoles.

Gazpacho (gahz PAH choh)—A cold vegetable soup, one that usually includes onions, garlic, green peppers, tomatoes and cucumbers.

Gratinée (grah tee NAY)—A dish that has been sprinkled with cheese or bread crumbs, then replaced in the oven until the top becomes crisp and golden.

Guacamole (gwa cah MOH lay)—A paste made from avocados. It is served on lettuce as a salad, as a filling, or as a dip.

Huevo (WAY boh)—The Spanish word for egg.

Jalapeño (hah lah PAIN yoh)—A kind of chile pepper that is frequently used in Tex-Mex recipes. Jalapeños are dark green peppers, with flavor from medium hot to extremely hot.

Longhorn cheese—A form of mellow Cheddar cheese which takes its name from the Longhorn breed of cow.

Madeira (mah DEER ah)—A Portugese wine. Rainwater Madeira has a light straw color, but a relatively full flavor and bouquet.

Masa (MAH zah)—A coarse corn flour used to make tortillas.

Mexican peppers—Fleshy fruits with many degrees of hotness. Some of the peppers used in Mexican cooking are: anchos, jalapeños, serranos, poblanos, chili pequins, pimentos, bell peppers.

Molcajete (mohl cah HAY tay)—A mortar used to grind ingredients.

Mole (MOH lay)—A Mexican hot sauce of chili, spices, and sometimes chocolate.

Monterey Jack—A mild, semi-soft cheese generally classified as a Cheddar, but also very similar to Muenster cheese. Although Monterey Jack originated in Monterey County, California, its name is sometimes spelled like the name of the Mexican city of Monterrey. Also called just Monterey or just Jack.

Mornay (more NAY)—A traditional French sauce made with white sauce and one or more kinds of melted cheese.

Mousse (MOOSE)—A French term which refers to light, airy dishes prepared with whipped cream or egg whites.

MSG—Monosodium glutamate, a powder taken from glutamic acid in plants. Used as a flavor enhancer. Some recipes use the brand, Accent.

Nachos (NAH chohs)—A popular Tex-Mex snack. They are fried tortilla chips that can be topped off with melted cheese, slices of pepper, or refried beans.

Pavlova—A light, whipped dessert, made with fruit, which has been called "as light on the stomach as the Russian ballerina was on her feet."

Persillade (per seh LAHD)—A French word which tells that a dish contains parsley or is garnished with parsley.

Picadillo (pee cah DEE yoh)—A Spanish or Mexican dish of chopped or ground pork and veal cooked together and then mixed with tomatoes, garlic, onion, olives, and other ingredients.

Picante (pee CAHN tay)—A Spanish word meaning spicy hot.

Piquant (pee CAHNT)—A French word meaning lively or tangy. Most often used to describe a sauce made with tomatoes and/or roux.

Pimento or *pimiento* (pee MAIN toh)—A sweet Spanish pepper.

Pistou (pehs TOO)—A kind of soup, with Italian origins, made with string beans, tomatoes, potatoes, and a variety of seasonings.

Poblanos (poh BLAH nohs)—Mild to hot, bright green chiles also called green chiles. They are sometimes stuffed and served like bell peppers.

Pollo (POY yoh)—The Spanish word for chicken.

Puréed (pure RAID)—Put through a sieve or blender and made into a pulp-like consistency.

Roux (ROO)—Flour carefully browned in fat, butter or oil, used to thicken sauces and gravies.

Salsa (SAHL sah)—Spanish for sauce. Salsa cruda is a red sauce consisting of uncooked tomatoes, green chilies, and herbs. Salsa verde is uncooked hot sauce.

Scallion—A small bulbless onion, also called a Welsh onion.

Schnecken (SHNAY ken)—Fruit-filled or nut-filled sweet rolls, named for the German word for snails because of their shape.

Serrano (say RAH noh)—Literally, "of the sierra" in Spanish. A kind of chile that is small, dark green (turns red when very mature), and very hot. Key ingredient in salsa cruda.

Shallot—A member of the lily family, something like an onion, but with a series of small sections instead of one main bulb.

Sopa (SOH pah)—The Spanish word for soup.

Sopapilla (soh pah PEE yah)—A dessert made of deep-fried dough, usually served with honey.

Succotash—The name of an American dish which is a mixture of sweet corn kernels and lima beans.

Suet—A firm kind of cooking fat from cattle and sheep used in cooking and making tallow.

Taco (TAH coh)—A kind of Tex-Mex sandwich, filled with combinations of ground meat, chile peppers, cheese, tomatoes, lettuce, and refried beans. Tacos are enclosed in a folded or rolled tortilla and served with salsa cruda.

Tamales (tah MAH lays)—Made by spreading a thick layer of masa on dried corn husks, then filling with shredded meat and cooking until soft.

Tart—A small pie filled with either sweet or unsweet filling, generally prepared without a top crust.

Tex-Mex—The term used to describe Texans' version of Mexican cooking.

Torte—A rich cake.

Tortilla (tor TEE yah)—A thin pancake of masa.

Tostada (tohs TAH dah)—A crisp, fried tortilla that is garnished.

Index

Pumping crude. Near San Angelo.

INDEX

Mexican Refried 117
Navy Beans for Writers 119
Ranger Nine-Bean Soup 106
Sweet and Sour Bean Casserole 116
Beef:
  After Theatre Steak 220
  Anticucho Sauce 221
  Aunt Martha's Tamale Pie 229
  Barbecued Beef Brisket 216
  Caldillo 213
  Cantonese Beef 222
  Carne Asada 222
  Cheeseburger Pie 236
  Cheesy Meat Loaf 234
  Cholent 212
  Crazy Crust Pizza 233
  Deluxe Cherry Brisket 215
  Easy Enchilada Casserole 227
  Fajitas 224
  French Stew 209
  Galveston Island Chili 206
  Gourmet Chili 207
  Gourmet Pot Roast 219
  Green Enchiladas 228
  Husband's Delight 232
  Italian Cutlets 225
  Italian-Style Cabbage Rolls 237
  Jalapeno Cheeseburgers 235
  Juicy Pig Sandwiches 236
  Lone Star Chicken-Fried Steak 223
  Marinated Beef Tender 214
  Mini-Mex Meat Loaves 235
  Noodle Stroganoff 232
  Party Tenderloin 217
  Pepper Steak 221
  Picadillo 32, 33
  Pick Pocket Tacos 226
  Pot Roast 219
  Salpicon 213
  Sam's Chili 208
  Sherry Beef and Rice 144
  Sombrero Spread 22
  Sour Cream Enchiladas 227
  State Fair Chuck Roast 218
  Steak Burgundy 220
  Tacos 226
  Tacos al Carbon 225
  Taco Salad 57
  Texas Brisket 215
  Texas Chili 207
  Texas Tamale Pie 231
  Wailiki Meatballs 40
  Wibb's Beef Tender 217
Beer Batter 174
Better Than Sex Cake 251
Betty Ewing's Jalapeno Corn Bread 93
Beverages:
  Festive Holiday Spiced Tea 15
  Gluhwein 15
  Hot Buttered Rum 16
  Libba's Bloody Marys 18
  Mint Tea 14
  Slush Punch 17
  Tequila Slush 17
  Wassail 16
  White Sangria 14
  Zippy, Eggnog Mix 18
Bing Cherry Pie 282
Bizcochos 272
Black Bottom Cupcakes 256
Black-Eyed Peas 130
Black-Eyed Pea Dip 19
Black Forest Cookies 270
Bleu Cheese Tarts 29
Bloody Marys, Libba's 18
Bongo Bongo 110
Bourbon Chocolate Pie 290
Boxty 132
Brandied Peaches 304
Bread:
  Annette's Cheesebread 88
  Apple Schnecken 80
  Betty Ewing's Jalapeno Corn Bread 93
  Bread 90
  Cherry Nut Muffins 81
  Cornbread Muffins 92
  Cream Cheese Braids 83
  Creole Cheese Sticks 89
  Easy Eggnog Bread 86
  Golden Sandwiches 96
  Hot Flitters 78
  Jalapeno Cornbread 93
  Jean's Garlic Bread 91
  Lemon and Lime Bread 86
  Maple Nut Cinnamon Rolls 94
  Mexican Cornbread 93
  Monkey Bread 87
  Mushroom Bread 88
  Popovers 89
  Pull-Apart Coffee Cake 78
  Ribbon Sandwich Loaf 95
  Sausage-Spinach Loaf 94
  Schnecken 80
  Sour Cream Coffee Cake 79
  Sugar Twist 81
  Sunflower Seed Bread 85
  Sweet Potato Rolls 82
  Very Special Southern Batter Bread 92
Breakfast Enchiladas 68
Breast of Chicken in Cream and
  Apples 184
Brie Soup 100
Broccoli-Cheese Soup 104
Broccoli Chicken 186
Broccoli Dip 20
Broccoli Supreme Casserole 119
Brownies, Deluxe 268
Brownies, Peppermint 269
Brunch Eggs 65
Bubble and Squeak 133
Buttermilk Pie 289

INDEX

INDEX

INDEX

INDEX

INDEX

Catalog of
Contributing
Cookbooks

River rafting on the Rio Grande. Big Bend National Park in Southwest Texas.

CATALOG OF CONTRIBUTING COOKBOOKS

All recipes in this book have been submitted from the Texas cookbooks shown on the following pages. Individuals who wish to obtain a copy of any particular book can do so by sending a check or money order to the address listed. Prices are subject to change. Please note the postage and handling charges that are required. Texas residents add tax only when requested. Retailers are invited to call or write to same address for wholesale information.

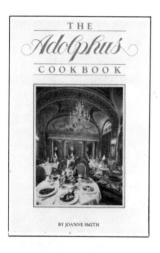

THE ADOLPHUS COOKBOOK

by Joanne Smith
Taylor Publishing Company
1550 West Mockingbird Lane
Dallas, TX 75235   214/637-2800

The Adolphus Cookbook combines the story of the Adolphus Hotel's heritage and hospitality with a collection of more than 140 recipes and ideas for elegant entertaining. Includes chef's suggestions for preparing, serving, and decorating, plus wine recommendations. 208 pages, 7x10 hardcover, black & white and full color photographs.

$24.95 Retail price
$ 1.50 Postage and handling
Make check payable to Taylor Publishing Co.
ISBN 0-87833-339-8

AMARILLO JUNIOR LEAGUE COOK-BOOK

Amarillo Junior League
P. O. Box 381
Amarillo, TX 79105   806/374-6661

The Amarillo Junior League Cookbook contains 656 recipes, each twice-tested. There are 330 pages in the sunny yellow book. The cover is decorative, with ribbon-tied green asparagus, and is a 3-ring looseleaf notebook with pages that lie flat. It is a top notch, kitchen-proven, eye-appealing, self-selling cookbook.

$12.50 Retail price
$ 1.50 Postage and handling
$ .64 Tax for Texas residents
Make check payable to Amarillo Junior League Publications
ISBN 0-9604102-0-1

AN AMERICAN GUMBO

by Linda West Eckhardt
Texas Monthly Press, Inc.
P. O. Box 1569
Austin, TX 78767   512/476-7085

 Everything in this book is good and cheap. Easy and
foolproof. Nothing costs more than $1.00 a serving and
some cost a whole lot less. No processed foods. Recipes
that are quick, delicious, and nutritious. Cook from this
book and you can be a gourmet every day.

$12.95 Retail price
$ 2.00 Postage and handling
$ .66 Tax for Texas residents
Make check payable to Texas Monthly Press
ISBN 0-932012-60-4

BECKY'S BRUNCH & BREAKFAST BOOK

by Rebecca Walker
P. O. Box 5892
Austin, TX 78763   512/443-7950

 Over 200 recipes and delightful menus for the most
important meal of the day—and the one most likely to
stump even the best and most creative cooks! Chapters
for every excuse given for not eating breakfast—dieting,
not enough time, etc. Plenty of easy-to-follow recipes
guaranteed to entice even the sleepyhead and "breakfast hater"!!

$ 7.95 Retail price
$ 1.50 Postage and handling
$ .41 Tax for Texas residents
Make check payable to *Becky's Brunch & Breakfast Book*
ISBN 0-9612284-0-7

THE BLUE DENIM GOURMET

Junior League of Odessa Publications
P. O. Box 7273
Odessa, TX 79760-7273   915/368-0031

 A real eye-catcher, the book measures 7"x9" with a
heavy paper cover of simulated blue denim with a bright
red comb. With more than 1,000 recipes (including a
special Mexican Food section), the book is alphabeti-
cally indexed and has eighteen pen-and-ink illustrations.

$ 8.95 Retail price
$ 1.60 Postage and handling
$ .46 Tax for Texas residents
Make check payable to Junior League of Odessa
ISBN 0-9612508-0-1

BRAVO, CHEF!

The Dallas Opera Guild
c/o Nancy Plamann
15151 Kingstree Drive
Dallas, TX 75248   214/239-9977

Expect an ovation when you cook with *Bravo, Chef!*, the 400-page Dallas Opera Guild Cookbook. *Bravo, Chef!* contains over 400 recipes including 100 contributions from international opera stars and is splendidly illustrated with color photographs of Dallas Opera productions. *Bravo Chef!* is an opera lover's best companion in the kitchen.

$16.95 Retail price
$ 2.00 Postage and handling
$ 1.04 Tax for Texas residents
Make check payable to The Dallas Opera
ISBN 0-9612306-0-6

CALF FRIES TO CAVIAR

by Janel Franklin and Sue Vaughn
Jan-Su Publications
1012 North 9th
Lamesa, TX 79331   806/998-5010

A collection of over 600 *true* Texas recipes. The simple, step-by-step instructions enable even a beginner to turn out taste-tempting treats, consistently and easily. The perfect gift for all occasions, a delight for the cook and the collector. The popular cover makes it suitable for men also. OLDIES, but GOODIES.

$11.95 Retail price
$ 1.75 Postage and handling
$ .60 Tax for Texas residents
Make check payable to Jan-Su Publications
ISBN 0-9610956-0-1

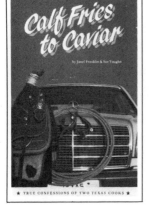

CHINESE COOKING THE AMERICAN WAY

By Catherine Liu
Catherine's Art of Cooking
P. O. Box 5734
Richardson, TX 75080   214/931-9318

Catherine Liu's new edition is the most comprehensive, best illustrated Chinese cookbook in print. One of the foremost Chinese cooking authorities in Dallas, Catherine is imaginative, creative, thorough and precise. Her book is written for the simple and the sophisticate. 300 pages. Illustrated.

$ 9.95 Retail price
$ 1.00 Postage and handling
$ .50 Tax for Texas residents
Make check payable to Catherine's Art of Cooking
ISBN 0-9604990-0-8

COLLECTIBLES II

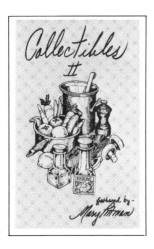

by Mary Pittman
P. O. Box 1008
Van Alstyne, TX 75095   214/433-2665

Collectibles II is 128 pages chocked full of recipes, some new, some old, some borrowed, but no blue— the emphasis is definately on delicious. Filled with "goodies" that are mealtime experiences from Mary Pittman's Tea House and family, all recipes are easy-do to help make entertaining a pleasure in today's servantless society.

$ 6.98 Retail price
$ 1.50 Postage and handling
$ .37 Tax for Texas residents
Make check payable to Mary Pittman

COMPANY'S COMING

The Institute of Texan Cultures
P. O. Box 1226
San Antonio, TX 78294   512/226-7651

Company's Coming has 166 tried and true holiday recipes, a festive collection from The Institute of Texan Cultures' volunteer group, The Alliance. Most of these recipes have been cherished by families for years. Many are typically Texan. All are sure to please. Handy household tips are sprinkled throughout. 115 pages.

$ 6.95 Retail price
$ 1.50 Postage and handling
$ .39 Tax for Texas residents
Make check payable to The Institute of Texan Cultures
ISBN 0-86701-025-8

COOK 'EM HORNS

The Ex-Students' Association of The University of
  Texas
P. O. Box 7278
Austin, TX 78713   512/476-6271

A literary cookbook, *Cook 'em Horns* is chock-full of University of Texas history and 700-plus tested, selected recipes from Texas Exes around the world. Perfect for kitchen, coffee table and gifts. Now in its fourth printing, it is an over-sized 7 ¾"x10½", 439-page book with a full-color hardback cover.

$19.95 Retail price
$ 2.00 Postage and handling
$ 1.01 Tax for Texas residents
Make check payable to The Ex-Students' Asscciation

327

COOKING TEXAS STYLE
by Candy Wagner and Sandra Marquez
University of Texas Press
Box 7819
Austin, TX 78712   512/471-7233

For over 100 years, the ancestors of Wagner and Marquez (who are sisters) have lived in Texas and have passed down their most cherished family recipes from one generation to the next. A unique collection of traditional recipes (over 200) which captures the historical flavor of the varied origins of Texas cuisine. 194 pages.

$12.95 Retail price
$ 1.50 Postage and handling
$ .70 Tax for Texas residents
Make check payable to University of Texas Press
ISBN 0-292-71082-8

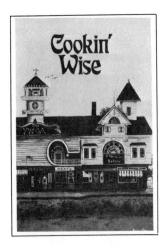

COOKIN' WISE
YWCA
3410 Magnolia
Texarkana, TX 75503   214/793-6769

A nostalgic, colorfully illustrated cover that makes it a "show off" cookbook in any kitchen. 550-plus diverse, *tested* recipes, well organized, explicit, easy to read; 12 well-organized food sections, each set off with a pen-and-ink illustration; and, a detailed, cross-filed index for simple finger-tip location of every recipe.

$ 7.95 Retail price
$ 1.25 Postage and handling
$ .41 Tax for Texas residents
Make check payable to *Cookin' Wise*

THE COTTAGE KITCHEN COOKBOOK
The Heritage Association of San Marcos, Inc.
308 East Hopkins Street
San Marcos, TX 78666   512/392-9997

This book of treasured recipes includes popular dishes served each Friday at the Cottage Kitchen in the Charles S. Cock House, a building on the National Register of Historic Places, which have drawn people to San Marcos from throughout the United States. This treasury of favorite recipes reflects the hospitality of the Heritage Association and San Marcos.

$ 6.95 Retail price
$ 1.50 Postage and handling
Make check payable to Heritage Association of San Marcos

COWTOWN CUISINE

St. Joseph's Hospital Guild Volunteer Office
1401 South Main
Fort Worth, TX 76104   817/336-9371 Ext. 5541

The traditional Texas blends with the cosmopolitan in *Cowtown Cuisine*. Members of St. Joseph's Hospital Guild share their favorite recipes for entertaining and for family meals. The hardcover book contains 270 pages and over 700 of the very best home-tested recipes for delicious eating!

$10.95 Retail price
$ .59 Tax for Texas residents
Make check payable to St. Joseph's Hospital Guild
   Publications, Inc.
ISBN 087833-323-1

CREATIVE MEXICAN COOKING

By Anne Lindsay Greer
Texas Monthly Press
P. O. Box 1569
Austin, TX 78767   512/476-7085

Anne Greer, author of *Cuisine of the Southwest*, has put together this cookbook from recipes of great Texas chefs. The recipes represent the best Tex-Mex that Texas restaurants have to offer.

$19.95 Retail price
$ 2.00 Postage and handling
$ 1.02 Tax for Texas residents
Make check payable to Texas Monthly Press
ISBN 0-9607740-1-7

CRÈME OF THE CROP

by Jane Neely Winchell
P. O. Box 5336
Waco, TX 76708   817/772-2262

A TEXAS STAR—written with love and care for beginners and gourmets—over 400 recipes, each one as used at the family table (see at Neiman-Marcus, Marshall Field's, etc.) A gift with all the right ingredients. Easy-to-read type. Cross referenced index. Spiral bound. 252 pages.

$ 8.95 Retail price
$ 1.00 Postage and handling
$ .46 Tax for Texas residents
Make check payable to *Crème of the Crop*
ISBN 0-9610978-0-9

CUCKOO TOO

by Nancy Allen, Kay Bruce, Fran Fauntleroy, Pat
Glauser, Isla Reckling, and Mary Whilden
5142 Green Tree
Houston, TX 77056   713/621-3197

A family cookbook including easy, delicious family
recipes for bachelors, yound singles, children's parties,
some even exotic! 349 pages, indexed, about 1,000
recipes, excellent Mexican foods, soul food, old time
favorites, "put-togethers," barbecue, salads—something for everyone!

$ 9.95 Retail price
$ 1.55 Postage and handling
Make check payable to Isla Reckling, Cuckoo Too
ISBN 0-89716-110-6

THE DALLAS PECAN COOKBOOK

Zonta Club of Dallas I
6412 Patrick
Dallas, TX 75214   214/821-8601

The Dallas Pecan Cookbook is full of wonderful
pecan recipes compiled by members and friends of
Zonta, a classified club of executive and professional
women. It has over 250 recipes in 130 pages.

$ 7.50 Retail price
$ .75 Postage and handling
$ .39 Tax for Texas residents
Make check payable to Zonta Club of Dallas I

THE DALLAS SYMPHONY COOKBOOK

Junior Group of the Dallas Symphony Orchestra League
P. O. Box 8472
Dallas, TX 75205   214/565-9100

A treasure for special entertaining. Recipes for
novices and gourmands. Fresh herbs used throughout.
Recipes for light, fresh approach. More than 350
specially selected and tested recipes. Hardback book.
224 pages.

$12.95 Retail price
$ 2.00 (1-3 copies) Postage and handling $5.00 (6-12)
$ .79 Tax for Texas residents
Make check payable to Junior Group Publications
ISBN 0-9611216-0-2

A DIFFERENT TASTE OF PARIS

McCuistion Regional Medical Center Auxiliary
865 Deshong Drive
Paris, TX 75460   214/737-1124

   This is a unique book with an easy-to-read format
containing everything from basic recipes and instructions for the beginner to sophisticated recipes for the
experienced cook. A delightful chapter focuses on
brunches and picnics complete with menus and recipes designed for the solo cook who desires to en-
tertain with style. 841 recipes in 322 pages.

$10.00 Retail price
$ 2.00 Postage and handling
$ .51 Tax forTexas residents
Make check payable to McCuistion Regional Medical
   Center Auxiliary

A DOCTOR'S PRESCRIPTION FOR GOURMET COOKING

by Reba Michels Hill, M.D.
6720 Bertner
Houston, TX 77030   713/791-3184 or 621-1787

   Five hundred elegant, easy, well-tested, make-ahead
recipes geared for the busy individual who wants a
gourmet meal in a few precious minutes. Funny vignettes made by guests make the book delightfully read-
able. Proceeds support Texas Medical Center Newborn
Research. Dedicated to the Pediatric house staff Baylor
College of Medicine who served as gourmet guinea pigs.

$ 9.95 Retail price
$ 2.00 Postage and handling
$ .61 Tax for Texas residents
Make check payable to A Doctor's Prescription for
   Gourmet Cooking

EASY DOES IT

Woman Time Management
2619 Amherst
Wichita Falls, TX 76308   817/691-1196

   All recipes are simple to make. Over 225 recipes are
included. A special section features time-saving tips on
organizing and cooking 12 meals in one day. The lay-
out is logical and easy to follow with clear, step-by-step
directions. This handy cookbook is protected by a stur-
dy, easy-to-clean laminated cover.

$ 9.95 Retail price
$ 1.50 Postage and handling
$ .51 Tax for Texas residents
Make check payable to Woman Time Management
ISBN 0-9610530-0-3

ELEGANT ELK - DELICIOUS DEER

by Judy Barbour
2305 Park Avenue
Bay City, TX 77414   409/245-7527 or 244-4398

"The Ultimate Authority" is for those who desire imaginative ideas for preparing wild game—elk, deer, moose, antelope, game birds and fish. Includes party ideas, appetizers, beverages, entrees, accompaniments, desserts. The perfect gift for hunters (and especially their wives). Brown leather-like cover with gold silhouettes of elk and deer. 196 pages. Hardbound.

$13.95 Retail price
$ 1.25 Postage and handling
$ .70 Tax for Texas residents
Make check payable to Judy Barbour
ISBN 0-686-33178-8

ENJOY!

Women's Symphony League of Austin
1101 Red River
Austin, TX 78701   512/476-6064

Enjoy!—a Texas cookbook that is not just chili and barbecue! With over 700 recipes—270 pages—it is a delightful cookbook filled with innovative and delicious ideas and recipes. Included is a guide listing 100 table wines arranged by type, color, body and price range.

$12.50 Retail price
$ 1.80 Postage and handling
$ .77 Tax for Texas residents
Make check payable to Women's Symphony League

ENTERTAINING AT ALDREDGE HOUSE

Dallas County Medical Society Auxiliary
P. O. Box 141231
Dallas, TX 75214   214/823-2972

Entertaining at Aldredge House has everything. 313 pages filled with 493 tasty recipes and party ideas will make any hostess "The Talk of the Town." The historical Aldredge House is the setting for social galas and television series. The mansion was used as Southfork for the pilot of *Dallas.*

$12.95 Retail price
$ 2.00 Postage and handling
$ .79 Tax for Texas residents
Make check payable to Aldredge House Publications
ISBN 0-87833-326-6

ENTERTAINING IN TEXAS
Junior League of Victoria
P. O. Box 2741
Victoria, TX 77902   512/573-4508

Experience the unique elegance of *Entertaining in Texas*! This 244-page special collection consists of over 400 selected and tested recipes from the South Texas area, which includes an entire section devoted to Tex-Mex foods. The wide range of recipes offered makes it the perfect gift—a must for the gourmet!

$ 9.95 Retail price
$ 2.00 Postage and handling
$ .51 Tax for Texas residents
Make check payable to *Entertaining in Texas*
ISBN 0-9608608-0-0

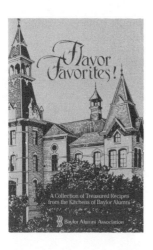

FLAVOR FAVORITES
Baylor University Alumni Association
Campus Box 378
Waco, TX 76798   817/755-1121

Crackerjack sharp, this outstanding collection of favorite recipes of Baylor alumni will be one of your most used cookbooks. Bright new second printing has popular comb binding. Historic Baylor photos highlight section division pages. More than 7,000 copies sold. Edited by Marilyn Wyrick Ingram, the book has more than 800 carefully tested recipes in 400 pages.

$ 9.95 Retail price
$ 1.50 Postage and handling
$ .51 Tax for Texas residents
Make check payable to B.A.S.E. (Baylor Alumni
   Service Enterprises)

FLAVORS
Junior League of San Antonio, Inc.
819 Augusta Street
San Antonio, TX 78215   512/225-1861

Flavors is an elegant 7¼"x10½" cookbook with 860 tested recipes ranging from gourmet to everyday fare, as unique and diversified as the city from which its flavors are derived. A proven best-seller, a must for collectors and a perfect gift for brides as well as gourmet cooks. *Flavors* is a standout on the shelf!

$14.95 Retail price
$ 1.75 Postage and handling
$ .84 Tax for Texas residents
Make check payable to Junior League of San Antonio
ISBN 0-9610416-0-9

FROM MY APRON POCKET

by Suzanne L. Collins
4701 Cedar Springs Road - 105
Dallas, TX 75219   214/528-3274 or 890-6807

Country French and Dutch traditions add richness
and flavor to an incomparable 230-page cookbook with
over 470 recipes, cookin'-how tips, and deriva-
tives for your reading pleasure. A blending of the old
and the new, different nationalities, countries and cus-
toms, makes it a prerequisite for the collector or the
cook.

$ 9.00 Retail price
$ 1.50 handling charge
$ .45 Tax for Texas residents
Make check payable to S. L. Collins

GALLERY BUFFET SOUP COOKBOOK

Dallas Museum of Art League
1717 North Harwood
Dallas, TX 75201   214/922-0220 Ext. 249

A collection of soup recipes ranging from simple to
exotic, featuring specialties of the house, hearty soups,
broths, stocks, clear soups, vegetable soups, cream soups,
chilled soups, quick soups, seafood soups, exotic soups,
foreign soups. 10 full-color reproductions featuring
portraits of women and children from the collection
of the Dallas Museum of Art.

$12.50 Retail price
$ 1.75 Postage and handling
$ .75 Tax for Texas residents
Make check payable to *Gallery Buffet Soup Cookbook*
ISBN 0-9609622-1-2

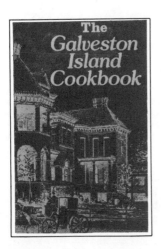

THE GALVESTON ISLAND COOKBOOK

The Women of Trinity Episcopal Church
2216 Ball
Galveston, TX 77550   409/765-6317

When the Women of Trinity Church compiled this
cookbook, they attempted to reflect the varied ethnic
and religious groups that have lived and prospered
together here for more than a hundred years. An added
treat are the historical salutes to our city among the
over 500 recipes.

$ 9.50 Retail price
$ .75 Postage and handling
$ .49 Tax for Texas residents
Make check payable to *Galveston Island Cookbook*

GUTEN APPETIT!

Sophienburg Memorial Association
401 West Coll
New Braunfels, TX 78130   512/629-1572

This 279-page cookbook is filled with German recipes, old home remedies, and table graces passed down from generation to generation. There are approximately 550 recipes in the book.

$11.43 Retail price
$ 1.25 Postage and handling
$ .57 Tax for Texas residents
Make check payable to Sophienburg Memorial Assn.
ISBN 0-87833-310-X

HOSPITALITY

Harvey Woman's Club
P. O. Box 1058
Palestine, TX 75801   214/723-7342

Reflects a meld of various influences from country to Cajun and other ethnic sources. Hardback, over 500 tested recipes, 312 pages. Dish categories logically separated, index clear and complete, and recipes are straightforward and easy-to-follow. Designated as an official Anderson County Sesquicentennial Cookbook in celebration of Texas' 150th birthday.

$11.95 Retail price
$ 2.00 Postage and handling
$ .61 Tax for Texas residents
Make check payable to *Hospitality*
ISBN 0-9611654-0-5

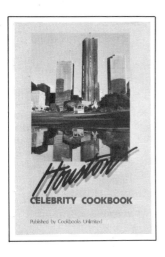

HOUSTON CELEBRITY COOKBOOK

Cookbooks Unlimited
1 Wind Poppy Court
Woodlands, TX 77381   713/363-2661

The Houston Celebrity Cookbook contains recipes from two hundred famous Houstonians (Vic Damone, ZZ Top and others). Robert Sakowitz wrote the introduction. This award-winning book is one of Hammermill's top ten for "Creative Inking." Proceeds benefit Texas Children's Hospital. 256 pages.

$17.95 Retail price
$ 1.00 Postage and handling
$ 1.08 Tax for Texas residents
Make check payable to Cookbooks Unlimited

HOUSTON FINE ARTS COOKBOOK
University of Texas Press
Box 7819
Austin, TX 78713   512/471-7233

For nearly a decade, the restaurant of Houston's Museum of Fine Arts has been a favorite of busy Houstonians. Its harmonious blending of fine art, delicious food, and exquisite garden setting has inspired this beautiful book of 50 menus (300 recipes) with full color pictures of artwork in 272 pages.

$19.95 Retail price
$ 2.00 Postage and handling
$ 1.02 Tax for Texas residents
Make check payable to University of Texas Press
ISBN 0-292-73024-1

HULLABALOO IN THE KITCHEN
Dallas A&M University Mothers' Club
P. O. Box 796212
Dallas, TX 75379   214/980-6488

Hullabaloo in the Kitchen proudly presented by the Dallas A&M Mothers' Club, is a zesty new collection of over 600 prized and proven recipes for beginners to gourmets. It contains a complete cross-referenced index, attractive dividers, with a microwave section, celebrity recipe section, and a special food section within its 384 elegant pages.

$12.95 Retail price
$ 2.00 Postage and handling
$ .66 Tax for Texas residents
Make check payable to *Hullabaloo in the Kitchen*
ISBN 0-9612446-0-7

"I'M GLAD I ATE WHEN I DID, 'CAUSE I'M NOT HUNGRY NOW"
Crazy Sam Enterprises
8301 Ambassador Row
Dallas, TX 75247   800/527-5267; 800/442-2439 TX

It's new. It's innovative. It's different. There has never been a cookbook quite like it, and there may never be one again. For the reading is as fascinating as the cooking. It's a real collector's item for the collectors of great home-made recipes. 310 pages. Full-color divider pages. Hardcover over wire ring.

$19.95 Retail price
$ 2.25 Postage and handling
$ 1.20 Tax for Texas residents
Make check payable to Crazy Sam Enterprises
ISBN 0-918865-00-X

IT'S A LONG WAY TO GUACAMOLE: THE TEX-MEX COOKBOOK

by Rue Judd and Ann Worley
P. O. Box 983
Arlington, VA 22216   703/538-2393

The Tex-Mex Cookbook has more than 100 highly acclaimed recipes and includes everything from cocktails and appetizers through desserts. All recipes—mild to super spicy—are easy to follow with ingredients specially selected for ready availability in local supermarkets. Features complete menus for every occasion. Spiral bound, 106 pages, now in 7th printing.

$ 6.00 Retail price
$ .75 Postage and handling
Make check payable to J & W Tex-Mex
ISBN 0-9604842-0-5

KEEPERS!

by Helene Randolph Moore
810 Oak Lane
New Braunfels, TX 78130   512/625-6844

Keepers is a wonderful cookbook of 550 recipes in a collection worth keeping. These are tested favorites for more than 40 years. Large type for easy reading. Simple enough for beginners and fancy enough for special guests.

$ 9.95 Retail price
$ 1.50 Postage and handling
$ .50 Tax for Texas residents
Make check payable to *Keepers!*

LA GALERIE PERROQUET FOOD FARE

by Carolyn M. Abney
205 Pinecrest West
Marshall, TX   75670   214/935-1952 or 938-9987

La Galerie Perroquet Food Fare is a new culinary lifestyle for the entire family. These gourmet recipes are all low cholesterol, low fat, including party planning and edible garnishes to help you with the preparation and presentation of meals.

$ 8.75 Retail price
$ 1.00 Postage and handling
$ .45 Tax for Texas residents
Make check payable to Carolyn M. Abney

LAGNIAPPE

Junior League of Beaumont
P. O. Box 7031
Beaumont, TX 77706   409/832-2709

Lagniappe (lan yap', lan'yap) n. something given with a purchase to a customer, for good measure. A unique cookbook resulting from six years of monthly gourmet luncheons hosted by Junior League of Beaumont members. 55 complete menus from the luncheons including 287 recipes. 282 additional proven recipes. 350 pages.

$12.95 Retail price
$ 1.50 Postage and handling
$ .65 Tax for Texas residents
Make check payable to Junior League of Beaumont
ISBN 0-9609604-0-6

Junior Service League of McAllen, Texas

LA PIÑATA

The Junior Service League of McAllen, Inc.
P. O. Box 2465
McAllen, TX 78502   512/682-0071

The McAllen Junior Service League presents this cookbook in the spirit of the piñata. It is a gaily decorated paper container filled with all sorts of surprises and good things. You have but to "break it open" and share its contents with others. Viva la Fiesta—Viva la Piñata! 436 pages.

$ 9.95 Retail price
$ 2.00 Postage and handling
$ .61 Tax for Texas residents
Make check payable to *La Piñata*
ISBN 0-9604548-0-2

For people who love good food
...but don't know how to cook
...are too tired to cook
...or don't want to cook.

LEAVING HOME

by Louise P. Grace
8338 San Leandro
Dallas, TX 75218   214/327-5207 or 327-4299

This cookbook is for people who love good food but don't know how to cook, are too tired to cook, or don't want to cook. No recipe has more than seven steps, all of which are numbered. *Leaving Home* is a cookbook for any age, gender, and degree of culinary talents.

$11.95 Retail price
$ 1.75 Postage and handling
$ .73 Tax for Texas residents
Make check payable to *Leaving Home*
ISBN 0-9613652-0-X

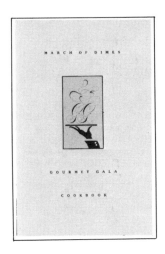

MARCH OF DIMES GOURMET GALA COOKBOOK

Women's Auxiliary of the March of Dimes
P. O. Box 12092
Dallas, TX 75225   214/869-2401

The Culinary Institute of America created the American Regional Cuisine Award for the outstanding recipes in the *Gourmet Gala Cookbook* prepared by celebrities of entertainment, sports and political fame during Gourmet Galas held across the United States. Begins with letter and recipes by Nancy Reagan. Color picture section of celebrities and contestants. 640 pages.

$25.00 Retail price
$ 2.50 Postage and handling
$ 1.32 Tax for Texas residents
Make check payable to Women's Auxiliary - Cookbook
ISBN 0-9613852-0-0

THE MELTING POT

The Institute of Texan Cultures
P. O. Box 1226
San Antonio, TX 78294   512/226-7651

Texas settlers brought from foreign lands recipes handed down by their ancestors. You can recreate these international dishes from 27 cultural groups— from Indian fry bread to Scottish clottie dumpling. Each section is devoted to a different ethnic group and contains a brief history of the culture. 275 recipes in 244 pages.

$10.95 Retail price
$ 1.50 Postage and handling
$ .62 Tax for Texas residents
Make check payable to The Institute of Texan Cultures
ISBN 0-86701-006-1

MICRO QUICK!

by CiCi Williamson and Ann Steiner
MicroScope
P. O. Box 79762
Houston, TX 77279   713/468-8455

A quick and easy microwave cookbook by nationwide newspaper columnists, CiCi Williamson and Ann Steiner. Includes 314 recipes "Quick"-er than 20 minutes plus special sections on herb and flower drying, microwave to grill, and baby food. This 224-page book is a "must" for cooks "living in the fast lane!"

$10.95 Retail price
$ 1.50 Postage and handling
$ .67 Tax for Texas residents
Make check payable to MicroScope
ISBN 0-9607740-1-7

MICROWAVE KNOW-HOW
by CiCi Williamson and Ann Steiner
MicroScope
P. O. Box 79762
Houston, TX 77279   713/468-8455

This 224-page microwave technique cookbook (formerly *MicroScope Savoir Faire*) tells it like it is. By the authors of "MicroScope," the nationally syndicated microwave column, the book features fast "Panic Button" recipes for the 5:00 rush, divider tabs, and 23 extensive defrosting and microwaving charts. Family-tested. Answers everyday microwave questions.

$10.95 Retail price
$ 1.50 Postage and handling
$ .67 Tax for Texas residents
Make check payable to MicroScope
ISBN 0-9607740-2-5

MORNING, NOON AND NIGHT COOK-BOOK
by Gerald Ramsey
SMU Press
P. O. Box 415, Dept. P
Dallas, TX 75275   214/692-2263

Roast Duck with Velvet Sauce, Chicken Breast Cadillac, Grasshopper Pie . . . these are but a few of the mouth-watering recipes found in this standard cookbook. Ramsey, the award-winning director of food service at SMU, offers complete menus for every occasion. A new section includes longtime favorite recipes from around the country. 272 pages.

$12.50 Retail price
$ .75 Tax for Texas residents
Make check payable to SMU Press
ISBN 0-87074-178-0

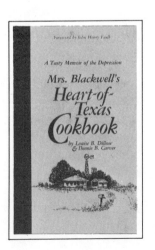

MRS. BLACKWELL'S HEART-OF-TEXAS COOKBOOK
by Louise B. Dillow and Deenie B. Carver
Corona Publishing Company
1037 S. Alamo
San Antonio, TX 78210   512/227-1771

A "tasty memoir of the Depression" that has captured hearts all over America (over 18,000 in print) . . . guaranteed to rekindle old memories of evenings in the farm kitchen. 130 pages. Illustrated. 122 recipes.

$ 6.95 Retail price
$ .80 Postage and handling
$ .38 Tax for Texas residents
Make check payable to Corona Publishing Company
ISBN 0-931722-06-3

NATURE'S KITCHEN
by Dr. Donald R. Whitaker and Barbara Durham
Flournoy
P. O. Box 1117
Lufkin, TX 75901   409/875-2981

Scriptural principles for total health. Over 200 selected and tested recipes to aid in prevention of cancer,
heart disease, arthritis, diabetes . . . great information
for preparing and eating a healthier, more natural diet.
Can be your ticket to a rich and healthy life—the kind
of life God so wants us all to enjoy. 269 pages.

$11.97 Retail price
$ 2.00 Postage and handling
$ .61 Tax for Texas residents
Make check payable to *Nature's Kitchen*

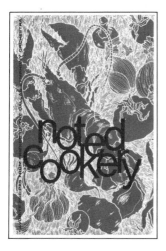

NOTED COOKERY
Junior Group of the Dallas Symphony Orchestra League
P. O. Box 8472
Dallas, TX 75205   214/565-9100

Time honored recipes of Texas delights. More than
750 tested recipes. Well chosen recipes for simple and
not-so-simple menus. Celebrity recipes included. Hardback book. 400 pages. Complete index.

$12.95 Retail price
$ 2.00 (1-3 copies) Postage and handling $5.00 (6-12)
$ .79 Tax for Texas residents
Make check payable to Junior Group Publications

OF MAGNOLIA AND MESQUITE
by Suzanne Corder and Gay Thompson
Su-Ga Publications
416 Mesa Circle
Plainview, TX 79072   806/293-5608

Of Magnolia and Mesquite is about families and neighbors, our children and friends. It is about sharing and
creating food and gracious entertaining. The menus
assure the successful blending of tastes, textures and
color, allowing you to be the perfect hostess.

$12.95 Retail price
$ 2.00 Postage and handling
$ .67 Tax for Texas residents
Make check payable to Su-Ga Publications
ISBN 0-9614184-0-0

Linda West Eckhardt

THE ONLY TEXAS COOKBOOK
by Linda West Eckhardt
Texas Monthly Press
P. O. Box 1569
Austin, TX 78767   512/476-7085

No one knows Texas cuisine so well as Linda West
Eckhardt, and no one has ever written about it with
such authority and charm. In a prose as lively as her
recipes are delicious (and authentic!), Eckhardt draws
on a lifetime of cooking, eating, and researching the
best food Texas has to offer.

$15.95 Retail price
$ 2.00 Postage and handling
$ .82 Tax for Texas residents
Make check payable to Texas Monthly Press
ISBN 0-932012-19-1

From Zapata, Texas

OUR FAVORITE RECIPES
Women of the United Methodist Church
Box 5218
Zapata, TX 78076   512/765-6674

Unique recipes (350) from a unique community on
the Mexican border. Compiled by the women of the
United Methodist Church from recipes gathered from
native Texans and winter residents, it features 177
pages of authentic Texas favorites, many unusual
recipes, traditional foods from old Mexico, and treasured family secrets.

$ 5.00 Retail price
$ 1.50 Postage and handling
Make check payable to United Methodist Church of
  Zapata
ISBN 0-932012-60-4

A COLLECTION OF RECIPES FROM
TFWC CLUBS
Compiled by
Texas Federation of Women's Clubs
Historical Foundation Trustees

THE PRIDE OF TEXAS
Texas Federation of Women's Clubs Historical Foundation Trustees
2312 San Gabriel
Austin, TX 78705   512/472-1456

A collection of recipes representing the big State of
Texas submitted by Texas Federation of Women's
Clubs. The cover features a color plate of the exterior
of TFWC Headquarters and dividers for food sections
show interior of building. The book has a labeled spiral binding for easy use and contains about 1200 recipes
(333 pages) in eight sections including microwave.

$14.00 Retail price
$ 1.00 Postage and handling
Make check payable to Texas Federation of Women's
  Clubs Historical Foundation

RARE COLLECTION

Junior League of Galveston County, Inc.
212 Kempner
Galveston, TX 77550   409/765-7646

Rare Collection presents 320 pages of over 450 collector quality recipes, refined for even the beginning gourmet. The unique cover and 16 full page illustrations reflect Galveston County's vivid past and vibrant future. With invaluable glossary and cross referenced index, the book is a hardbound volume with concealed wiro-binding.

$15.95 Retail price
$ 1.50 Postage and handling
$ .82 Tax for Texas residents
Make check payable to J.L.G.C. Publications.
ISBN 0-961-37790-9

READY TO SERVE

National Guard Auxiliary of Austin
P. O. Box 5733
Austin, TX 78763   512/454-7300 or 346-0674

These recipes are presented with pride in the same spirit that is the heritage of the state militia, the Texas National Guard, which stand *Ready To Serve*. Vignettes of Texas military history and ten color illustrations depicting flags carried in early Texas battles make this book truly unique. "Top Brass" and "Cooking For The Troops" sections. 384 pages.

$12.95 Retail Price
$ 2.00 Postage and handling
$ .65 Tax for Texas residents
Make check payable to *Ready To Serve*
ISBN 0-9612502-0-8

REPAST

Harris County Heritage Society
1100 Bagby
Houston, TX 77002   713/759-9217

The Harris County Heritage Society, dedicated to historic preservation and restoration in the City of Houston and Harris County has gathered in this beautiful cookbook treasured recipes from supporting and enthusiastic society members. 370 pages. Ring Bound. The book has beautiful cover-quality full color divider pictures throughout.

$12.95 Retail price
$ 1.50 Postage and handling
$ .79 Tax for Texas residents
Make check payable to Harris County Heritage Society

ROLLING IN DOUGH

by Hilda Eicher Higley
5915 Fair Lane Drive
Austin, TX 78731   512/452-4203

This book is spiral-bound and includes 160 kitchen-tested bread recipes specifically catagorized under: Basic, International, US Regional, and Eggless. The author, a bread-making instructor for many years, realized the need for such a book, listing simple recipes as well as more involved doughs.

$ 8.95 Retail price
$ 1.00 Postage and handling
$ .49 Tax for Texas residents
Make check payable to Hilda Higley
ISBN 0-938934-08-2

SAN ANGELO JUNIOR LEAGUE COOKBOOK

San Angelo Junior League, Inc.
P. O. Box 3033
San Angelo, TX 76902   915/942-1003

San Angelo Junior League Cookbook is a culmination of 1,000 recipes tested many times for excellence and accuracy. It is 272 pages of delicious West Texas recipes guaranteed to make you wish that you could be a West Texan! Our cookbook is our way of life.

$10.95 Retail price
$ 1.50 Postage and handling
$ .60 Tax for Texas residents
Make check payable to San Angelo Junior League, Inc.

SAN ANTONIO CONSERVATION SOCIETY COOKBOOK

San Antonio Conservation Society
107 King William Street
San Antonio, TX 78204   512/224-6163

The San Antonio Conservation Society Cookbook reflects the cuisine of the Alamo City and the heritage of its people. Now in its third printing in less than three years, the colorful cookbook features five full color watercolors by noted Texas artist, Caroline Shelton, and contains outstanding Mexican Food and South Texas Wild Game sections.
$12.95 Retail price
$ 1.80 Postage and handling
$ .65 Tax for Texas residents
Make check payable to San Antonio Conservation
    Society

San Antonio Cookbook II

SAN ANTONIO COOKBOOK II

The San Antonio Symphony League
P. O. Box 17412
San Antonio, TX 78217   512/492-2578

The taste of Texas and the spice of San Antonio from the finest kitchens and restaurants of the Alamo City. Explore the toast of Texas from coastal favorites to the wild game óf the Hill Country in 500 recipes on 300 pages with 20 full-page lithographs on sand paper.

$ 9.95 Retail price
$ 1.00 Postage and handling
$ .55 Tax for Texas residents
Make check payable to *San Antonio Cookbook II*
ISBN 0-9612470-0-2

SCRUMPTIOUS

Houston Junior Forum
P. O. Box 13502
Houston, TX 77219   713/528-5395

Scrumptious is a beautiful hardbound collection containing over 1,000 tested and edited recipes from Houston kitchens. Features Texas specialities plus other ethnic favorites. *Scrumptious* has elegant recipes for the accomplished cook and simple ones for the beginner. A delight for anyone—a must for the serious collector! 373 pages. 1,003 recipes.

$11.98 Retail price
$ 1.50 Postage and handling
$ .73 Tax for Texas residents
Make check payable to Houston Junior Forum

SEASONED WITH SUN

Junior League of El Paso, Inc.
520 Thunderbird Drive
El Paso, TX 79912   915/584-3511

Seasoned With Sun is one of the finest cookbooks ever compiled on southwestern cooking. It is a rich collection of over 500 recipes on 266 spiral-bound pages. It includes over 150 original Mexican recipes with "how to" instructions. *Seasoned With Sun* has been featured in *Ladies Home Journal* and *Cuisine*.

$ 9.95 Retail price
$ 1.50 Postage and handling
$ .51 Tax for Texas residents
Make check payable to The Junior League of El Paso, Inc.
ISBN 0-9607974-0-8

SPINDLETOP INTERNATIONAL COOKS

Spindletop Oilmen's Golf Charities, Inc.
2900 North Loop West, Suite 1200
Houston, TX 77092   713/956-0920

Over a thousand recipes from Spindletop oil people from all over the world, plus recipes from famous Houston restaurants. Traditional regional fare to innovative haute cuisine, bringing you exciting dining ideas, menu suggestions and helpful hints. Includes suggestions for the right wine to enhance any meal. Spindletop International supports Houston area youth charities.

$25.00 Retail price
$ 2.00 Postage and handling
$ 1.53 Tax for Texas residents
Make check payable to *Spindletop International Cooks*

SQUARE HOUSE MUSEUM COOKBOOK

Carson County Square House Museum
Box 276
Panhandle, TX 79068   806/537-3118

Now in its fourth printing, this 325-page book includes family favorites used for 150 years as well as recipes for gourmet dining. Early in the support of the museum, the board baked cakes and pastries and served benefit meals for the museum. Requests from pleased patrons brought about publication of the book.

$10.00 Retail price
$ 1.50 Postage and handling
$ .50 Tax for Texas residents
Make check payable to Carson County Square House
    Museum

SWEETS. . . . FROM MARINA WITH
LOVE . . . .

by Marina Reed Gonzalez
9714 Laurel Oaks
San Antonio, TX 78240   512/696-0243

This beautifully illustrated hardback dessert cookbook began as a collection of recipes for a local homemaker's family and friends. 319 unique recipes and 225 illustrations in 285 pages. Each chapter is introduced with a poem and a full-page color illustration. Overall, the collection is eclectic and international, including many of Marina's Mexican specialties. Watercolor illustrated cover.

$19.95 Retail price
$ 2.00 Postage and handling
$ 1.05 Tax for Texas residents
Make check payable to *Sweets . . . . From Marina
    With Love . . . .*

TASTEFUL TRADITIONS

Women for Abilene Christian University
ACU Station Box 7122
Abilene, TX 79699   915/673-3429

Tasteful Traditions has more than 800 recipes submitted by WACU members nationwide that have been carefully selected. This beautifully written, organized and indexed book was an immediate best seller. The cover and divider pages were designed by a well-known West Texas artist, Juanita Tittle Pollard.

$13.95 Retail price
$ 1.50 Postage and handling
$ .70 Tax for Texas residents
Make check payable to *Tasteful Traditions*
ISBN 0-9611750-0T1

A TASTE OF VICTORIA

Nazareth-St. Joseph Schools Project
P. O. Box 3503
Victoria, TX 77903   512/575-5594

Now in its fourth printing, this cookbook commemorated the Sesquicentennial of the town of Victoria. 500 favorite recipes of old families, some shared for the first time. Includes men's favorite recipes, game cookery, everyday family favorites, and great desserts. Photography of this area by Louise O'Conner.

$ 7.95 Retail price
$ 1.25 Postage and handling
$ .45 Tax for Texas residents
Make check payable to *A Taste of Victoria*

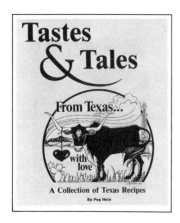

TASTES & TALES FROM TEXAS . . . WITH LOVE

Hein & Associates
5321 Industrial Oaks Blvd. No. 123
Austin, TX 78735   512/892-5650

A collection of best-loved recipes contributed by great cooks from all over the Lone Star State combined with fascinating short tales about Texas people, places and history. The book is illustrated and has 188 pages.

$ 8.95 Retail price
$ 1.07 Postage and handling
$ .43 Tax for Texas residents
Make check payable to Hein & Associates
ISBN 0-9613881-0-2

FANNIN COUNTY, TEXAS COOKBOOK

TEMPTING TRADITIONS

Fannin County Historical Commission
P. O. Box 338
Bonham, TX 75418   214/583-8042

Nostalgic and traditional, *Tempting Traditions* is filled with today's Texas specialties. With six beautiful color photographs, it depicts six decades of Texas history. With over 500 tested recipes, on 278 pages, it shares a small touch of history and a large taste of Texas dining pleasure.

$11.95 Retail price
$ 1.50 Postage and handling
$ .60 Tax for Texas residents
Make check payable to *Tempting Traditions*
ISBN 0-9609602

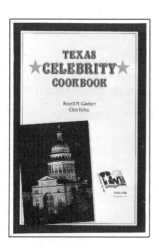

TEXAS
★CELEBRITY★
COOKBOOK

Russell H. Gardner
Chris Farkas

TEXAS CELEBRITY COOKBOOK

Gardner-Farkas Press, Inc.
P. O. Box 33229
Fort Worth, TX 76162   817/870-2113

An officially-sanctioned project of the Texas 1986 Sesquicentennial, celebrating 150 years of Texas independence, the *Texas Celebrity Cookbook* has over 300 recipes collected from some of Texas' most prominent personalities. Eight full-color photo inserts depict famous scenes from the state of Texas. 256 pages.

$14.95 Retail price
$ 2.00 Postage and handling
$ .77 Tax for Texas residents
Make check payable to Gardner-Farkas Press
Visa/MC ordering available
ISBN 0-9613874-0-8

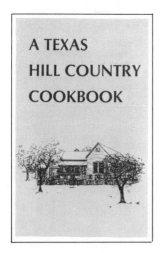

A TEXAS
HILL COUNTRY
COOKBOOK

A TEXAS HILL COUNTRY COOKBOOK

Rt. 3, Box 629
Marble Falls, TX 78654   512/598-5727

A book of favorites from the legendary Texas Hill Country. Featured are 680 recipes in 408 pages of ancestral German, French, Mexican, ranch and wild game cooking. Pen-and-ink drawings of Hill Country landmarks. Now in its 10th printing. Comb binding, washable cover in beige, rust and black.

$10.95 Retail price
$ 1.50 Postage and handling
$ .45 Tax for Texas residents
Make check payable to *A Texas Hill Country Cookbook*
ISBN 0-9609210-1

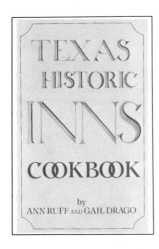

TEXAS HISTORIC INNS COOKBOOK

by Ann Ruff and Gail Drago
Texas Monthly Press
P. O. Box 1569
Austin, TX 78767   512/476-7085

    A compendium of history and recipes from the heritage inns and hotels of the Lone Star State. The authors have traveled the interstates and the byways of Texas and gathered a delightful collection of reputation-making recipes and anecdotes, along with the enchanting stories behind the historic inns they visited.

$16.95 Retail price
$ 2.00 Postage and handling
$ .87 Tax for Texas residents
Make check payable to Texas Monthly Press
ISBN 0-932012-45-0

THE TEXAS MICROWAVE COOKBOOK

by Carolyn H. White
Home Economist Consulting Services
P. O. Box 13112
Arlington, TX 76013   817/451-9699

    Recipes developed and tested for microwave classes for adults requesting delicious, simple recipes for the most typically Texan foods. Hardcover, 176 pages, with Flavor of Texas scenic illustrations and Almanac of Microwave Menus for Texas. Preface information on oven cooking wattage and variable power levels.

$ 9.95 Retail price
$ 1.00 Postage and handling
$ .45 Tax for Texas residents
Make check payable to Home Economist Consulting
   Services
ISBN 0-941294-00-5

THROUGH OUR KITCHEN DOOR

Dallas County Heritage Society Guild
Old City Park
1717 Gano
Dallas, TX 75215   214/421-5141

    "Preserving the best of yesterday for today" is the commitment of Old City Park. It, too, is the story of *Through Our Kitchen Door*, a cookbook of 282 pages containing 591 recipes. Guild volunteers are happy to share the long-loved heirloom recipes and family favorites that reflect the sturdy heritage of our North Texas area. Enjoy!

$ 9.95 Retail price
$ 2.50 Postage and handling
$ .61 Tax for Texas residents
Make check payable to Dallas County Heritage Society

TRADING SECRETS

Beaumont Heritage Society
2985 French Road
Beaumont, TX 77706   409/898-0348

A keepsake collection of special recipes, glimpses of historical Beaumont, and photographs, old and new. Presented by the members and friends of the Beaumont Heritage Society. There are 142 pages in the book and 338 recipes.

$ 7.95 Retail price
$ 1.00 Postage and handling
$ .40 Tax for Texas residents
Make check payable to The Beaumont Heritage Society

WILD-N-TAME FISH-N-GAME

by Lynn M. Moore
P. O. Box 368
Cypress, TX 77429   713/469-6911 or 469-1950

Traditional and newly devised recipes compiled, adapted, and entertainingly presented by Lynn Mitchell Moore, Home Economist. Preceding each game section are pages titled "About," which offer helpful information on the care, preservation, and cooking of fish and game. Includes camp foods, microwave dishes and how to field dress for better flavor.

$11.95 Retail price
$ 1.95 Postage and handling
$ .60 Tax for Texas residents
Make check payable to Richard S. Moore, Inc.
ISBN 0-918464-31-5

THE WOODLANDS CELEBRITY COOKBOOK

Cookbooks Unlimited
1 Wind Poppy Court
Woodland, TX 77381   713/363-2661

The Woodlands Celebrity Cookbook is as unique as its hometown. Celebrities from throughout the United States have settled here. Two hundred recipes are introduced with the celebrity's background and origin of their recipe. Award-winning color photos introduce the seven major food categories. 256 pages.

$17.95 Retail price
$ 1.00 Postage and handling
$ 1.08 Tax for Texas residents
Make check payable to Cookbooks Unlimited